easy Computer Basics

Windows® Edition

Michael Miller

QUE®

800 East 96th Street
Indianapolis, In 46240

CONTENTS

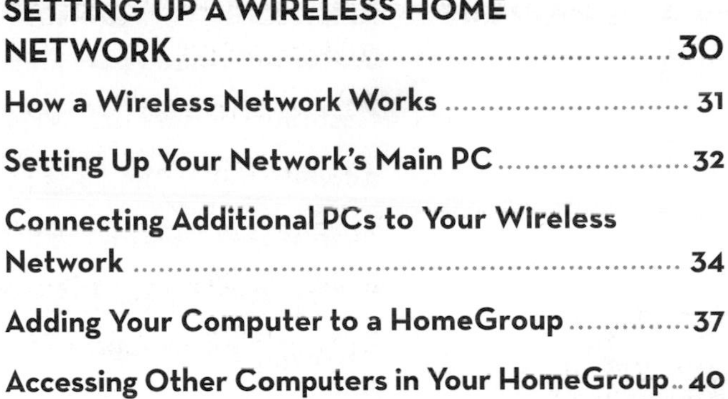

From:
To:
Cc:
Subject:

EASY COMPUTER BASICS, WINDOWS® 8 EDITION

ISBN-13: 9780789750051
ISBN-10: 0789750058

The Library of Congress cataloging-in-publication data is on file.

Printed in the United States of America

First Printing: September 2012

TRADEMARKS

All terms mentioned in this book that are known to be trademarks or service marks have been appropriately capitalized. Que Publishing cannot attest to the accuracy of this information. Use of a term in this book should not be regarded as affecting the validity of any trademark or service mark.

WARNING AND DISCLAIMER

Every effort has been made to make this book as complete and as accurate as possible, but no warranty or fitness is implied. The information provided is on an "as is" basis. The author and the publisher shall have neither liability nor responsibility to any person or entity with respect to any loss or damages arising from the information contained in this book.

BULK SALES

Que Publishing offers excellent discounts on this book when ordered in quantity for bulk purchases or special sales. For more information, please contact

U.S. Corporate and Government Sales
1-800-382-3419
corpsales@pearsontechgroup.com

For sales outside of the U.S., please contact

International Sales
international@pearsoned.com

Associate Publisher
Greg Wiegand

Acquisitions Editor
Michelle Newcomb

Development Editor
Keith Cline

Managing Editor
Kristy Hart

Project Editor
Jovana Shirley

Technical Editor
Vince Averello

Copy Editor
Keith Cline

Indexer
Cheryl Lenser

Publishing Coordinator
Cindy Teeters

Compositor
Bronkella Publishing

ABOUT THE AUTHOR

Michael Miller is a successful and prolific author with a reputation for practical advice, technical accuracy, and an unerring empathy for the needs of his readers.

Mr. Miller has written more than 100 best-selling books over the past two decades. His books for Que include *Absolute Beginner's Guide to Computer Basics, Easy Facebook, Facebook for Grown-Ups, My Pinterest,* and *The Ultimate Digital Music Guide*.

He is known for his casual, easy-to-read writing style and his practical, real-world advice—as well as his ability to explain a variety of complex topics to an everyday audience.

You can email Mr. Miller directly at easycomputer@molehillgroup.com. His website is located at www.molehillgroup.com.

DEDICATION

To Sherry—life together is easier.

ACKNOWLEDGMENTS

Thanks to the usual suspects at Que, including but not limited to Greg Wiegand, Michelle Newcomb, Jovana Shirley, Keith Cline, and technical editor Vince Averello.

WE WANT TO HEAR FROM YOU!

As the reader of this book, you are our most important critic and commentator. We value your opinion and want to know what we're doing right, what we could do better, what areas you'd like to see us publish in, and any other words of wisdom you're willing to pass our way.

We welcome your comments. You can email or write to let us know what you did or didn't like about this book—as well as what we can do to make our books better.

Please note that we cannot help you with technical problems related to the topic of this book.

When you write, please be sure to include this book's title and author as well as your name and email address. We will carefully review your comments and share them with the author and editors who worked on the book.

Email: feedback@quepublishing.com

Mail: Que Publishing
ATTN: Reader Feedback
800 East 96th Street
Indianapolis, IN 46240 USA

READER SERVICES

Visit our website and register this book at quepublishing.com/register for convenient access to any updates, downloads, or errata that might be available for this book.

IT'S AS EASY AS 1-2-3

Each part of this book is made up of a series of short, instructional lessons, designed to help you understand basic information.

1. Each step is fully illustrated to show you how it looks on screen.
2. Each task includes a series of quick, easy steps designed to guide you through the procedure.
3. Items that you select or click in menus, dialog boxes, tabs, and windows are shown in bold.

Tips, notes, and cautions give you a heads-up for any extra information you may need while working through the task.

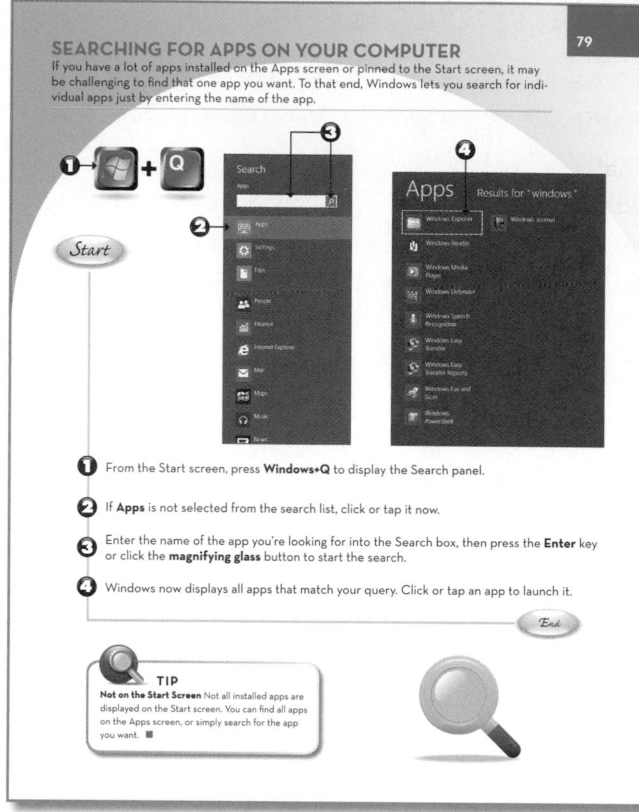

79

SEARCHING FOR APPS ON YOUR COMPUTER

If you have a lot of apps installed on the Apps screen or pinned to the Start screen, it may be challenging to find that one app you want. To that end, Windows lets you search for individual apps just by entering the name of the app.

1. From the Start screen, press **Windows+Q** to display the Search panel.
2. If **Apps** is not selected from the search list, click or tap it now.
3. Enter the name of the app you're looking for into the Search box, then press the **Enter** key or click the **magnifying glass** button to start the search.
4. Windows now displays all apps that match your query. Click or tap an app to launch it.

End

TIP

Not on the Start Screen Not all installed apps are displayed on the Start screen. You can find all apps on the Apps screen, or simply search for the app you want.

INTRODUCTION

Computers don't have to be scary or difficult. Computers can be *easy*—if you know what to do.

That's where this book comes in. *Easy Computer Basics, Windows 8 Edition* is an illustrated, step-by-step guide to setting up and using your new computer. You'll learn how computers work, how to connect all the pieces and parts, and how to start using them. All you have to do is look at the pictures and follow the instructions. Pretty easy.

After you learn the basics, I show you how to do lots of useful stuff with your new PC. You learn how to use Microsoft Windows to copy and delete files; use Windows 8's Mail app to send and receive email messages; use Microsoft Word to write letters and memos; use Internet Explorer to search for information on the Internet; and use Facebook, Pinterest, and Twitter to keep up with what your friends are doing. We even cover some fun stuff, including listening to music, viewing digital photographs, and watching movies and TV shows online.

If you're worried about how to keep your PC up and running, we cover some basic system maintenance, too. And, just to be safe, I show you how to protect your computer when you're online, too. It's not hard to do.

To help you find the information you need, I've organized *Easy Computer Basics, Windows 8 Edition* into 16 parts.

Chapter 1, "Understanding Personal Computers," discusses all the different types of personal computers out there and describes the pieces and parts of a typical computer system. Read this part to find out all about desktops, all-in-ones, notebooks, and tablets—and the things like hard drives, keyboards, mice, and printers that make them tick.

Chapter 2, "Setting Up Your PC," shows you how to connect all the pieces and parts of a typical PC and get your new computer system up and running.

Chapter 3, "Setting Up a Wireless Home Network," helps you connect all the computers in your house to a wireless network and share a broadband Internet connection.

Chapter 4, "Using Microsoft Windows 8," introduces the backbone of your entire system—the Microsoft Windows 8 operating system—including how it works and how to use it.

Chapter 5, "Personalizing Windows 8," shows you how to customize Windows 8's Lock screen, how to change system colors, how to add and delete tiles from the Start screen, and how to add new users to your system.

Chapter 6, "Working with Windows 8 Apps," walks you through everything you know to launch, use, and switch between useful apps—including the Maps and Weather apps included with Windows 8.

Chapter 7, "Working with Traditional Desktop Apps," shows you how to move beyond the Windows 8 interface and use the Windows 8 desktop—and apps that run on the desktop.

Chapter 8, "Using Microsoft Word," shows you how to use both the desktop and online versions of Microsoft's popular word processor to create letters and other documents.

Chapter 9, "Using the Internet," is all about how to get online and what to do when you're there—including how to use Internet Explorer to surf the Web, search for information, shop for items online, and find news, sports, and weather online.

Chapter 10, "Communicating with Email," is all about using email to communicate with friends, family, and co-workers. The focus is on Windows 8's new Mail app, as well as the Gmail web-based email service.

Chapter 11, "Sharing with Facebook and Other Social Networks," introduces you to the fascinating world of social networking—and shows you how to share with friends on Facebook, Pinterest, and Twitter.

Chapter 12, "Watching TV and Movies Online," shows you how to use your computer to watch television programming, movies and other videos from YouTube, Hulu, and Netflix.

Chapter 13, "Playing Digital Music," shows you how to download and play digital music files, listen to CDs on your PC, and copy songs from your PC to your Apple iPod.

Chapter 14, "Viewing Digital Photos," helps you connect a digital camera to your PC, transfer your photos to your PC, and view them on your computer screen.

Chapter 15, "Working with Files and Folders," shows you how to use Windows Explorer to manage all the computer files you create—by moving, copying, renaming, and deleting them.

Chapter 16, "Protecting Your Computer," is all about defending against online menaces, keeping your PC running smoothly, backing up your important files, and recovering from serious crashes.

And that's not all. At the back of the book you'll find a glossary of common computer terms—so you can understand what all the techie types are talking about!

(By the way, if something looks a little different on your computer screen than it does in your book, don't dismay. Microsoft is constantly doing little updates and fixes to Windows, so it's possible the looks of some things might have changed a bit between my writing this book and you reading. Nothing to worry about.)

So, is using a computer really this easy? You bet—just follow the simple step-by-step instructions, and you'll be computing like a pro!

UNDERSTANDING PERSONAL COMPUTERS

Chances are you're reading this book because you have a new computer. At this point you might not be totally sure what it is you've gotten yourself into. Just what is this mess of boxes and cables—how does it all go together, and how does it work?

We'll start by looking at the physical components of your system—the stuff we call computer *hardware*. A lot of different pieces and parts make up a typical computer system—and the pieces and parts differ depending on the type of computer you have.

You see, no two computer systems are identical. That's because there are several different types of configurations (desktops, notebooks, and such) and because you can always add new components to your system—or disconnect other pieces you don't have any use for.

DIFFERENT TYPES OF COMPUTERS

Traditional desktop PC

All-in-one desktop PC

Notebook PC

Tablet PC

GETTING TO KNOW DESKTOP PCs

A traditional desktop computer is one with a monitor designed to sit on your desktop, along with a separate keyboard and mouse and freestanding stereo speakers. The central component of traditional desktop system is the *system unit*, which contains the PC's central processing unit (CPU), memory, and motherboard. All the external components connect directly to the system unit.

Start

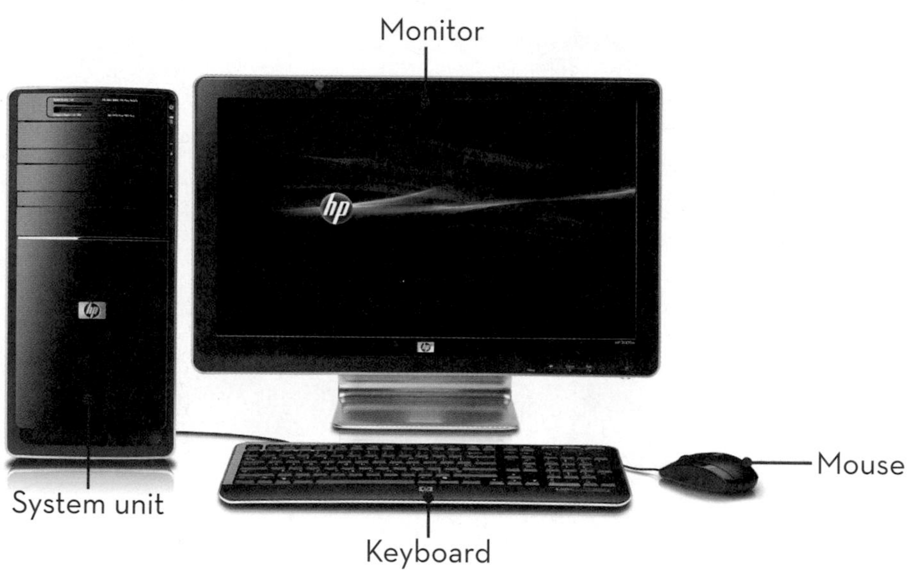

End

NOTE

Connecting Components The external components (called *peripherals*) of a desktop PC connect to the system unit via an assortment of different connectors. Most peripherals today connect via USB connectors, but some components use other types of connections. ■

NOTE

Desktop Front and Back On a desktop PC, most of the primary components connect to ports on the back of the system unit. ■

GETTING TO KNOW ALL-IN-ONE PCs

An all-in-one computer is a desktop model where the system unit is built in to the monitor. The monitor/system unit also includes built-in speakers, as well as all the ports you need to connect external peripherals. Many people like the easier setup and smaller space requirements of an all-in-one system.

Start

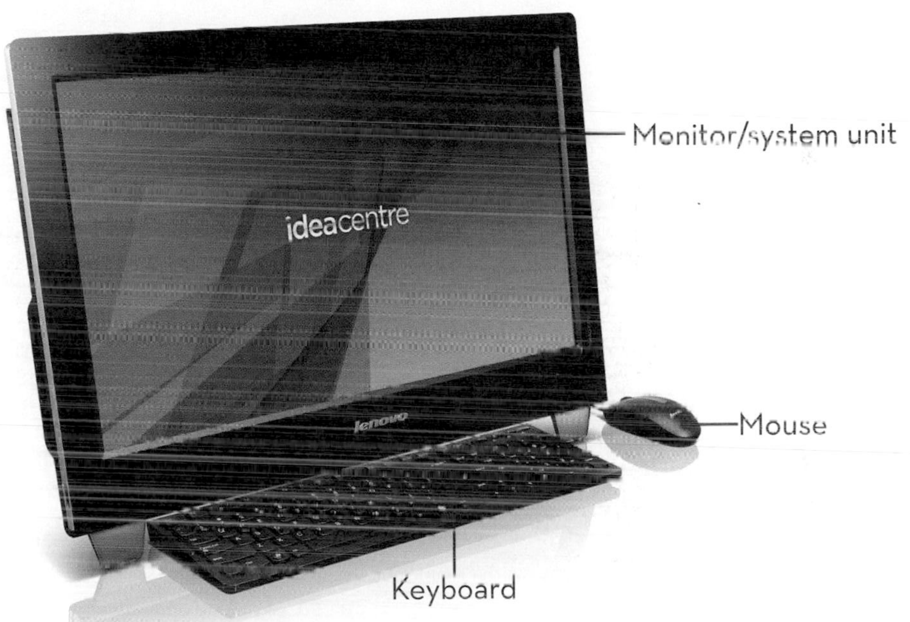

End

NOTE

Touchscreens Some of all-in-one PCs feature touchscreen monitors, so you can control them by tapping and swiping the monitor screen with your fingers. ■

CAUTION

All-in-One Drawbacks The chief drawbacks to all-in-one systems are the price (typically a bit more than traditional desktop PCs) and the fact that if one component goes bad, the whole system is out of commission. It's a lot easier to replace a single component than an entire system! ■

GETTING TO KNOW NOTEBOOK PCs

Most new computers today are notebook models—sometimes called *laptops*. A notebook PC differs from a desktop PC in that all the pieces and parts are combined into a single unit that you can take with you almost anywhere. The built-in battery provides power when you're not near a wall outlet.

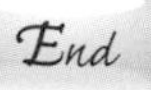

NOTE

Different Types of Notebooks There are four different types of notebook computers. *Traditional notebooks* have screens in the 14-inch to 16-inch range, 320GB or larger hard drives, and built-in CD/DVD drives. *Desktop replacement notebooks* have larger 17-inch screens, more powerful processors, but shorter battery life. *Netbooks* have small screens in the 10-inch to 12-inch range, smaller hard drives, no CD/DVD drive, but much longer battery life. *Ultrabooks* have 12-inch to 14-inch screens, are smaller and thinner than traditional notebooks, and use fast solid-state memory rather than hard drives. ■

TIP

External Peripherals Even though a notebook PC has the keyboard, mouse, and monitor built in, you can still connect external keyboards, mice, and monitors to the unit. This is convenient if you want to use a bigger keyboard or monitor or a real mouse (instead of the notebook's track pad). ■

GETTING TO KNOW TABLET PCs

A tablet PC is a self-contained computer you can hold in one hand. Think of a tablet as the real-world equivalent of one of those communication pads you see on *Star Trek*; it doesn't have a separate keyboard, so you operate it by tapping and swiping the screen with your fingers. The Windows 8 operating system is optimized for just this sort of touch operation.

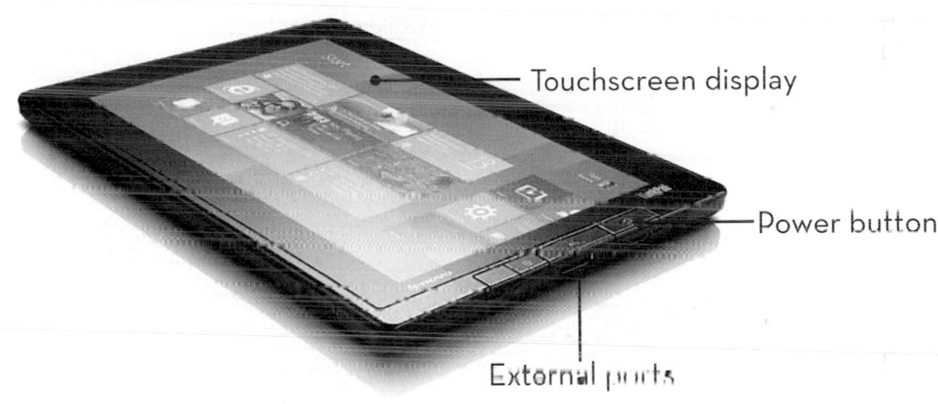

End

NOTE

Apple's iPad The most popular tablet PC today is the Apple iPad. The iPad, however, runs its own proprietary operating system (called iOS), and is therefore incompatible with the hundreds of millions of Windows-based computers currently in use. Microsoft expects several manufacturers to release Windows 8-compatible tablets in the near future—and Microsoft itself has announced its Surface tablet to compete directly with the iPad. ■

NOTE

Hybrid PCs Several manufacturers are planning to release Windows 8-compatible *hybrid PCs*. A hybrid PC is a blend of the ultrabook and tablet form factors; think of a hybrid PC as an ultrabook with a touchscreen, or a tablet with a keyboard. For example, Microsoft's Surface computer looks and works like a tablet, but has a keyboard built in to the unit's case. You can use the tablet's touchscreen display, or open the case and type on the keyboard, as you would a portable PC. ■

CONNECTORS

Every external component you plug into your computer has its own connector, and not all connectors are the same. This results in an assortment of jacks—called *ports* in the computer world. The USB port is probably the most common, used to connect all sorts of external peripherals, including printers, keyboards, mice, and disk drives.

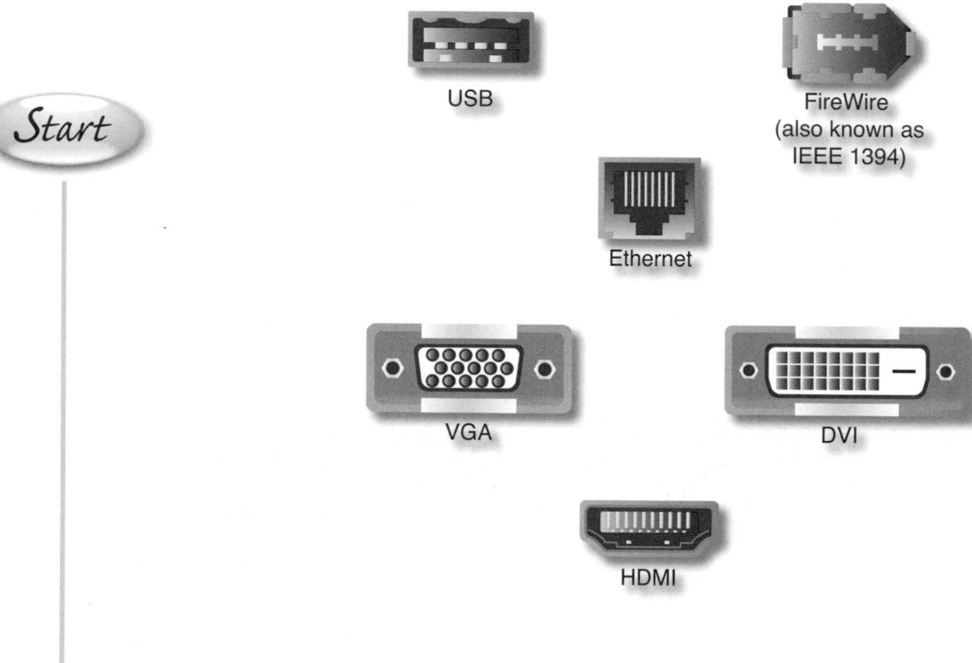

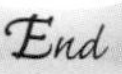

NOTE

Portable Devices Most portable devices that you connect to your computer, such as iPods and digital cameras, connect via USB—as do most larger peripherals. ■

TIP

HDMI If you want to connect your computer to your living TV, to watch videos over the Internet, look for a computer with an HDMI port. HDMI carries digital audio and high-definition video in a single cable. All of today's flat-screen TVs have multiple HDMI inputs. ■

HARD DISK DRIVES: LONG-TERM STORAGE

The hard disk drive inside your computer stores all your important data—up to 2 terabytes (TB) or more, depending on your computer. A hard disk consists of metallic platters that store data magnetically. Special read/write heads realign magnetic particles on the platters, much like a recording head records data onto magnetic recording tape.

Start

Hard disk light

End

TIP

Formatting the Drive Before data can be stored on a hard disk, the disk must first be *formatted*. When you format a hard disk, your computer prepares each track and sector of the disk to accept and store data magnetically. (Most new hard disks, such as the one in your new PC, come preformatted.) ■

NOTE

Ultrabook Storage Most ultrabook and tablet PCs use solid-state flash storage rather than hard disks. Solid-state storage is lighter and faster than hard disk storage—but more expensive and with a smaller storage capacity. ■

KEYBOARD

A computer keyboard looks and functions just like a typewriter keyboard, except that computer keyboards have a few more keys (for navigation and special program functions). When you press a key on your keyboard, it sends an electronic signal to your system unit that tells your machine what you want it to do.

Start

End

NOTE

Windows Key Many essential operations are triggered by use of the special Windows key on the computer keyboard. (For example, you open the Windows Start screen by pressing the **Windows** key.) This key is indicated by the Windows logo. ■

TIP

Wireless Keyboards If you want to cut the cord, consider a wireless keyboard or mouse. These wireless devices operate via radio frequency signals and let you work several feet away from your computer, with no cables necessary. ■

TOUCHPAD

On a desktop PC, you control your computer's onscreen pointer (called a *cursor*) with an external device called a *mouse*. On a notebook PC, you use a small *touchpad* instead. Move your finger around the touchpad to move the cursor, and then click the left and right buttons below the touchpad to initiate actions in your program.

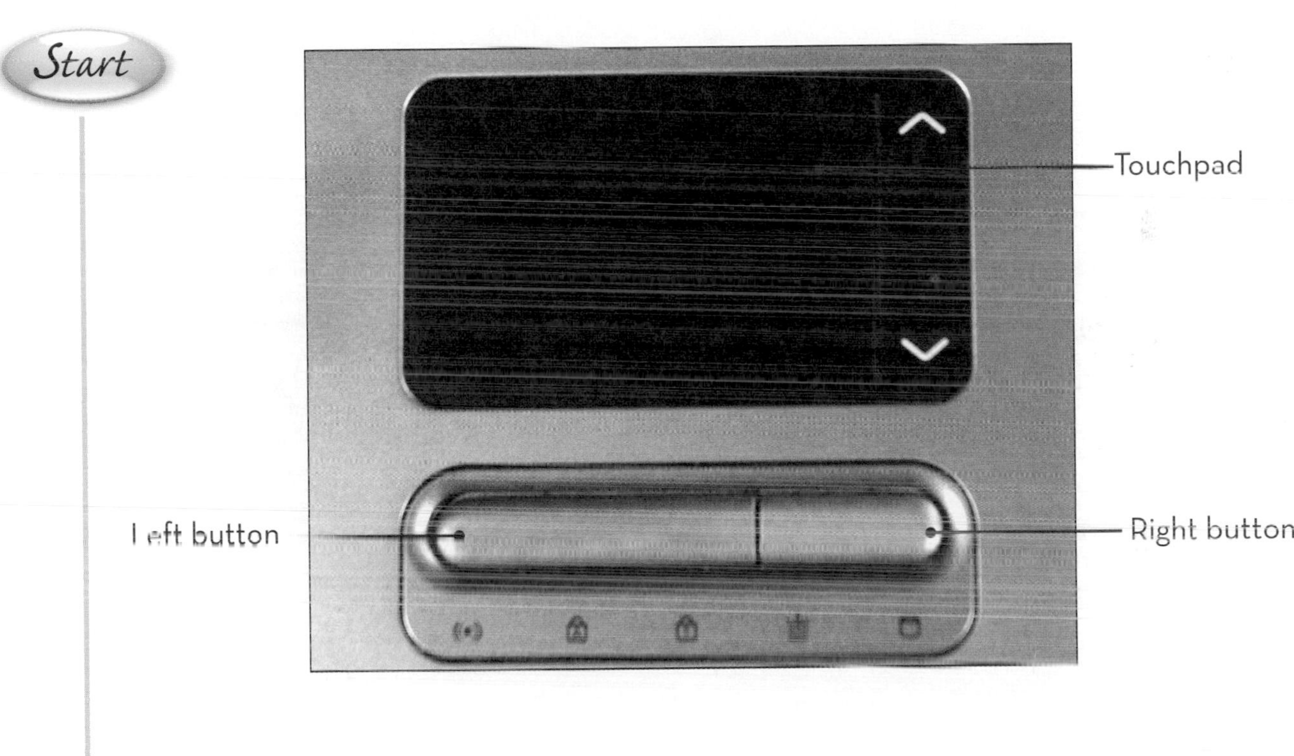

TIP

External Mice If you'd rather use a mouse than a touchpad, you can connect any external mouse to your notebook PC via the USB port. Some manufacturers sell so-called notebook mice that are smaller and more portable than normal models. ■

NOTE

Mouse Options Most external mice offer more control options than built-in touchpads. For example, some mice include a *scrollwheel* you can use to quickly scroll through a web page or word processing document. ■

MEMORY CARD READER

Many computers today include a set of memory card readers, usually grouped on the front or side of the unit. Memory cards store photos and movies recorded on digital cameras and camcorders. To read the contents of a memory card, simply insert the card into the proper slot of the memory card reader.

Start

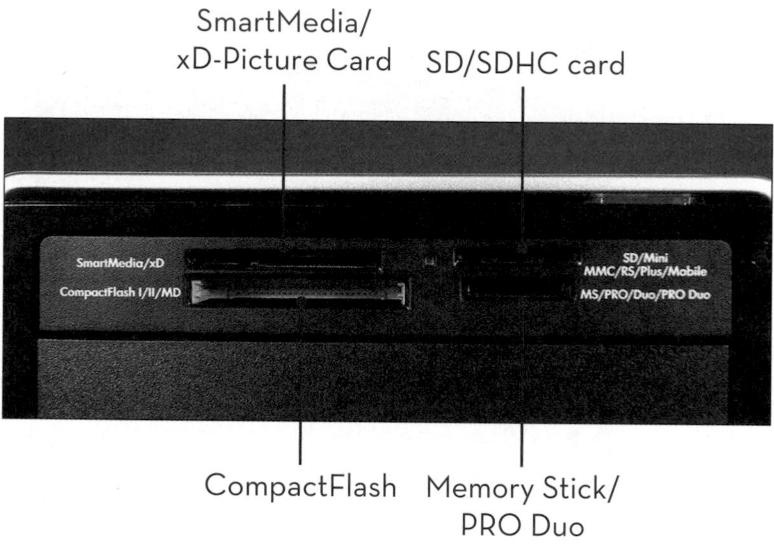

End

NOTE

Memory Card Formats Different portable devices use different types of memory cards—which is why your computer has so many memory card slots. The most popular memory cards today are the Secure Digital (SD), Secure Digital High Capacity (SDHC), CompactFlash (CF), Memory Stick, and xD-Picture Card formats. ■

CD AND DVD DRIVES

Computer or data CDs, DVDs, and Blu-ray discs look just like the compact discs and movies you play on your home audio/video system. Data is encoded in microscopic pits below the disc's surface and is read from the disc via a drive that uses a consumer-grade laser. The laser beam follows the tracks of the disc and reads the pits, translating the data into a form your computer can understand.

Start

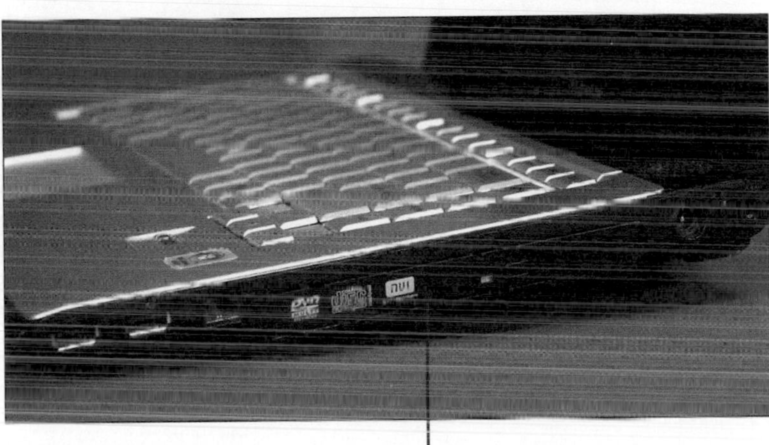

Disc tray

End

NOTE

CD, DVD, and Blu-ray Most new PCs come with combination CD/DVD drives that can read and write both CDs and DVDs. The advantage of a data DVD over a data CD is that a DVD disc can hold much more data—4.7 gigabytes (GB) on a DVD versus 700 megabytes (MB) for a typical CD. Blu-ray drives are even larger, with up to 33GB of storage. ■

NOTE

Music and Movies A computer CD drive can play back both data and commercial music CDs. A computer DVD drive can play back both data and commercial movie DVDs. ■

DISPLAY

Your computer electronically transmits words and pictures to the computer screen built in to your notebook, or to a separate video monitor on a desktop system. These images are created by a *video card* or chip installed inside the computer. Settings in Windows tell the video card or chip how to display the images you see on the screen.

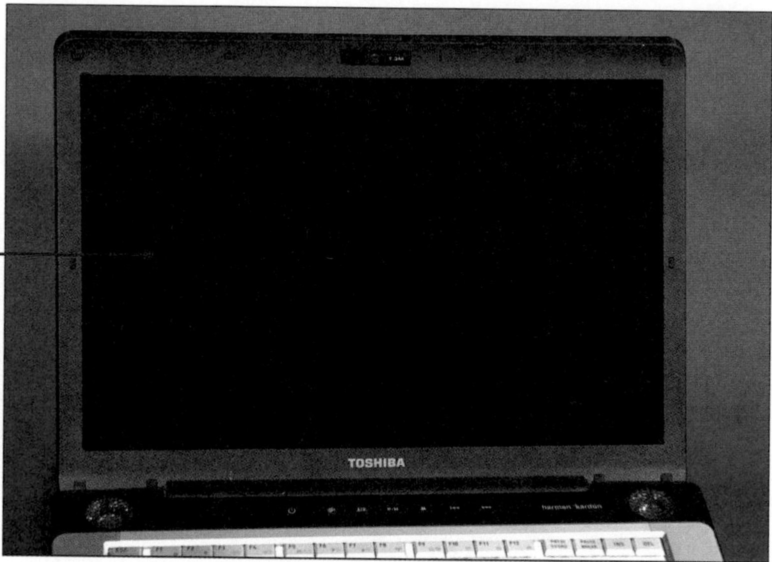

End

NOTE

CRT Versus LCD Many older computer systems used traditional cathode ray tube (CRT) monitors. Newer flat-screen monitors use an LCD display instead, which takes up less desk space. ■

NOTE

Touchscreen Displays Tablet PCs, along with some all-in-one and hybrid models, feature touchscreen displays. These displays function just like traditional displays but are also touch sensitive, so you can control your system by tapping and swiping the screen with your fingers. ■

PRINTERS

To create a hard copy of your work, you must add a printer to your system. The two most common types are *laser* printers and *inkjet* printers. Laser printers work much like copy machines, applying toner (powdered ink) to paper by using a small laser. Inkjet printers shoot jets of ink onto the paper's surface to create the printed image.

Start

End

TIP

Black and White Versus Color Black-and-white printers are faster than color printers and better if you're printing memos, letters, and other single-color documents. Color printers are essential if you want to print pictures taken with a digital camera. ■

NOTE

Multifunction Printers So-called multifunction printers offer copy, scan, and fax functionality, in addition to traditional printing. ■

SETTING UP YOUR PC

When you first get a new PC, you have to get everything set up, connected, and ready to run. If you're using a traditional desktop PC, setup involves plugging in all the external devices—your monitor, speakers, keyboard, and such. If you're using an all-in-one desktop, the task is a bit easier because the system unit, monitor, and speakers are all in a single unit; all you have to connect are the keyboard and mouse.

Setup is even easier if you have a notebook PC, as all the major components are built in to the computer itself. Same thing with a tablet; there's really nothing to connect.

If you're connecting a desktop PC, or even a notebook with external peripherals, start by positioning it so that you easily can access all the connections on the unit. You'll need to carefully run the cables from each of the external peripherals to the main unit, without stretching the cables or pulling anything out of place. And remember, when you plug in a cable, make sure that it's *firmly* connected—both to the computer and to the specific piece of hardware. Loose cables can cause all sorts of weird problems, so be sure they're plugged in really well.

THE WINDOWS 8 LOCK SCREEN

SETTING UP A TRADITIONAL DESKTOP PC

If you have a traditional desktop computer, you need to connect all the pieces and parts to your computer's system unit before powering it on. After connecting all your peripherals, you can then connect your system unit to a power source. Just make sure the power source is turned off before you connect!

1. Connect the mouse cable to a USB port on the back of your system unit.

2. Connect the keyboard cable to a USB port on the back of your system unit.

3. Connect the blue monitor cable to the blue monitor port on the back of your system unit; make sure the other end is connected to your video monitor.

NOTE

Mice and Keyboards Most newer mice and keyboards connect via USB. Some older models, however, connect to dedicated mouse and keyboard ports on your system unit. You should use whatever connection is appropriate. ■

TIP

Digital Connections Many newer computer monitors use a Digital Video Interface (DVI) or HDMI connection instead of the older Video Graphics Array (VGA) type of connection. If you have a choice, a DVI or HDMI connection delivers a crisper picture than the older analog connection . HDMI is preferred if you're connecting to a flat-screen TV or home theater system, because it transmits both video and audio. ■

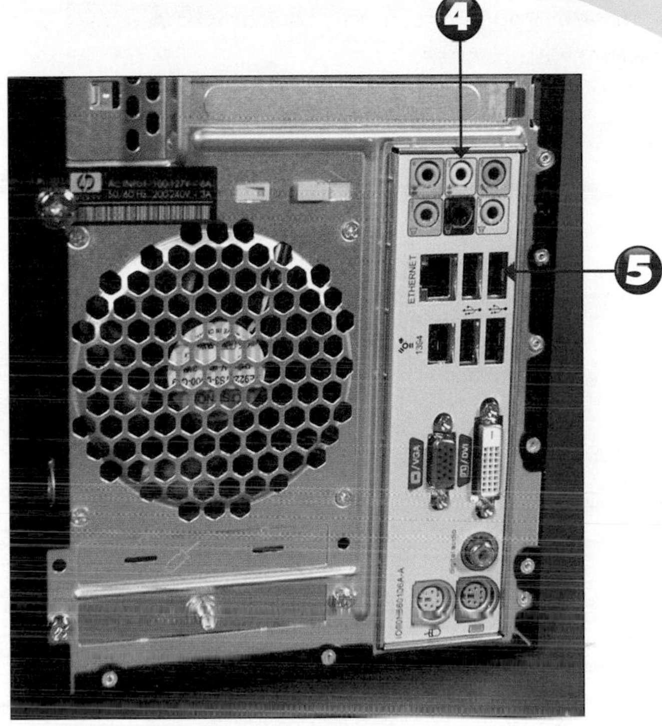

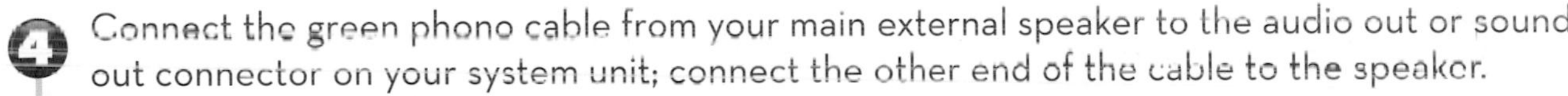

4. Connect the green phono cable from your main external speaker to the audio out or sound out connector on your system unit; connect the other end of the cable to the speaker.

5. Connect one end of your printer's USB cable to a USB port on the back of your system unit; connect the other end of the cable to your printer.

Continued

TIP

Your Connection Might Vary Not all speaker systems connect the same way. For example, many systems run the main cable to one speaker (such as the subwoofer) and then connect that speaker to the other speakers in the systems. Make sure you read your manufacturer's instructions before you connect your speaker system. ■

NOTE

Connect by Color Most PC manufacturers color-code the cables and connectors to make the connection even easier—just plug the blue cable into the blue connector and so on. ■

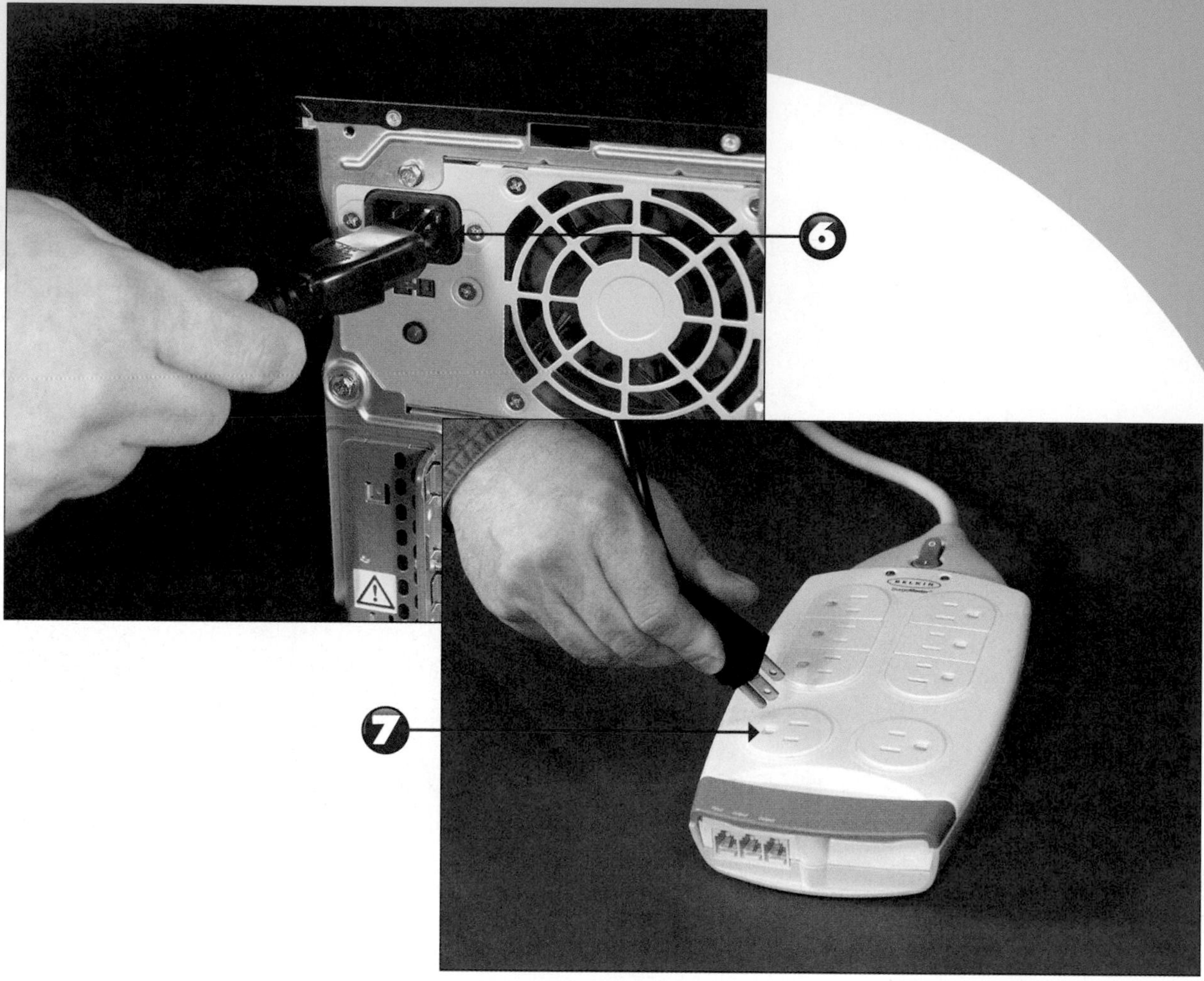

6 Connect one end of your computer's power cable to the power connector on the back of your system unit; connect the other end of the power cable to a power source.

7 Connect your printer, speakers, and other powered external peripherals to an appropriate power source.

End

TIP

Use a Surge Suppressor For extra protection, connect the power cable on your system unit to a surge suppressor rather than directly into an electrical outlet. This protects your PC from power-line surges that can damage its delicate internal parts. ■

CAUTION

Power Surges A power surge, whether from a lightning strike or an issue with your electric company, can do significant damage to a computer system. Too much power, even for just a second, can destroy your computer's microprocessor, memory chips, and other delicate components. In many instances, recovery from a power surge is either costly or impossible. ■

SETTING UP A NOTEBOOK PC

Setting up a notebook PC is much simpler than setting up a desktop model. That's because almost everything is built into the notebook—except external peripherals, such a printer. Just connect the printer, plug your notebook into a power outlet, and you're ready to go.

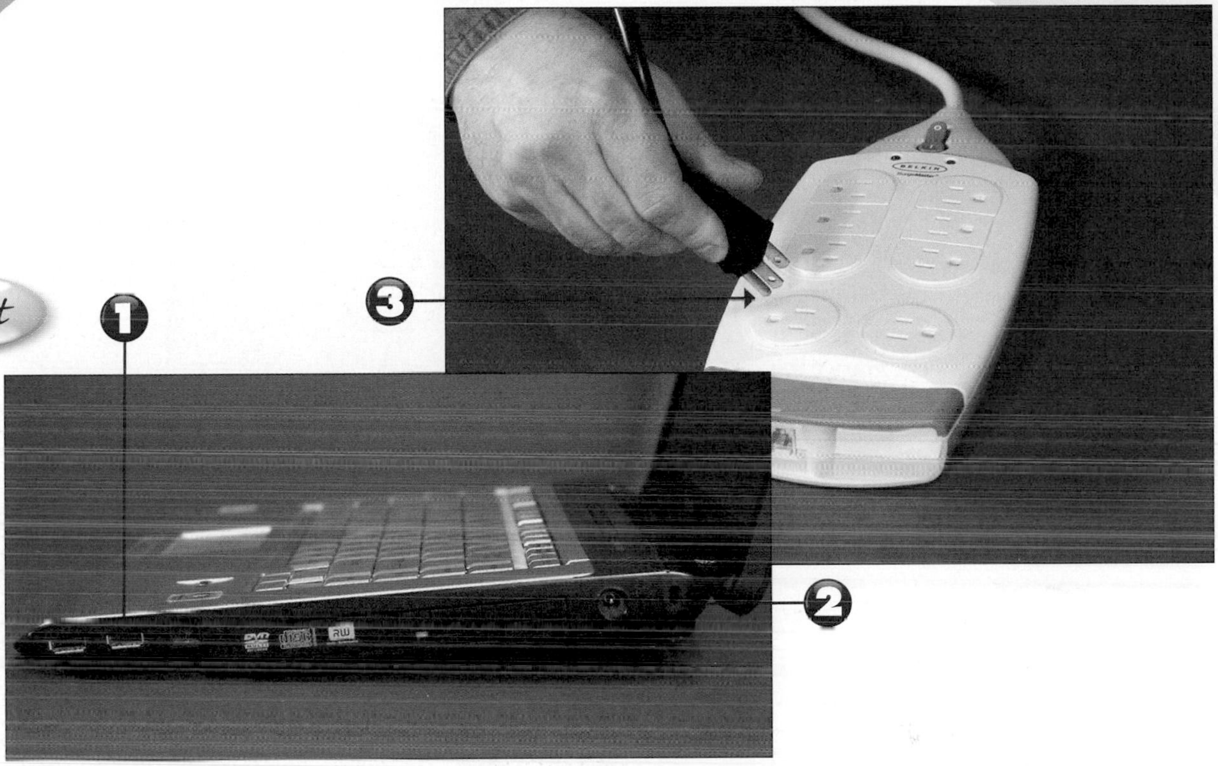

Start

1 Connect one end of your printer's USB cable to a USB port on your notebook; connect the other end of the cable to your printer.

2 Connect one end of your computer's power cable to the power connector on the side or back of your notebook; connect the other end of the power cable to a power source.

3 Connect your printer, speakers, and other powered external peripherals to an appropriate power source.

End

TIP

External Peripherals If you're using an external mouse or keyboard, connect it to a USB port on your notebook. If you're using an external monitor, connect it to your notebook's external video port.

SETTING UP AN ALL-IN-ONE DESKTOP PC

In an all-in-one desktop PC, the speakers and system unit are built in to the monitor, so you have fewer things to connect—just the mouse, keyboard, and any external peripherals, such as a printer. This makes for a much quicker and easier setup.

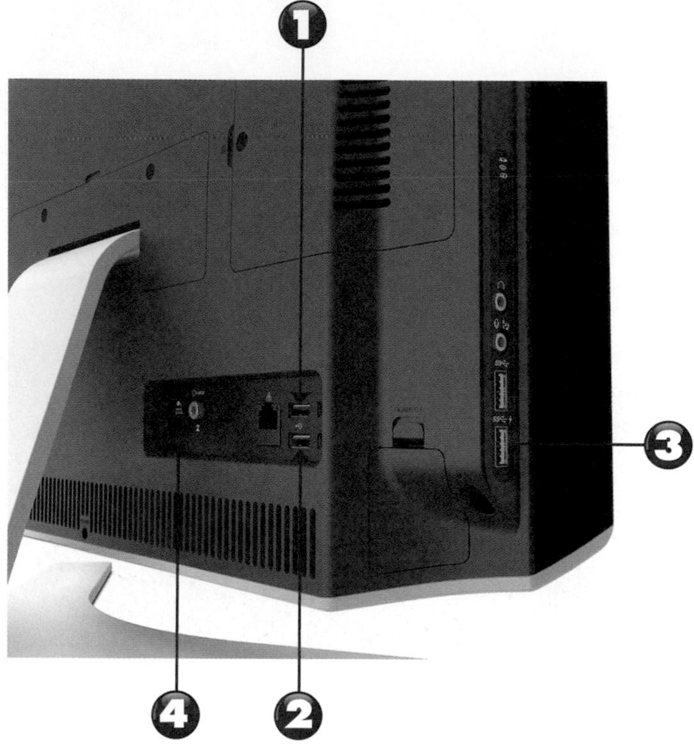

1. Connect the mouse cable to a USB port on the back of the monitor.
2. Connect the keyboard cable to a USB port on the back of the monitor.
3. Connect one end of your printer's USB cable to a USB port on the back or side of your system unit; connect the other end of the cable to your printer.
4. Connect one end of your computer's power cable to the power connector on the back of your system unit.

Continued

TIP

Back and Side Connections Most all-in-one PCs have USB ports on both the back and side of the unit. It doesn't matter which of these ports you use, although connecting to the back ports is usually a little cleaner looking—it does a better job of hiding the cables from view. ■

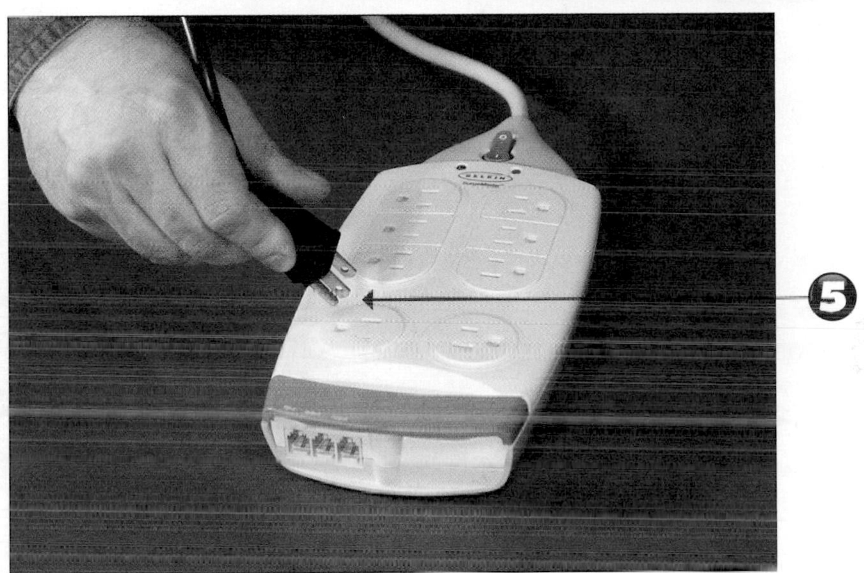

5 Connect the other end of the power cable to a power source, and then connect your printer and other powered external peripherals to the same power source.

End

NOTE

External Speakers Some all-in-one PCs feature a speaker output you can use to add additional external speakers, or perhaps a subwoofer (for better-sounding bass).

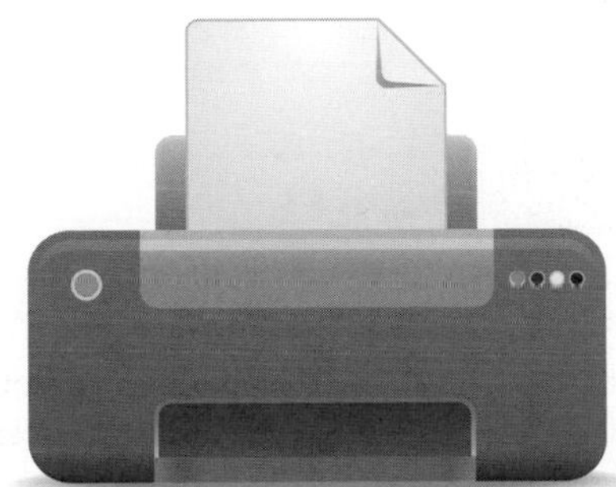

POWERING ON

Now that you have everything connected, sit back and rest for a minute. Next up is the big step—turning it all on!

1. Turn on your printer, monitor (for a traditional desktop PC), and other powered external peripherals.
2. If you're using a notebook PC, open the notebook's case so that you can see the screen and access the keyboard.
3. Press the power or "on" button on your computer.

End

NOTE

Booting Up Technical types call the procedure of starting up a computer *booting* or *booting up* the system. Restarting a system (turning it off and then back on) is called *rebooting*. ■

CAUTION

Go in Order Your computer is the *last* thing you turn on in your system. That's because when it powers on, it has to sense all the other components—which it can do only if the other components are plugged in and turned on. ■

LOGGING ON TO WINDOWS

Windows launches automatically as your computer starts up. After you get past the Windows Lock screen, you're taken directly to the Windows Start screen, and your system is ready to run.

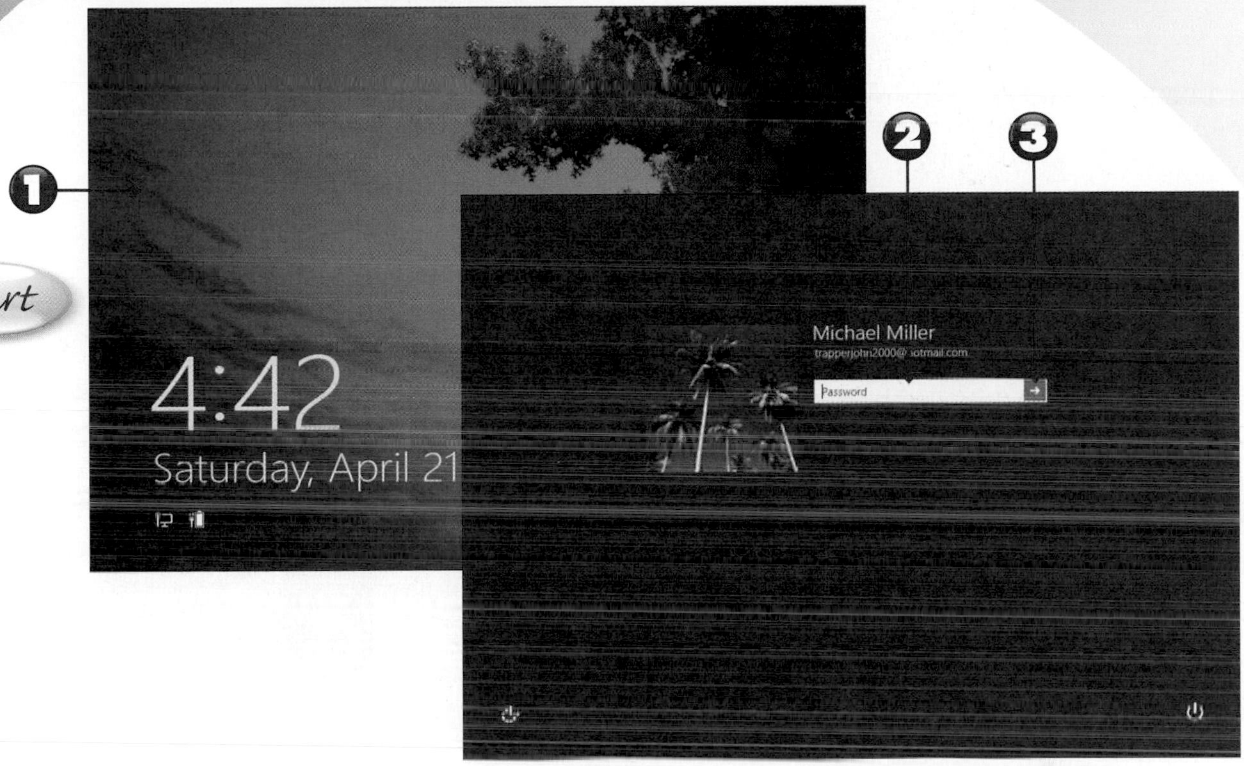

Start

1. When you start your PC, you see the Windows Lock screen; tap any key to display your logon information.

2. Enter your password (if necessary).

3. Press the **Enter** key on your keyboard or click the right arrow.

End

TIP

Starting Up for the First Time The first time you start your new PC, you're asked to perform some basic setup operations, including activating and registering Windows and configuring your system for your personal use. ■

NOTE

Lock Screen Information The Windows Lock screen displays a photographic background with some useful information on top—including the date and time, power status, and WiFi (connectivity) status. ■

SHUTTING DOWN

When you want to turn off your computer, you do it through Windows. In fact, you don't want to turn off your computer any other way—you *always* want to turn things off through the official Windows procedure.

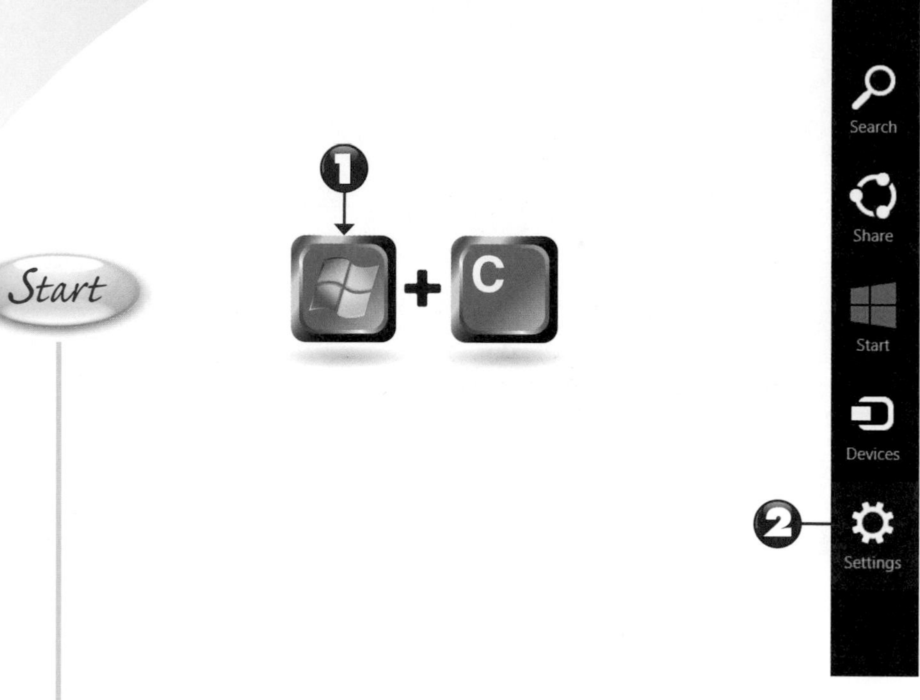

1. Press **Windows+C** to display the charms bar.
2. From the charms bar, click or tap **Settings**.

CAUTION

Always Use Windows to Shut Down Do *not* turn off a desktop computer without shutting down Windows. You could lose data and settings that are temporarily stored in your system's memory. (Using the power button to shut down a notebook computer, however, is typically okay; this just activates Windows' Sleep mode.) ■

TIP

Sleep Mode If you're using a notebook PC, Windows includes a special Sleep mode that keeps your computer running in a low-power state, ready to start up quickly when open the lid or turn it on again. In most instances, you enter Sleep mode by closing the lid of your notebook. ■

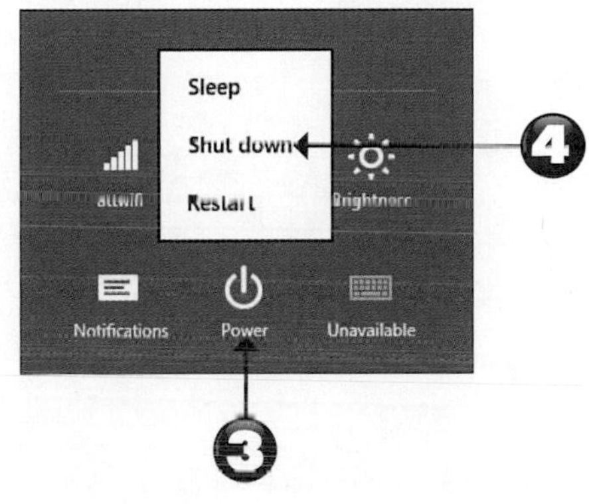

3 When the Settings panel appears, click or tap **Power** to display the pop-up menu.

4 Click or tap **Shut Down**.

End

TIP

Shutting Off the Rest of Your System If you have a desktop PC, you'll then want to manually turn off your monitor, printer, and other peripherals.

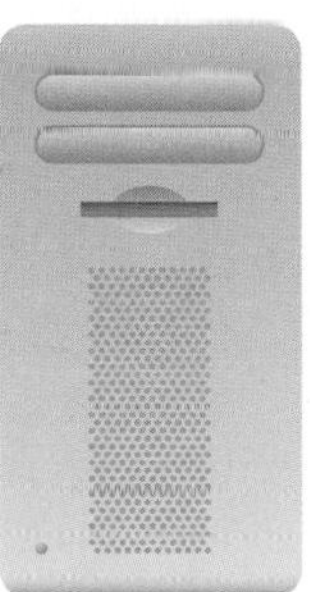

ADDING NEW DEVICES TO YOUR SYSTEM

At some point in the future, you might want to expand your system—by adding a second printer, a scanner, a webcam, or something equally new and exciting. Most of these peripherals are external and connect to your PC using a USB cable. When you're connecting a USB device, not only do you not have to open your PC's case, but you also don't even have to turn off your system when you add the new device.

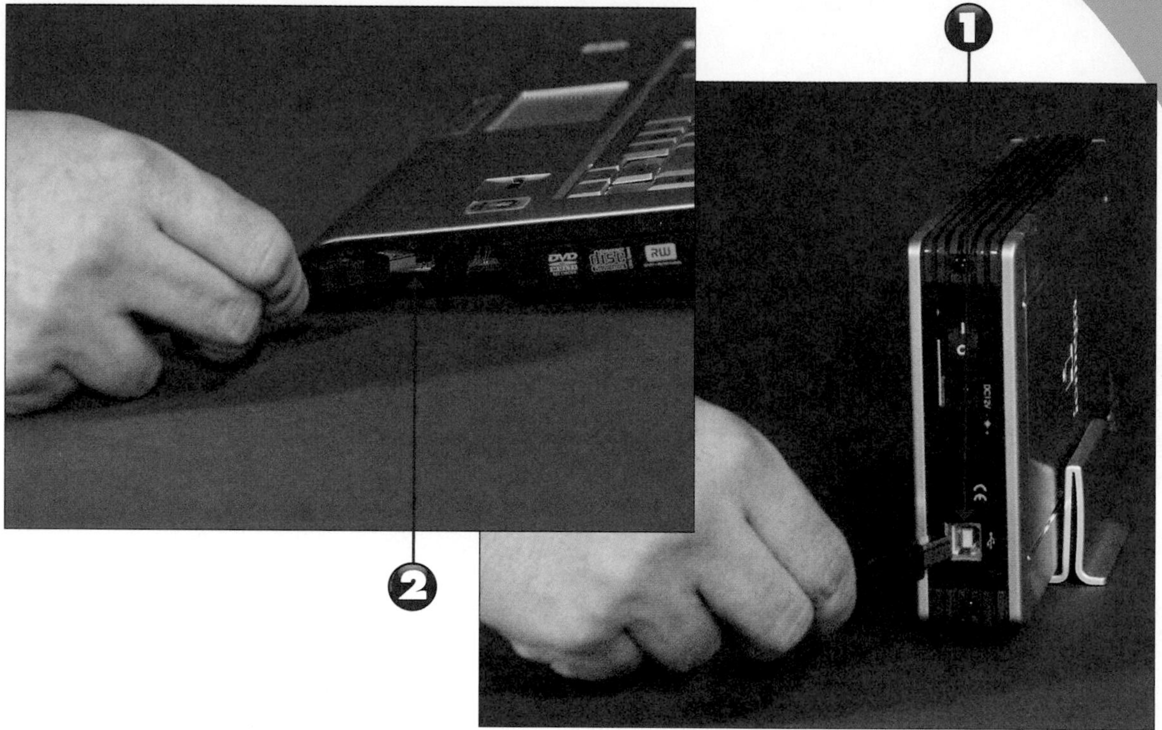

Start

1. Connect one end of the USB cable to your new device.
2. Connect the other end of the cable to a free USB port on your PC.

Continued

TIP

Follow Directions As easy as most USB devices are to connect, you should still read the device's instructions and follow the manufacturer's directions for installation. ■

NOTE

FireWire Connections Some external devices, such as fast hard drives and high-end video camcorders, connect via FireWire, a slightly faster connection than USB. Connecting a device via FireWire is similar to connecting it via USB; just connect to your PC's FireWire port. ■

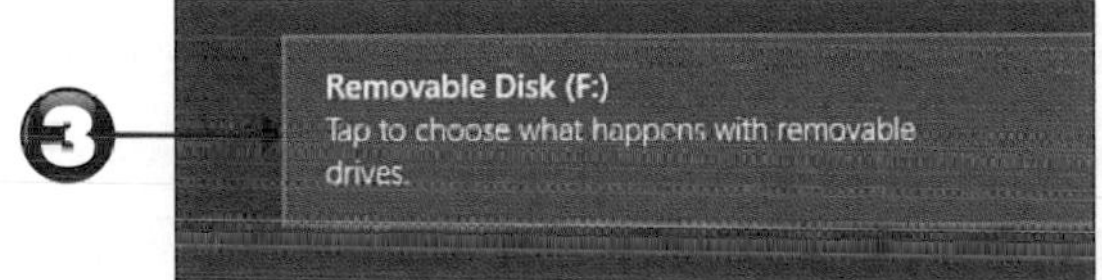

3 Depending on the device, Windows may ask you what action you want to perform. Click the notification message to make a choice.

End

CAUTION

Install Before Connecting? Windows normally detects a new USB device when you connect it and then installs the driver automatically. However, some devices require you to install the driver *before* connecting the device. Make sure you read the directions before you install any new device!

TIP

USB Hubs If you connect too many USB devices, you can run out of USB connectors on your PC. If that happens, buy an add-on USB hub, which lets you plug multiple USB peripherals into a single USB port.

SETTING UP A WIRELESS HOME NETWORK

When you want to connect two or more computers in your home, you need to create a computer *network*. A network is all about sharing; you can use your network to share files, peripherals (such as printers), and even a broadband Internet connection.

There are two ways to connect your network: wired or wireless. A wireless network is more convenient (no wires to run), which makes it the network of choice for most home users. Wireless networks use radio frequency (RF) signals to connect one computer to another. The most popular type of wireless network uses the WiFi standard and can transfer data at 11Mbps (802.11b), 54Mbps (802.11g), or 248Mbps (802.11n).

HOW A WIRELESS NETWORK WORKS

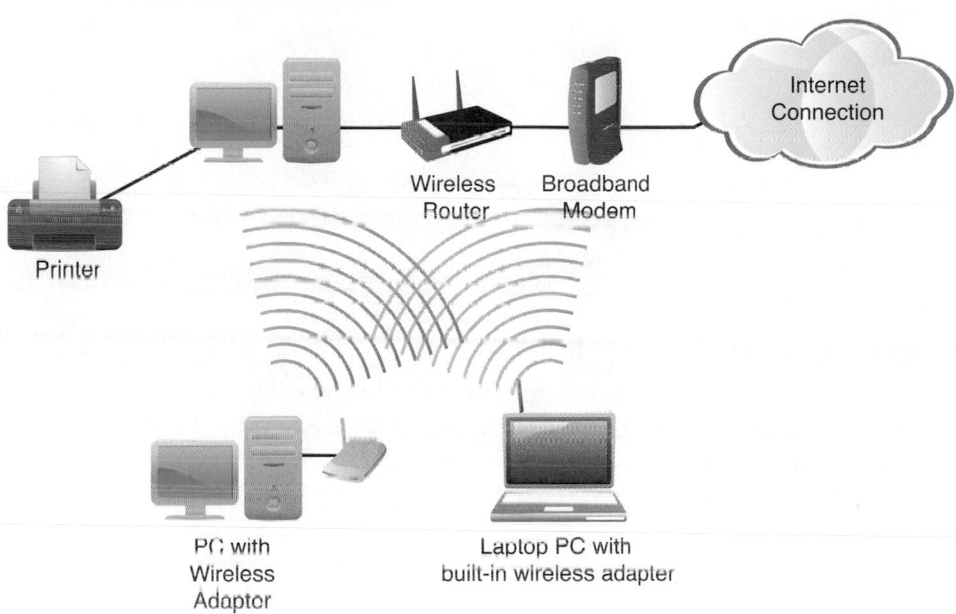

SETTING UP YOUR NETWORK'S MAIN PC

The focal point of your wireless network is the *wireless router*. The wireless PCs on your network must be connected to or contain *wireless adapters*, which function as mini-transmitters/receivers to communicate with the base station.

Start

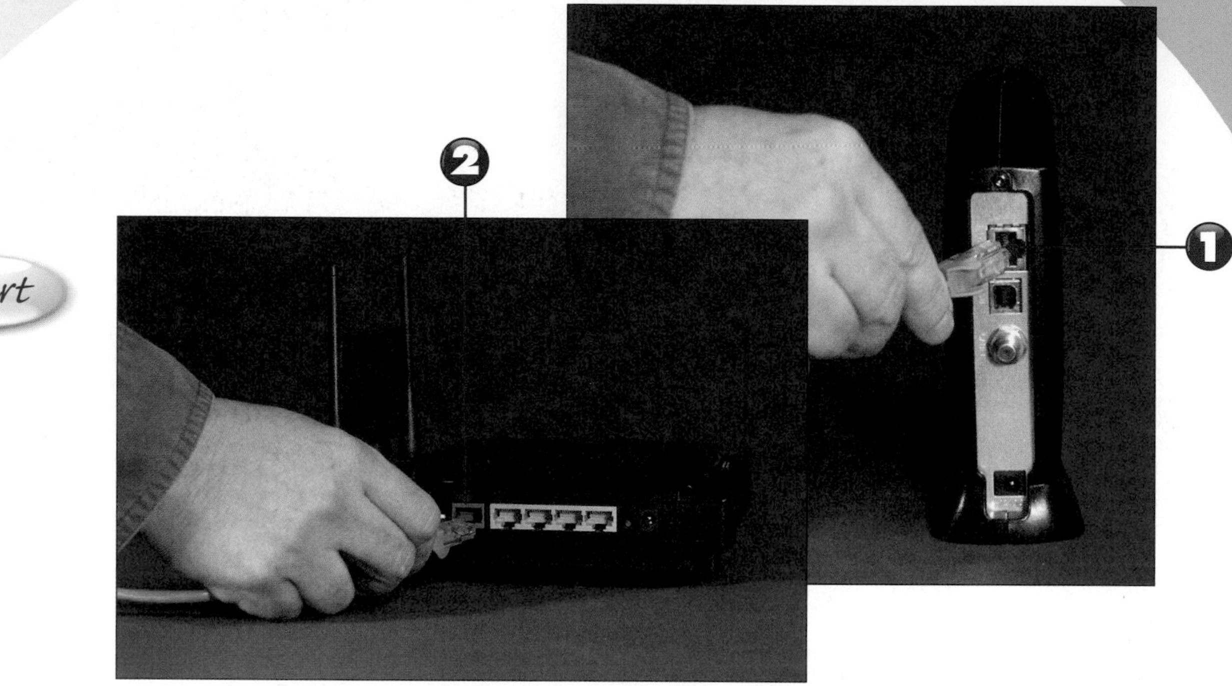

1. Connect one end of an Ethernet cable to the Ethernet port on your broadband modem.
2. Connect the other end of the Ethernet cable to one of the Ethernet ports on your wireless router—preferably the one labeled Internet or WAN.

Continued

TIP

Internet Port Most routers have a dedicated input for your broadband modem, sometimes labeled Internet—although the modem can be connected to any open Ethernet input on the router. ■

NOTE

Broadband Routers Some Internet service providers (ISPs) provide broadband modems that include built-in wireless routers. If you have one of these, you don't need to buy a separate router. ■

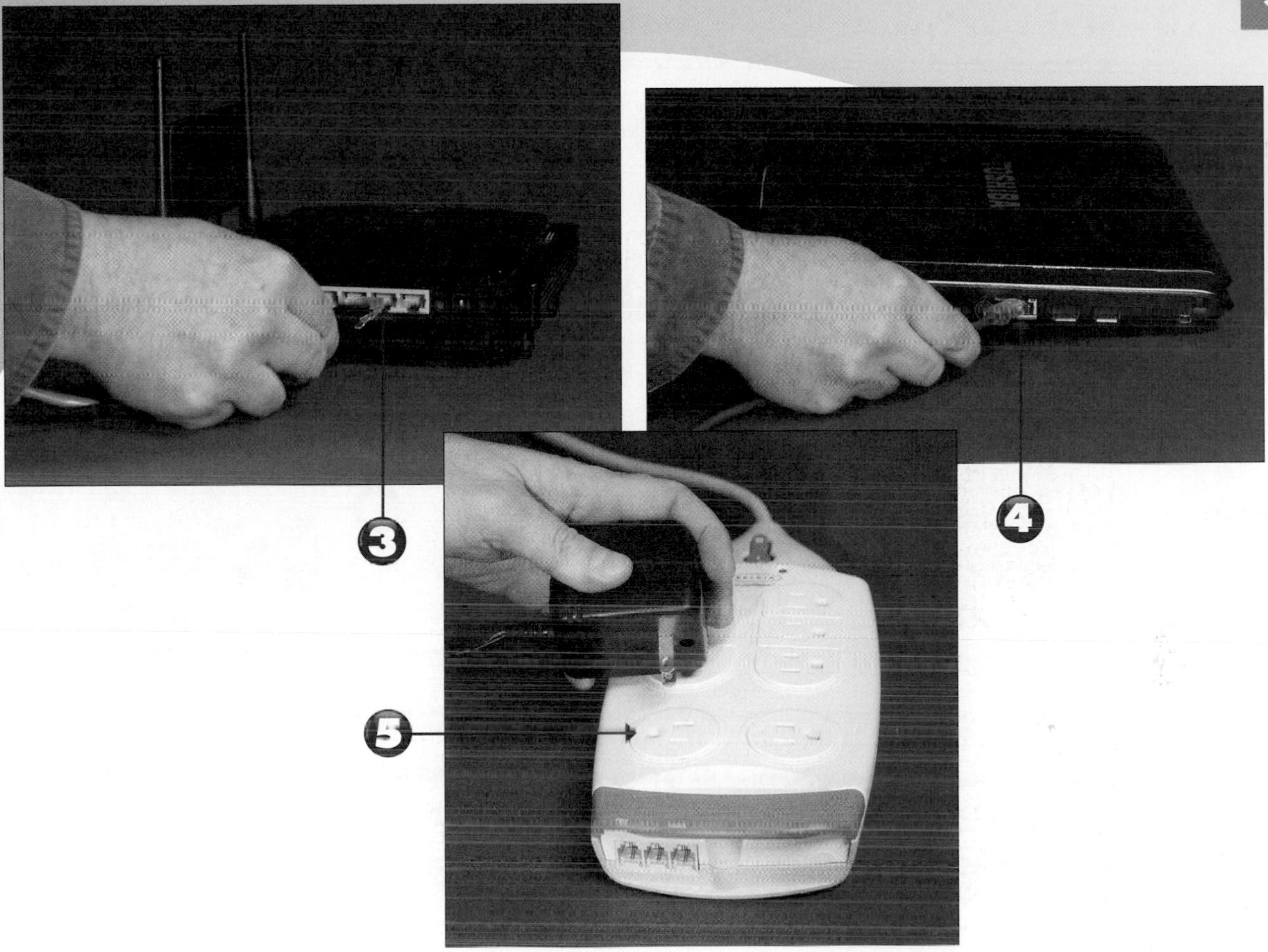

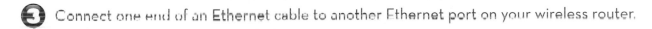

3 Connect one end of an Ethernet cable to another Ethernet port on your wireless router.

4 Connect the other end of the Ethernet cable to the Ethernet port on your main PC.

5 Connect your wireless router to a power source and, if it has a power switch, turn it on. Your computer should now be connected to the router and your network.

End

TIP

Router Configuration Some wireless routers require you to connect your main computer via Ethernet for initial configuration, as described here. Other routers will connect wirelessly to your main computer for the entire configuration process. When in doubt, follow the instructions that came with your router. ■

TIP

Wireless Security To keep outsiders from tapping into your wireless network, you need to enable wireless security for the network. This adds an encrypted key to your wireless connection; no other computer can access your network without this key. ■

CONNECTING ADDITIONAL PCs TO YOUR WIRELESS NETWORK

Each additional PC on your network requires its own wireless adapter. Most notebook and tablet PCs come with a wireless adapter built in. Some desktop PCs come with built-in wireless adapters, whereas others may require you to connect an external adapter.

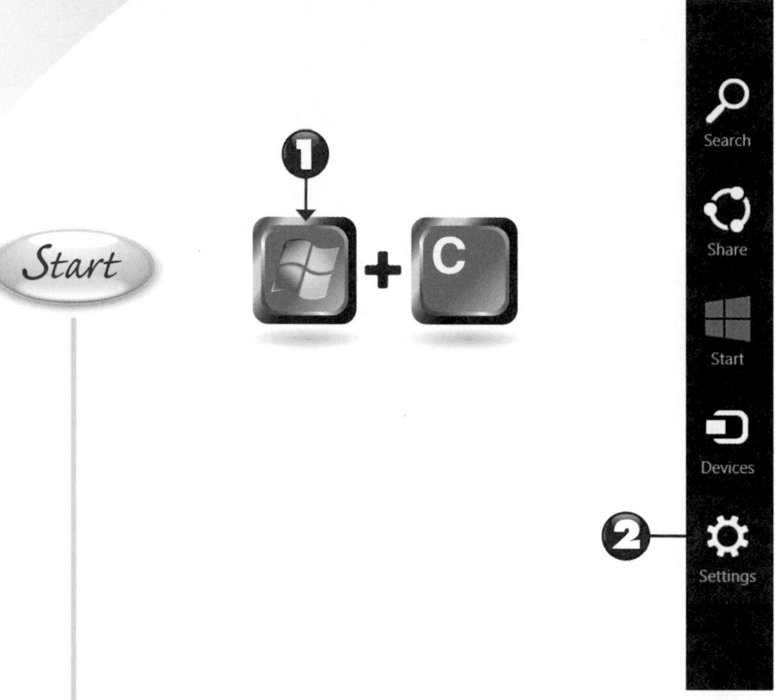

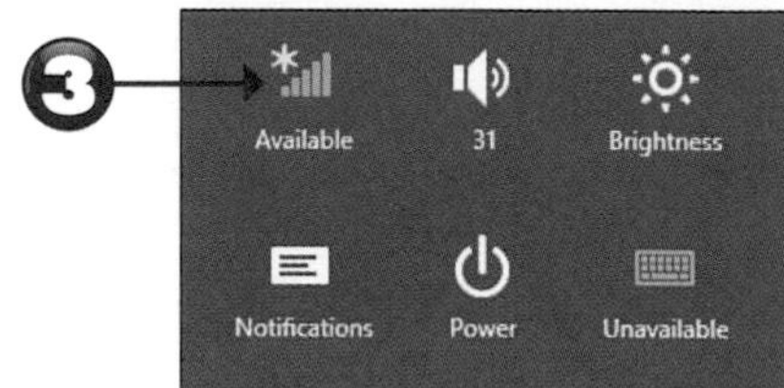

1. From within Windows, press **Windows+C** to display the charms bar.
2. Click or tap **Settings** to display the Settings panel.
3. Click or tap the **WiFi** ("Available") icon to display a list of available networks.

Continued

TIP

Wireless Adapters A wireless adapter can be a small external device that connects to the PC via USB, an expansion card that installs inside your system unit, or a PC card that inserts into a laptop PC's card slot. ■

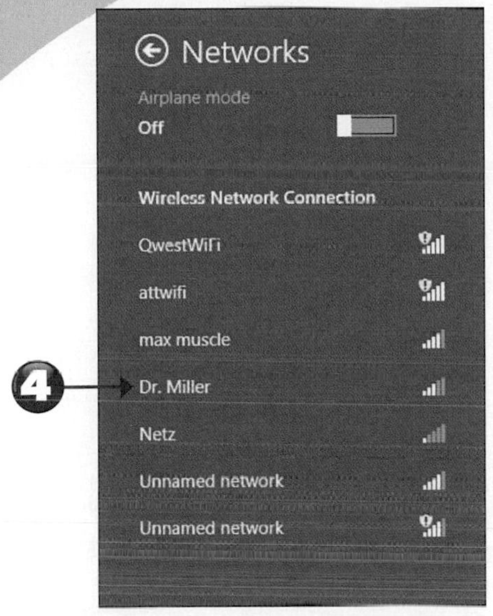

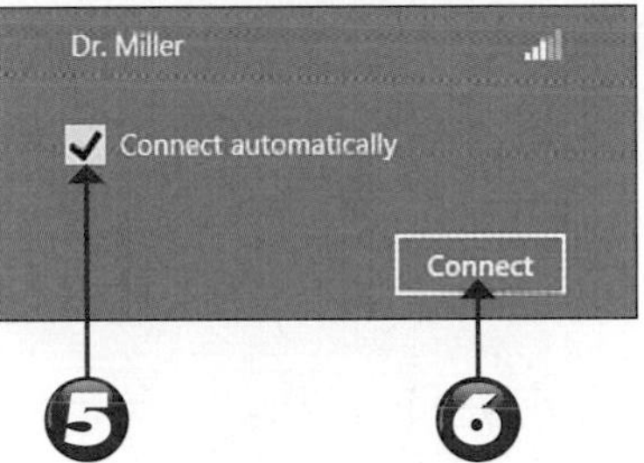

4. Click or tap your wireless network; this expands the panel for this network.
5. To connect automatically to this network in the future, check the **Connect Automatically** box.
6. Click **Connect**.

Continued

TIP

Connect Automatically When you're connecting to your home network, it's a good idea to enable the Connect Automatically feature. This lets your computer connect to your network without additional prompting or interaction on your part. ■

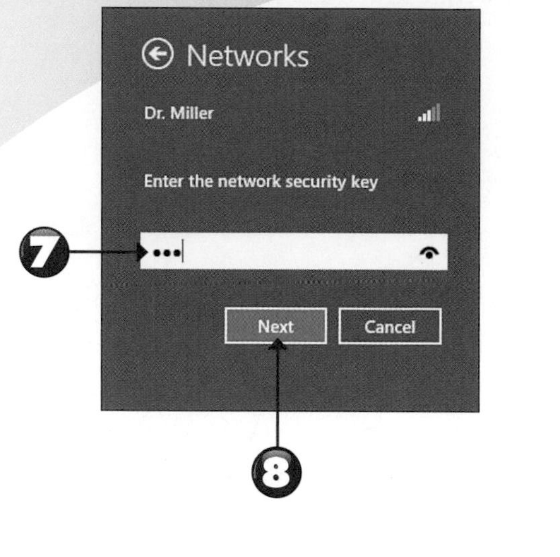

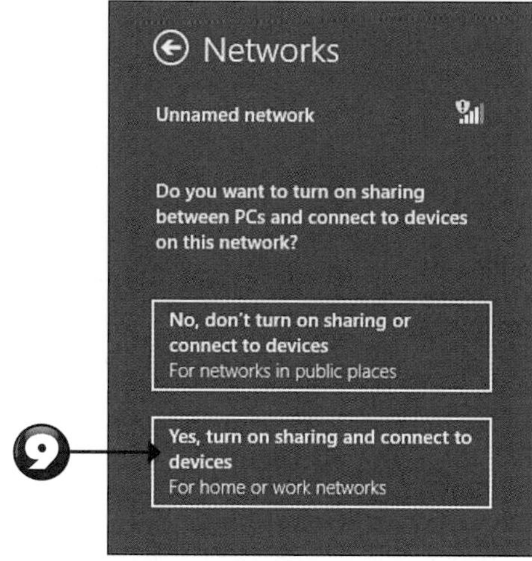

7 When prompted, enter the password (called the *network security key*) for your network.

8 Click **Next.**

9 When the next screen appears, click **Yes**, **Turn On Sharing and Connect to Other Devices on the Network**.

End

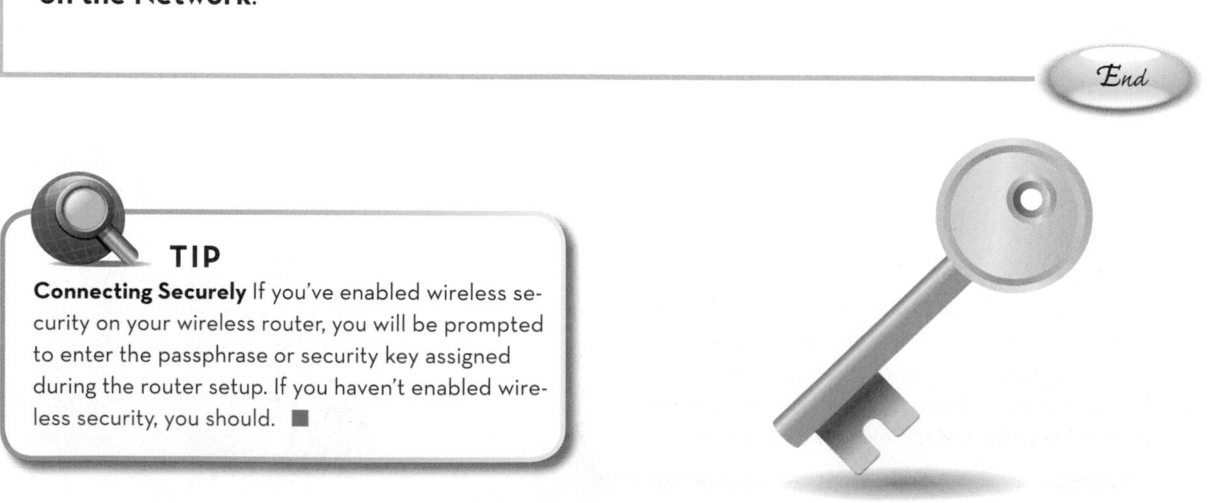

TIP

Connecting Securely If you've enabled wireless security on your wireless router, you will be prompted to enter the passphrase or security key assigned during the router setup. If you haven't enabled wireless security, you should. ■

ADDING YOUR COMPUTER TO A HOMEGROUP

The easiest way to connect multiple home computers is to create a HomeGroup for your network. A HomeGroup is kind of a simplified network that lets automatically share files and printers between connected computers.

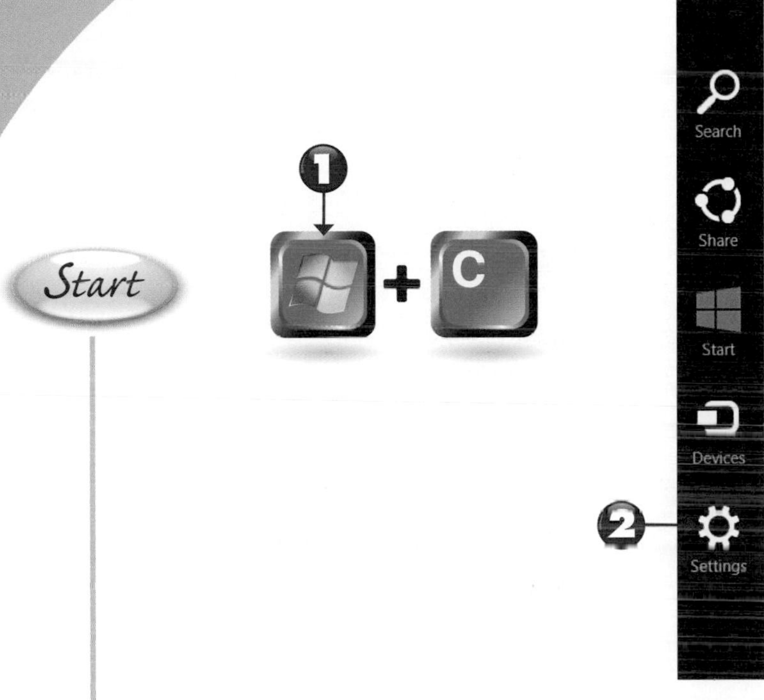

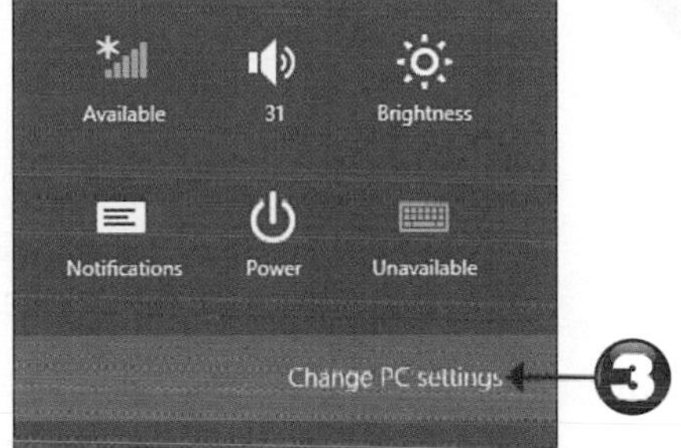

1. Press **Windows+C** to display the charms bar.
2. Click or tap **Settings** to display the Settings pane.
3. Click or tap **Change PC Settings** to display the PC Settings screen.

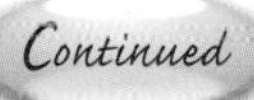

NOTE

Windows 7 and 8 Only PCs running Windows 7 or Windows 8 can be part of a HomeGroup. PCs running older versions of Windows do not have the HomeGroup feature and must use the normal Windows networking functions instead. ■

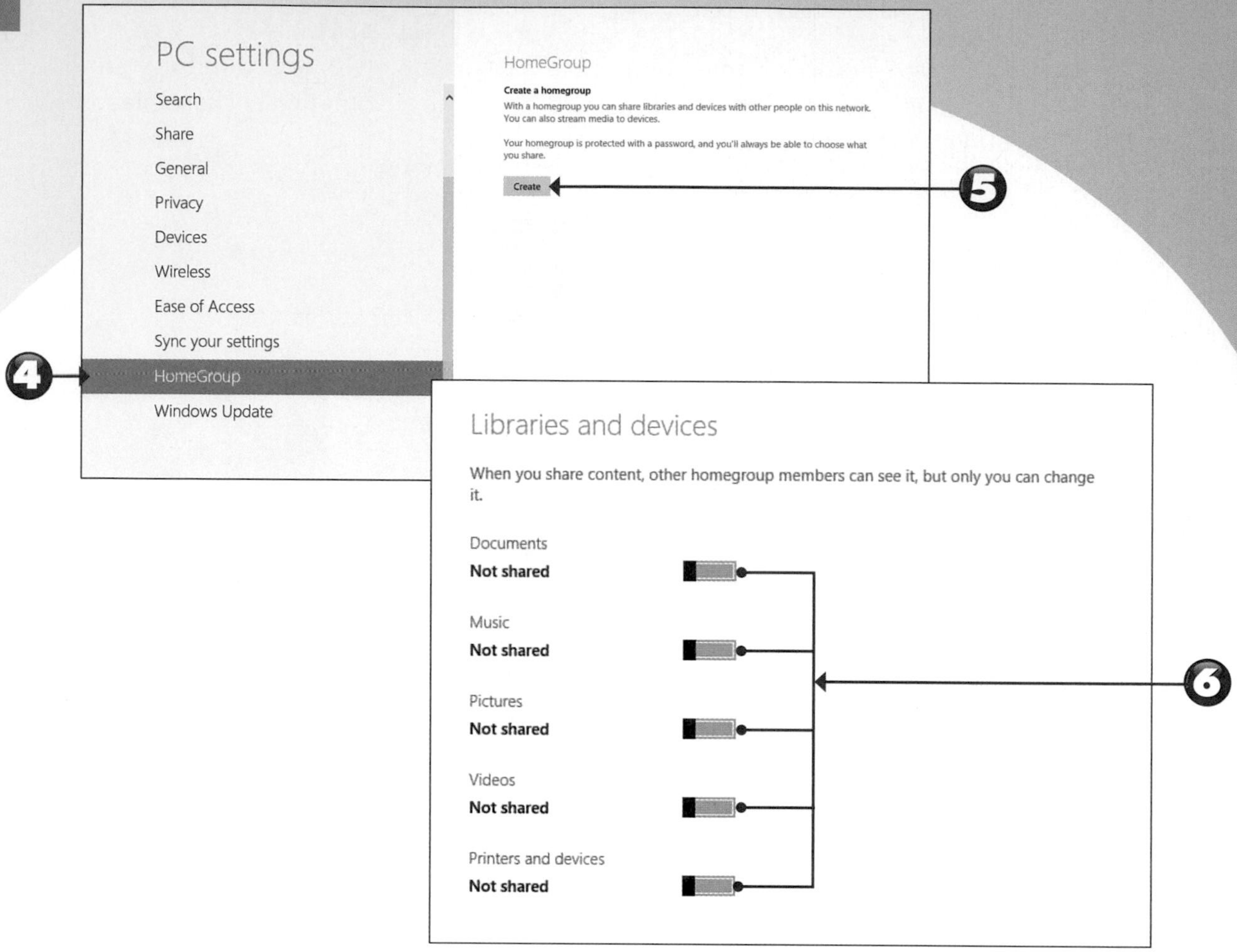

PC settings

Search
Share
General
Privacy
Devices
Wireless
Ease of Access
Sync your settings
HomeGroup
Windows Update

HomeGroup

Create a homegroup

With a homegroup you can share libraries and devices with other people on this network. You can also stream media to devices.

Your homegroup is protected with a password, and you'll always be able to choose what you share.

Create

Libraries and devices

When you share content, other homegroup members can see it, but only you can change it.

Documents
Not shared

Music
Not shared

Pictures
Not shared

Videos
Not shared

Printers and devices
Not shared

4. Scroll down the list on the left and select **HomeGroup**.

5. Click or tap the **Create** button.

6. When the Library and Devices section appears, click or tap "on" those items you want to share with other computers.

Continued

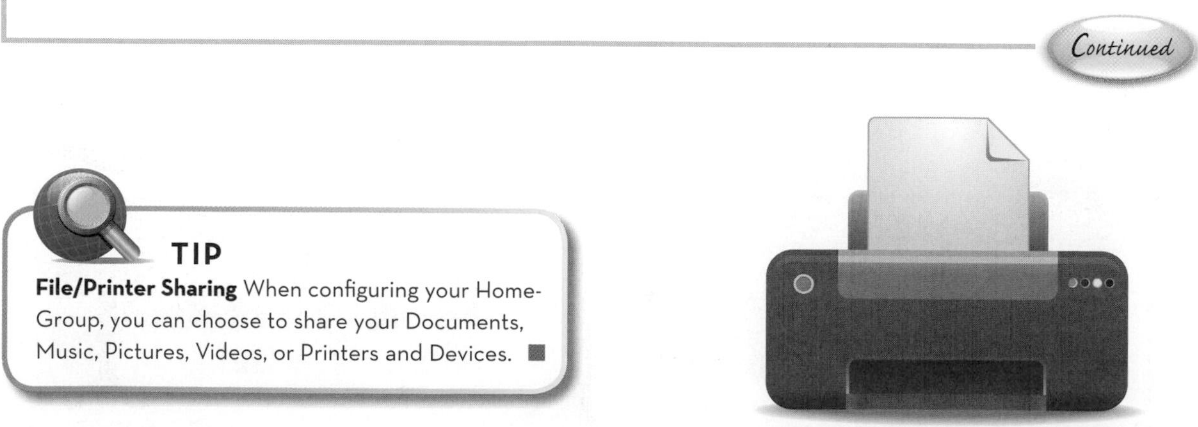

TIP

File/Printer Sharing When configuring your HomeGroup, you can choose to share your Documents, Music, Pictures, Videos, or Printers and Devices. ■

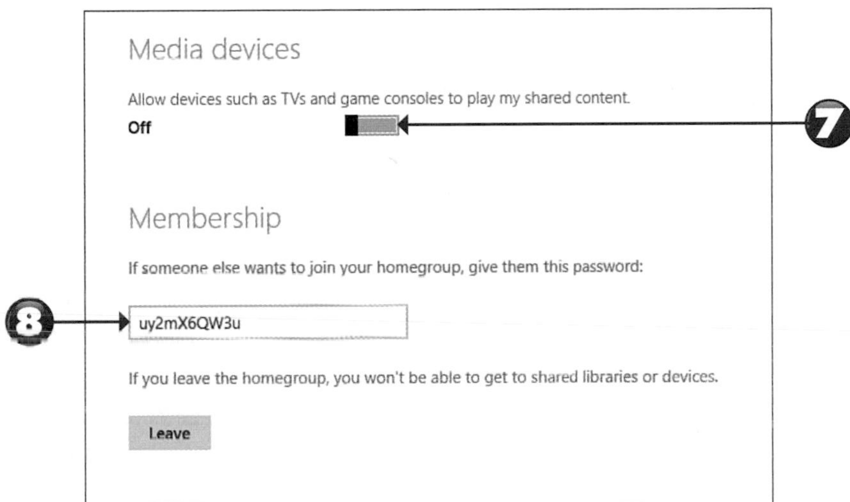

If you want noncomputers, such as network connected TVs or videogame consoles, to be able to access the content on this computer, go to the Media Devices section and click or tap "on" this option.

Go to the Membership section and write down the password. You'll need to provide this to users of other computers on your network who want to join your HomeGroup.

End

NOTE

Configuring Other PCs You'll need to configure each computer on your network to join your new HomeGroup. Enter the original HomeGroup password as instructed. ■

ACCESSING OTHER COMPUTERS IN YOUR HOMEGROUP

Once you have your home network set up, you can access shared content stored on other computers on your network. How you do so depends on whether the other computer is part of your HomeGroup. We'll look at HomeGroup access first.

Start

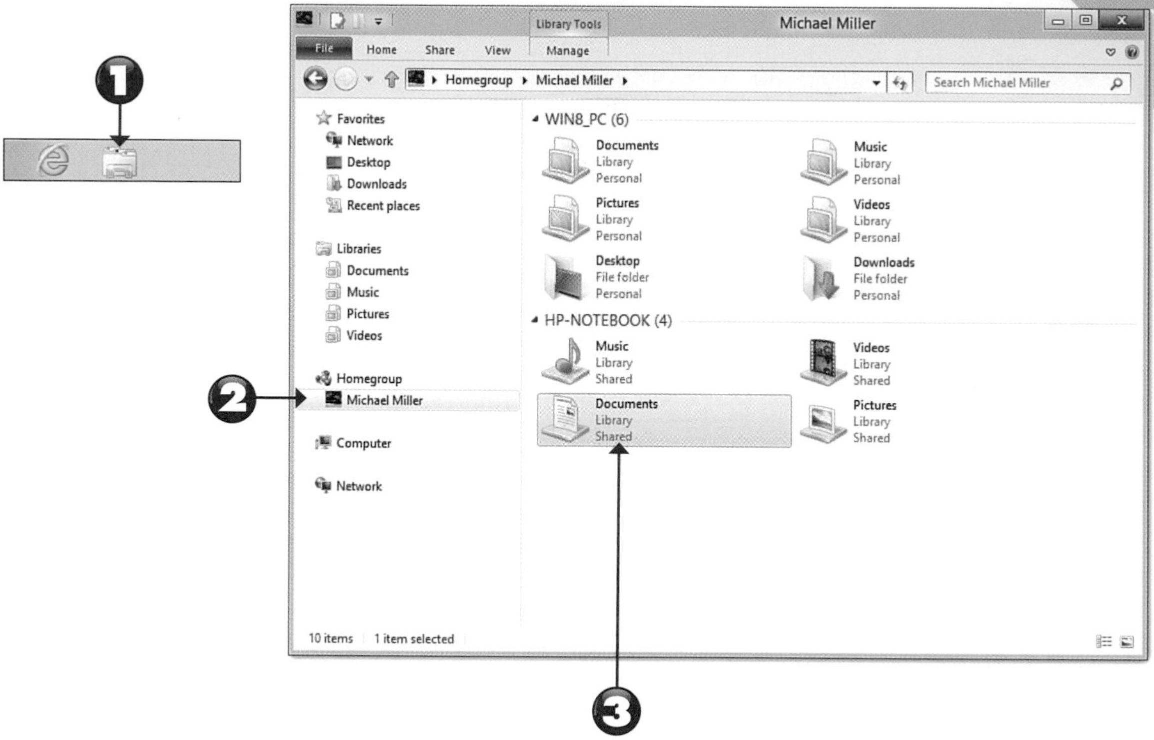

1. From the Windows desktop, click the **File Explorer** icon on the taskbar.
2. When File Explorer opens, go to the HomeGroup section of the navigation pane and click the HomeGroup you want to access.
3. Windows now displays the shared libraries on all the computers in your HomeGroup. Double-click a library to access that particular content.

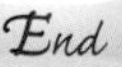

ACCESSING OTHER COMPUTERS ON YOUR NETWORK

A computer doesn't have to be connected to your HomeGroup for you to access its content. Windows lets you access any computer connected to your home network—although you can only share content the computer's owner has configured as sharable.

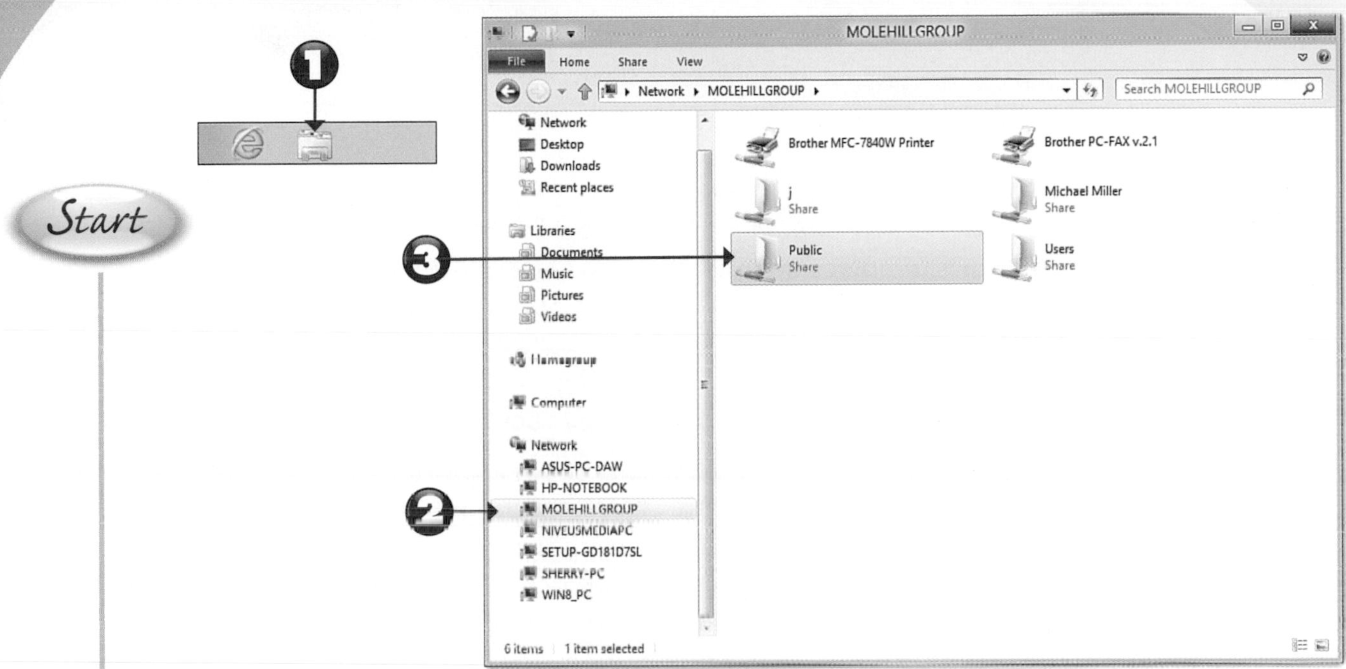

1. From the Windows desktop, click the **File Explorer** icon on the taskbar.
2. When File Explorer opens, go to the Network section of the navigation pane and click the computer you want to access.
3. Windows now displays the shared folders on the selected computer. Double-click a folder to view that folder's content.

End

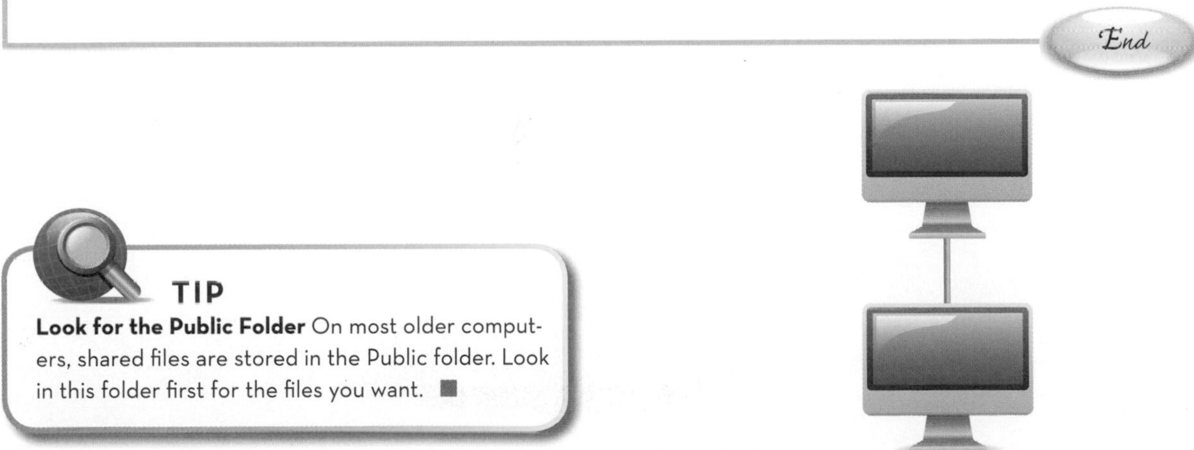

TIP

Look for the Public Folder On most older computers, shared files are stored in the Public folder. Look in this folder first for the files you want. ■

USING MICROSOFT WINDOWS 8

Microsoft Windows is a piece of software called an *operating system*. An operating system does what its name implies—it operates your computer system, working in the background every time you turn on your PC. The *desktop* that fills your screen is part of Windows, as is the taskbar at the bottom of the screen and the big menu that pops up when you click the Start button.

If you've used a previous version of Windows, or seen someone else using Windows, you might think that Windows 8 looks a lot different—and you'd be right. Windows 8 is the latest version of the Microsoft Windows operating system, with a completely different *user interface* than previous versions. The Windows 8 user interface (also known as the *Metro* interface) differs considerably from the traditional Windows desktop.

In Windows 8, everything starts on the Start screen (the home screen full of tiles for different apps) and goes from there. The traditional desktop is still there (as an app, and used to run older software programs), but you'll be spending most of your time with the new Windows 8 interface, and its tiled Start screen.

EXPLORING THE WINDOWS 8 START SCREEN

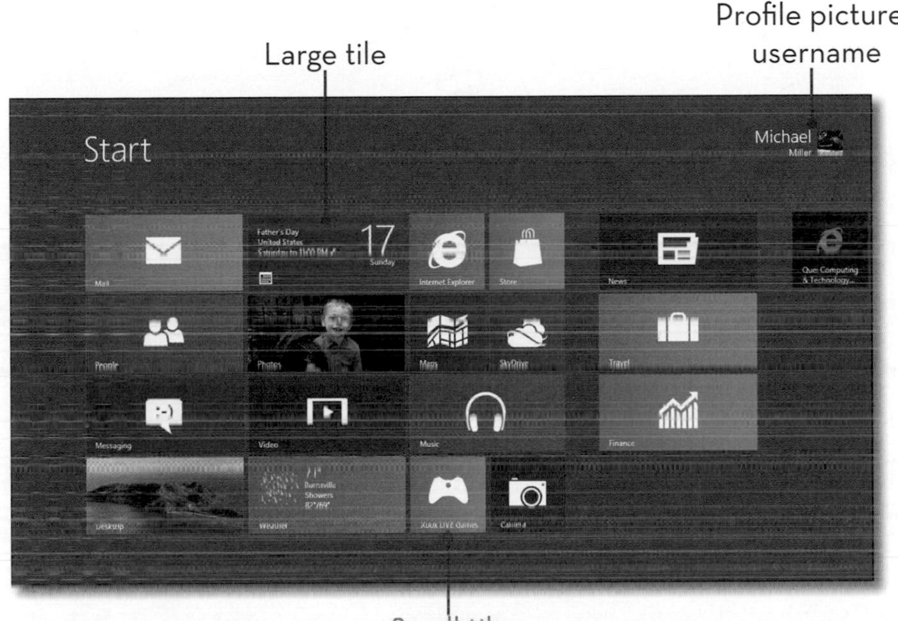

USING WINDOWS WITH A MOUSE

To use Windows efficiently, you must master a few simple operations, all of which you perform with your mouse. Most mouse operations include *pointing* and *clicking*. Normal clicking uses the left mouse button; however, some operations require that you click the right mouse button instead.

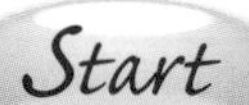

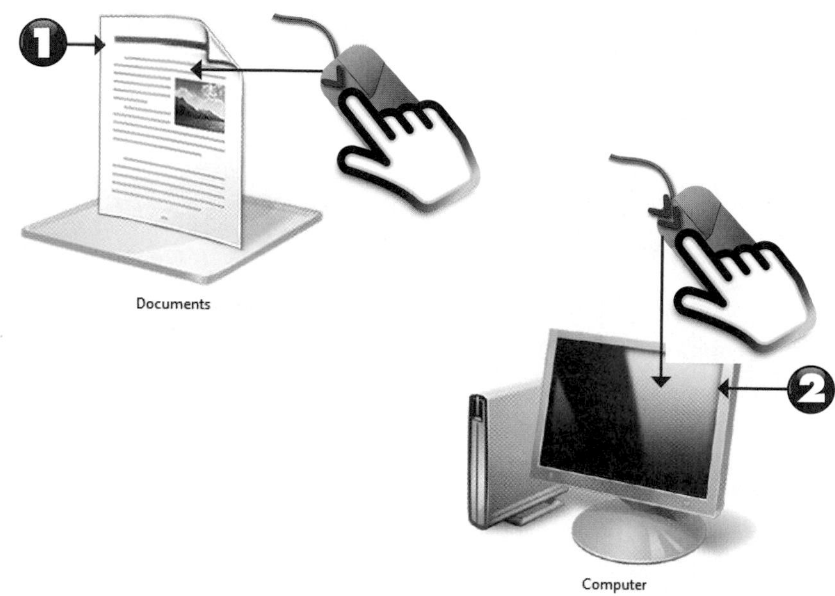

1. To single-click, position the cursor over the onscreen item and click the left mouse or touchpad button.
2. To double-click, position the cursor over the onscreen item and click the left mouse or touchpad button twice in rapid succession.

Continued

TIP

Click to Select Pointing and clicking is an effective way to select icons, menu items, directories, and files. ■

NOTE

Mouse Over Another common mouse operation is called the *mouse over*, or *hovering*, where you hold the cursor over an onscreen item without pressing either of the mouse buttons. For example, when you mouse over an icon or menu item, Windows displays a *ToolTip* that tells you a little about the selected item. ■

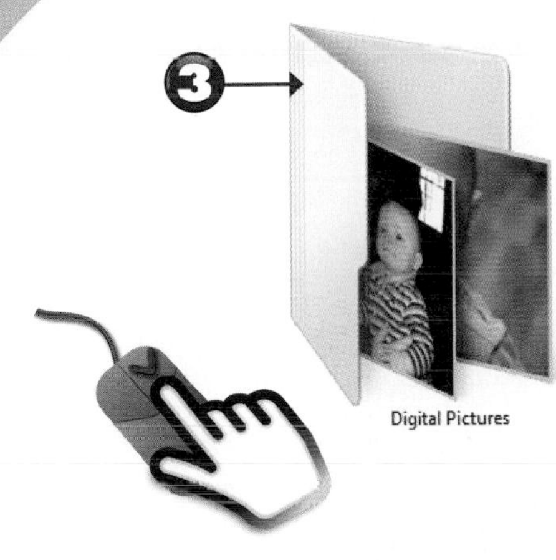

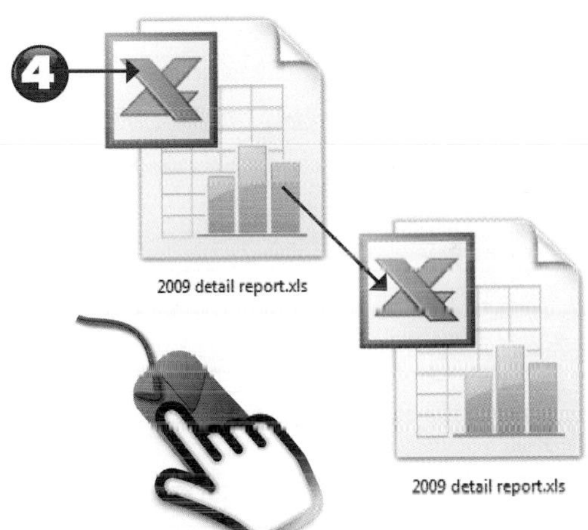

3. To right-click, position the cursor over the onscreen item, and then click the *right* mouse button.

4. To drag and drop an item from one location to another, position the cursor over the item, click and hold the left mouse button, drag the item to a new position, and then release the mouse button.

End

TIP

Pop-Up Menus Many items in Windows feature a context-sensitive pop-up menu. You access this menu or list by right-clicking the item. (When in doubt, right-click the item and see what pops up!) ■

TIP

Moving Files You can use dragging and dropping to move files from one folder to another or to delete files by dragging them onto the Recycle Bin icon. ■

USING WINDOWS WITH A TOUCHSCREEN DISPLAY

If you're using Windows on a computer or tablet with a touchscreen display, you'll be using your fingers instead of a mouse to do what you need to do. To that end, it's important to learn some essential touchscreen operations.

1. Tapping is the equivalent of clicking with your mouse. Tap an item with the tip of your finger and release.
2. To display additional information about any item, press and hold the item with the tip of your finger.

Continued

TIP

Right-Click = Press and Hold Pressing and holding is the touchscreen equivalent of right-clicking an item with your mouse. ■

NOTE

Metro Interface Throughout Windows 8's development, the new tiled interface was referred to as the Metro interface. Microsoft subsequently quit calling it Metro, although a lot of developers and evaluators still use that term. ■

3 To scroll down a page or perform many edge-centric operations, swipe the screen in the desired direction with your finger.

4 You can also scroll up, down, or sideways by touching and dragging the page with one or more fingers.

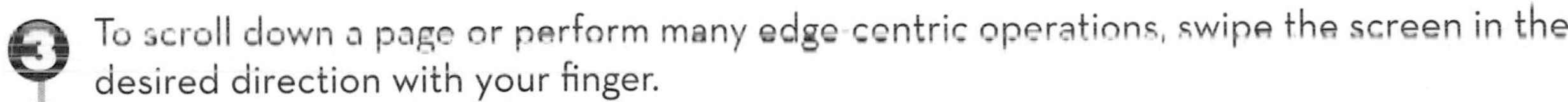

TIP

Zooming In To zoom into a given screen (that is, to make a selection larger), use two fingers to touch two points on the item, and then move your fingers apart.

TIP

Zooming Out To zoom out of a given screen (that is, to make a selection smaller and see more of the surrounding page), use two fingers—or your thumb and first finger—to touch two points on the item, and then pinch your fingers in toward each other.

NAVIGATING THE WINDOWS START SCREEN

Everything in Windows 8 revolves around the Start screen. The Start screen is where you start out and where you launch new apps and software programs.

Start

1 Press the **Windows** button on your keyboard at any time to return to the Start screen.

2 Click or tap your name to sign out of Windows, lock the screen, or change your account picture.

3 Click or tap any tile to launch the associated program.

End

TIP

Launching with the Keyboard To launch a program using your keyboard, use the keyboard's arrow keys to move to the appropriate tile, and then press the **Enter** key. ■

TIP

Returning to the Start Screen You can also return to the Start screen by displaying the charms bar and clicking **Start**. You can also move your mouse to the lower-left corner of any screen to display a thumbnail of the Start screen; click this thumbnail to return to the Start screen. ■

SCROLLING THROUGH THE START SCREEN

There are probably more tiles on your Start screen than can be displayed on a single screen of your computer display. To view all your Start tiles, scroll the screen left or right.

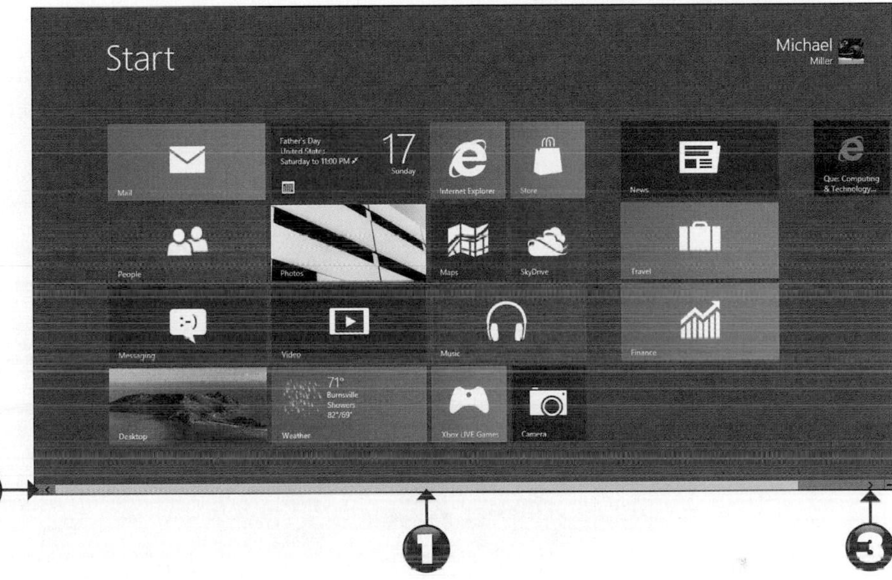

1. Mouse over or tap the bottom of the screen to display the horizontal scrollbar, and then click and drag the scrollbar to scroll left or right.
2. Click the left scroll arrow to scroll left.
3. Click the right scroll arrow to scroll right.

End

TIP

Scrolling with the Keyboard or Touchscreen To scroll through the Start screen with your keyboard, press the **PageDown** key to scroll right or **PageUp** key to scroll left. You can also scroll one tile at a time by pressing the **left arrow** or **right arrow** keys. To scroll on a touchscreen display, swipe the screen with your finger right to left to scroll right, or left to right to scroll left. ■

TIP

Zoom You can shrink the Start screen to see all the available tiles by clicking the **Zoom** button in the lower-right corner of the Start screen (when the scrollbar is visible). ■

USING THE CHARMS BAR

Windows 8 has more functions up its sleeve, although they're not obvious during normal use. These are a series of system functions, called *charms*, which are accessed from a charms bar that appears on the right side of the screen.

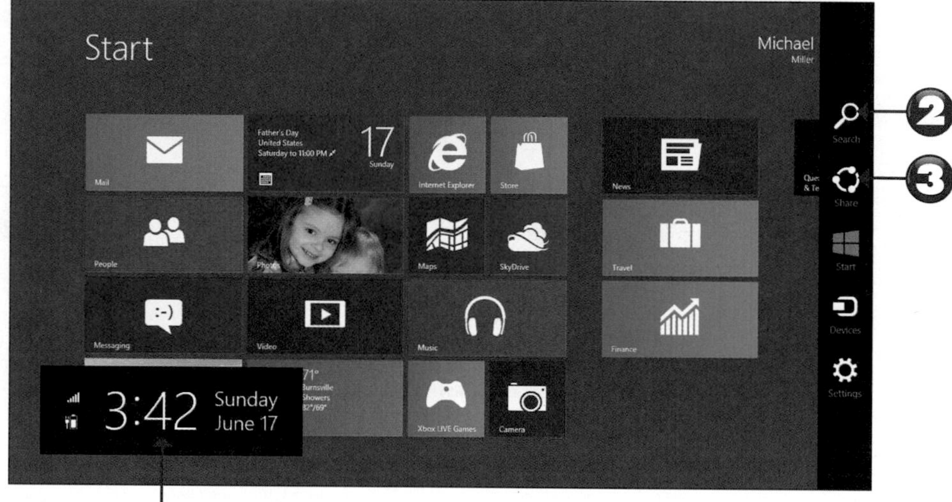

Information panel

1. To display the charms bar, press **Windows+C** on your keyboard.

2. Click the **Search** icon to search your computer for apps and documents.

3. Click the **Share** icon to share the content of the current app with other apps.

Continued

TIP

Charms Bar with the Mouse To display the charms bar with your mouse, move the mouse cursor to either the top-right or bottom-right corner of the screen. ■

TIP

Charms Bar on a Touchscreen To display the charms bar on a touchscreen display, swipe your finger from right edge of the screen to the left. ■

4. Click the **Start** icon to return to the Start screen from any other location in Windows.

5. Click the **Devices** icon to configure the settings of any external devices connected to your PC.

6. Click the **Settings** icon to access and configure various Windows settings.

End

TIP

Charms Bar from Any Screen You can access the charms bar from any screen in Windows 8, even if you have an app displayed full screen. All you have to do is click or tap appropriately, and the charms bar appears. ■

NOTE

Notification Panel Whenever the charms bar is displayed, Windows also displays a notification panel at the bottom left of the screen. This panel duplicates the information shown on the Windows Lock screen—current date and time, Internet connection status, and power status. ■

GETTING HELP IN WINDOWS

When you can't figure out how to perform a particular task, it's time to ask for help. In Windows 8, this is done through the Windows Help and Support Center.

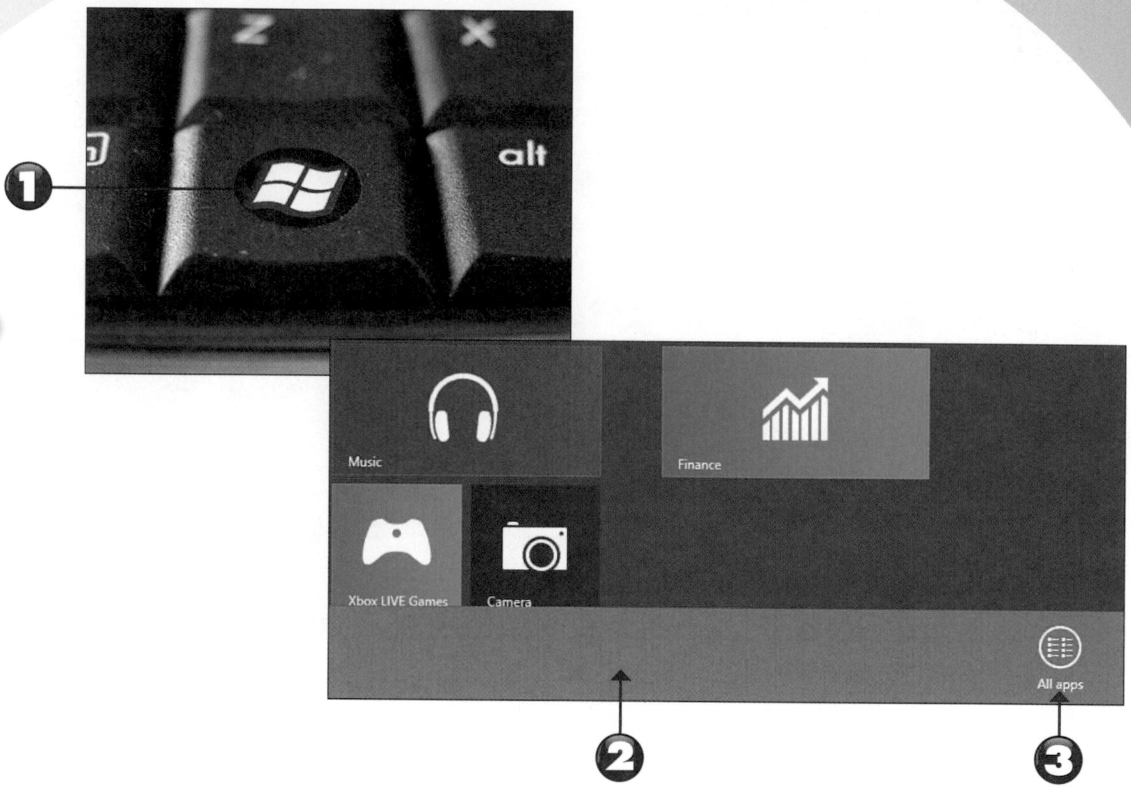

Start

1. Press the **Windows** key to display the Start screen.
2. Right-click anywhere on the Start screen to display the options bar at the bottom of the screen.
3. Click or tap **All Apps**.

Continued

TIP

More on the Web More help information is available on Microsoft's website, www.microsoft.com. ■

Narrator
Run
On-Screen Keyboard
Task Manager
Windows Speech Recognition
Windows Defender
Windows System
Windows Easy Transfer
Command Prompt
Computer
Control Panel
Default Programs
Help and Support

Windows Help and Support
Search
Help home | Browse help | Contact support
More to explore
Windows website
Check out the videos, articles, and other content on the Windows website.
Microsoft Answers website
Provide feedback and get answers to questions from Microsoft support professionals and other Windows users.

Windows Help and Support
start
Help home | Browse help | Contact support
Search results for "start" (58)
Show results from:
Windows (58)
Start your PC from a Windows To Go workspace
Get a brief explanation about the different ways to start your PC from a Windows To Go workspace.
Windows Firewall from start to finish
Learn about Windows Firewall: what it is, how to turn it on or off, and how to allow programs to communicate through it.
Troubleshoot problems with installing updates
Learn more about common problems with installing Windows updates, and steps you can take to solve them to help keep Windows up to date.
Get to know Windows 8
Learn about new features in Windows 8: the Search, Share, Start, Devices, and Settings charms, app commands, switching through open apps, and snapping apps.
Learn how safe mode can start Windows in a limited state, which can be useful for troubleshooting problems.
Online Help

4 Scroll to the Windows System section and tap or click **Help and Support**. This opens a Help and Support window on the Windows desktop.

5 Enter a description of your issue into the Search box, and then press **Enter**.

6 Windows now displays a list of topics that match your search query. Click an item to view it in its entirety.

End

TIP

Browse for Help You can also browse the topics in the Windows Help system. Click **Browse Help** at the top of the Help window, and then click the appropriate topic below. ■

CAUTION

Less Than Helpful Windows' Help system doesn't have all the answers. If you can't find what you need in the Help system, you can go online to the Microsoft Support website (support.microsoft.com), or access the technical support offered by your computer's manufacturer. Also useful are the other books and articles offered by this book's publisher, available online at www.quepublishing.com. ■

PERSONALIZING WINDOWS 8

When you first turn on your new computer system, you see the Windows Lock screen, and then the Start screen, as Microsoft (or your computer manufacturer) set them up for you. If you like the way these screens look, great. If not, you can change them.

Windows presents a lot of different ways to personalize the look and feel of your system. In fact, one of the great things about Windows is how quickly you can make Windows look like *your* version of Windows, different from anybody else's.

DIFFERENT WINDOWS LOCK SCREENS

CUSTOMIZING THE LOCK SCREEN PICTURE

The Lock screen is what you see when you first power on your computer or begin to log on to Windows. You can change the background picture of the Lock screen, and you can add information from specific apps, such as Weather or Calendar, to the screen.

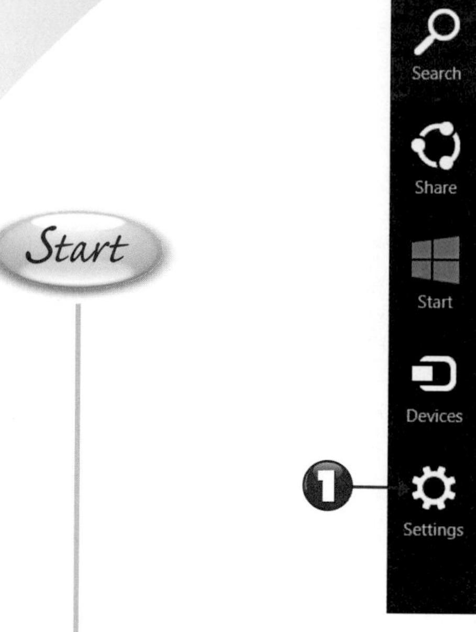

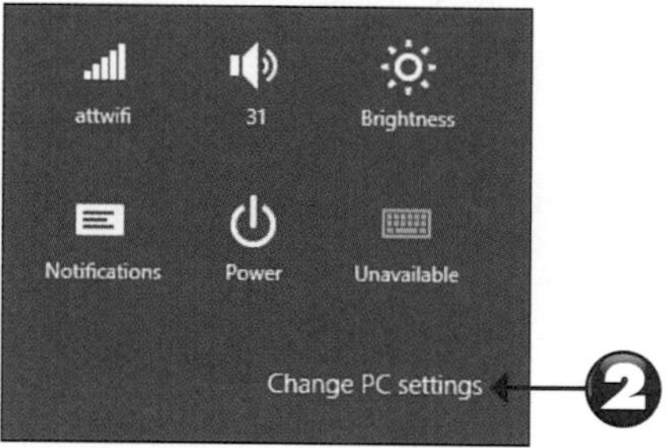

1. Display the charms bar and click or tap **Settings** to display the Settings panel.
2. Click or tap **Change PC Settings** to display the PC Settings page.

TIP

Lock Screen The Lock screen appears when you first power on your PC and any time you log off from your personal account or switch users. It also appears when you awaken your computer from sleep mode. ■

NOTE

Smartphone Lock Screens The Windows Lock screen is similar to the lock screens you see on various smartphones, such as the Apple iPhone, whenever you "wake up" the phone. ■

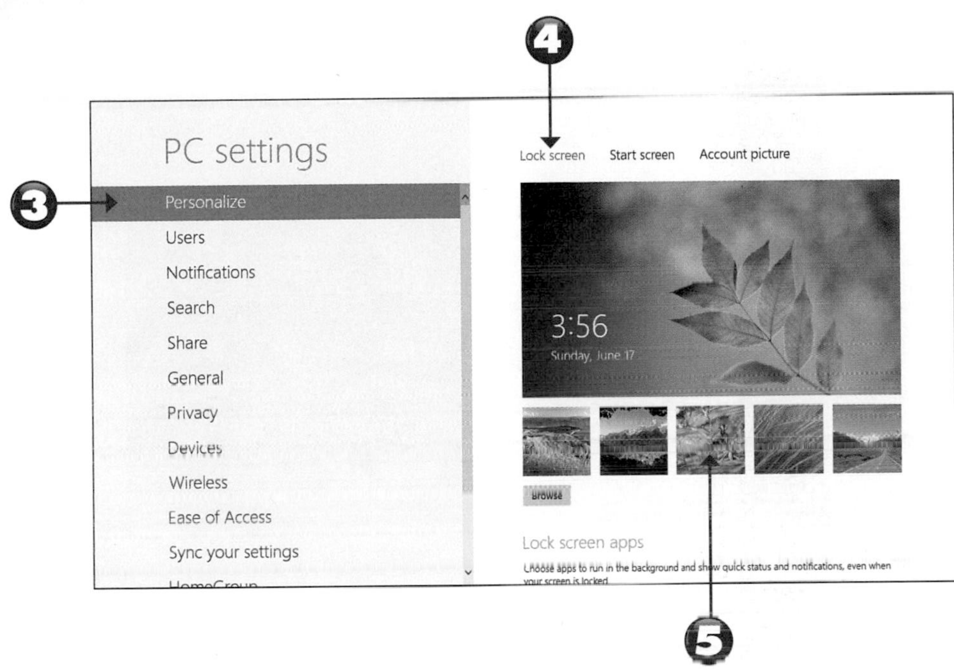

3. Click or tap **Personalize** in the left column.
4. Click or tap **Lock Screen** in the right panel.
5. Click or tap the thumbnail for the picture you want to use.

End

TIP

Personalize Your Picture To use your own picture as the background, click the **Browse** button. When the Files screen appears, navigate to and click or tap the picture you want to use, and then click or tap the **Choose Picture** button. ■

ADDING APPS TO THE LOCK SCREEN

The Lock screen can display a number of apps that run in the background and display useful or interesting information, even while your computer is locked. By default, you see the date/time, power status, and connection status, but it's easy to add other apps to the Lock screen.

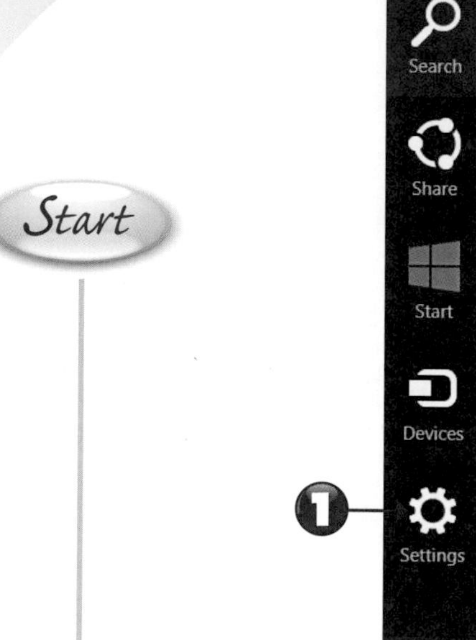

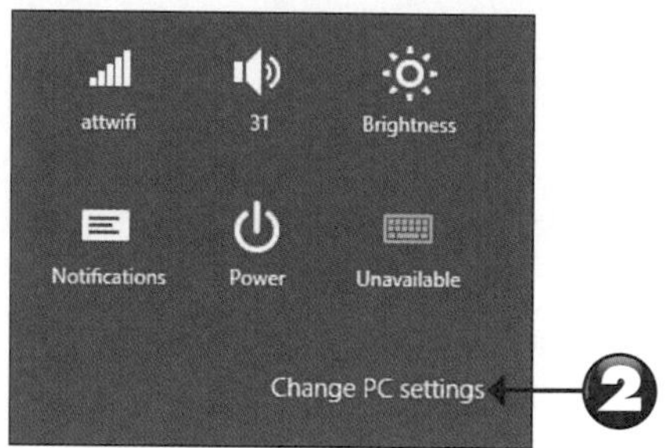

1. Display the charms bar and click or tap **Settings** to display the Settings panel.

2. Click or tap **Change PC Settings** to display the PC Settings page.

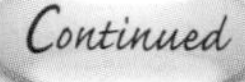

TIP

Lock Screen Apps You can add information from the following apps to the Lock screen: Calendar, Mail, Messaging, and Weather. ■

TIP

Real-Time Information The apps you see on the Lock screen display information in real time. ■

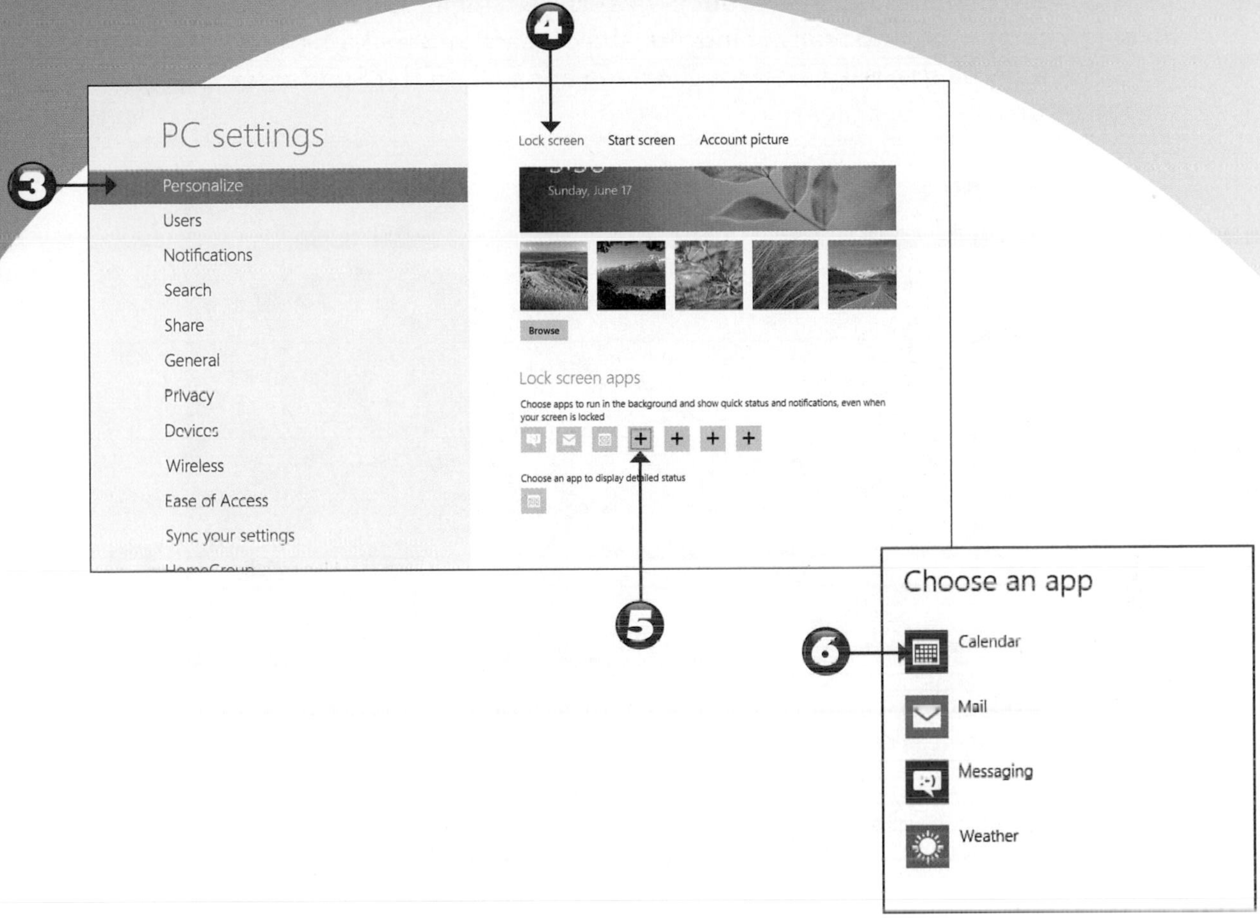

3. Click or tap **Personalize** in the left column.

4. Click or tap **Lock Screen** in the right panel.

5. Scroll down the Lock Screen panel to the Lock Screen Apps section and click a + button to display the Choose an App panel.

6. Click or tap the app you want to add.

End

TIP

Displaying Live Information You can also opt for one of the Lock screen apps to display detailed live information, such as unread messages or current weather conditions. To select which app displays detailed information, click or tap the app button in the Choose an App to Display Detailed Status section. When the Choose an App panel appears, click or tap the app you want. ■

REARRANGING TILES ON THE START SCREEN

As you know, the Start screen is your own personal home base in Windows 8. The Start screen is composed of dozens of individual tiles, each representing an app, program, operation, or file. If you don't like where a given tile appears on the Start screen, you can rearrange the order of your tiles.

Start

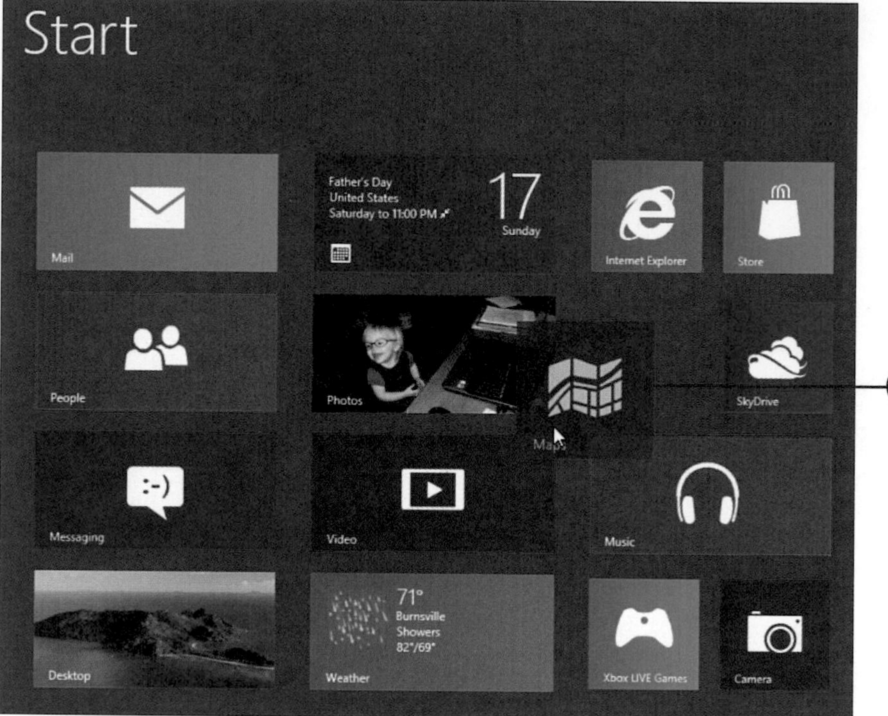

1 Click and drag the selected tile to a new position.

End

TIP

Using a Touchscreen Display To move a tile on a touchscreen display, use your finger to press and drag the tile to a new position. ■

...OR SMALLER

...d at either one- or two-column width. You can

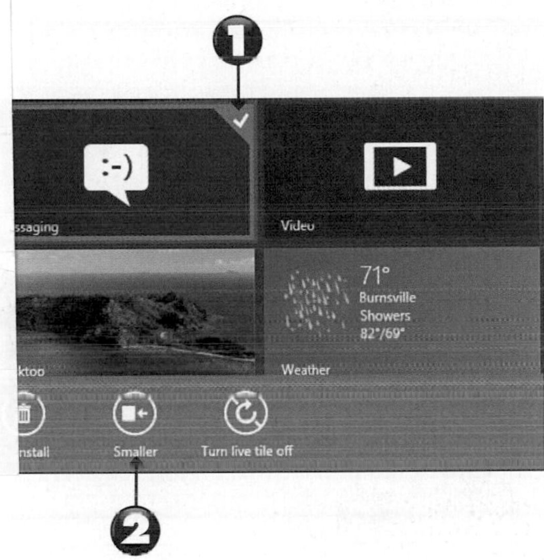

1. Right-click the tile you want to change. (On a touchscreen device, tap and hold the tile.) This adds a check mark to the tile and displays the options bar at the bottom of the screen.

2. Click or tap **Smaller** to make a large tile smaller; click or tap **Larger** to make a small tile larger.

End

TIP

Live Tiles Many tiles are "live," in that they display the current operation or information. For example, the Weather tile displays the current weather conditions, and the Photos tile displays a slideshow of pictures on your computer. ■

TIP

Turning Off Live Tiles To turn off a live tile (to display the default tile icon), right-click the tile to change; this adds a check mark to the tile and displays the options bar at the bottom of the screen. Click or tap **Turn Live Tile Off**. ■

REMOVING TILES

You may find that there are one or more tiles on your Start screen that you never use. You can remove unused tiles to get them out of your way and make room for additional titles.

1. Right-click the tile you want to delete. This adds a check mark to the tile and displays the options bar at the bottom of the screen.
2. Click or tap **Unpin from Start**.

End

TIP

Too Many Tiles Many new apps add tiles for actions associated with the app, such as deleting or configuring the app. You probably don't need these additional tiles, and can delete them—leaving only the main tile to launch the app itself. ■

ADDING NEW TILES TO THE START SCREEN

If you accidently remove a tile from the Start screen, or want to add a tile for an app or program or operation that isn't already there, it's easy to do so.

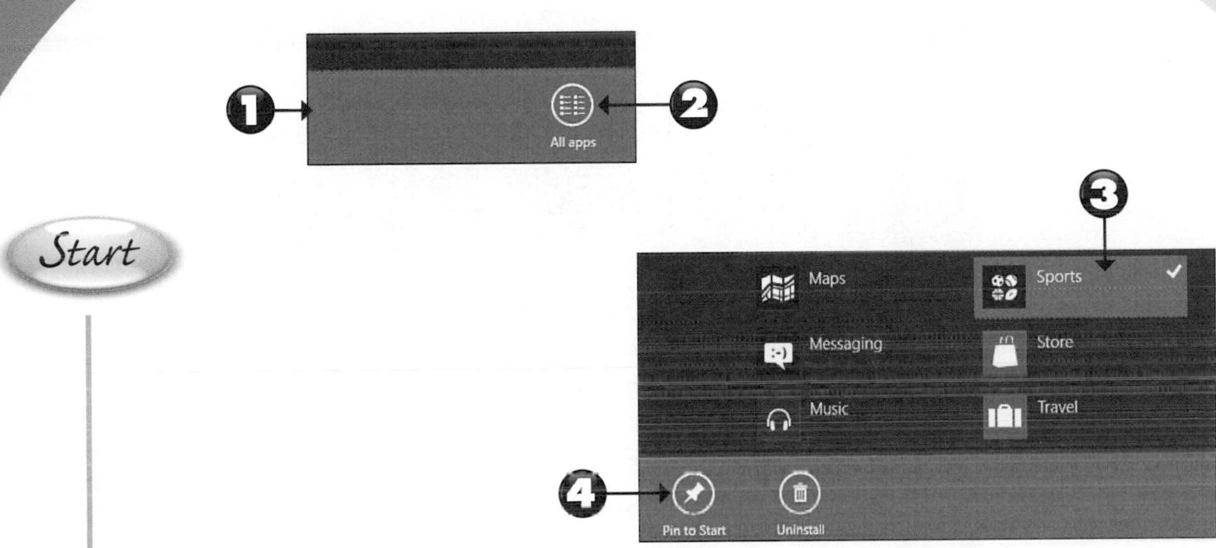

Start

1. Right-click anywhere on the Start screen (or press **Windows+Z**) to display the options bar at the bottom of the screen.
2. Click or tap **All Apps**.
3. When the Apps screen appears, right-click the item you want to add; this displays the options bar at the bottom of the screen.
4. Click or tap **Pin to Start**.

End

TIP

Tiles for New Apps When you download or install a new app on your system, a tile for that app should be automatically added to the Start screen. If it isn't, follow the steps on this page to add a tile for that app. ■

CHANGING WINDOWS COLORS

When you configured Windows when you first turned on your new computer, you were asked to choose a color scheme. Fortunately, you're not locked into your initial choice. You can change the color scheme for your Start screen (and subsidiary screens) at any time.

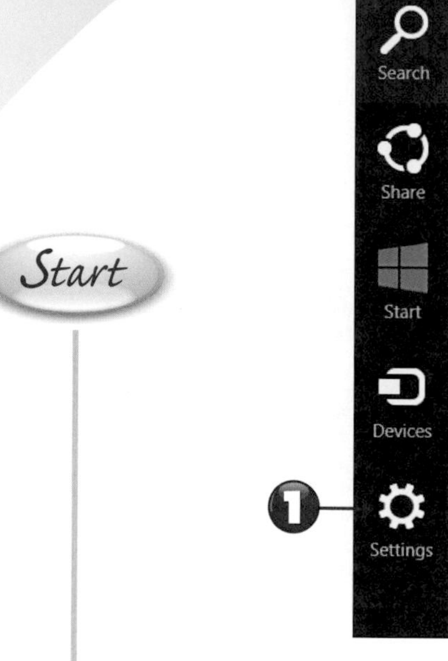

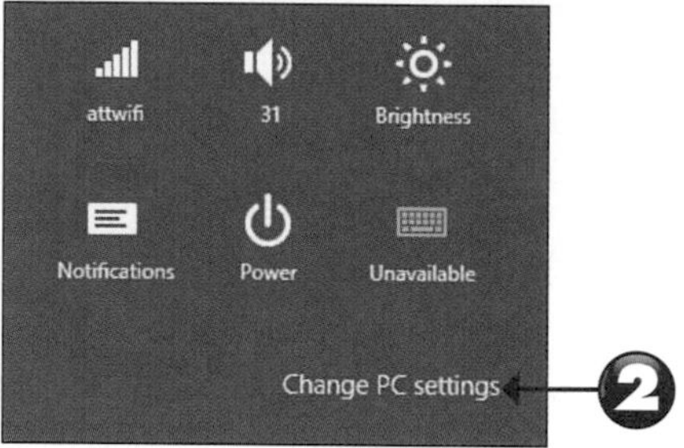

1. Display the charms bar and click or tap **Settings** to display the Settings panel.
2. Click or tap **Change PC Settings** to display the PC Settings page.

Continued

TIP

Background Pattern You can change both the background color and the pattern in the screen background. ■

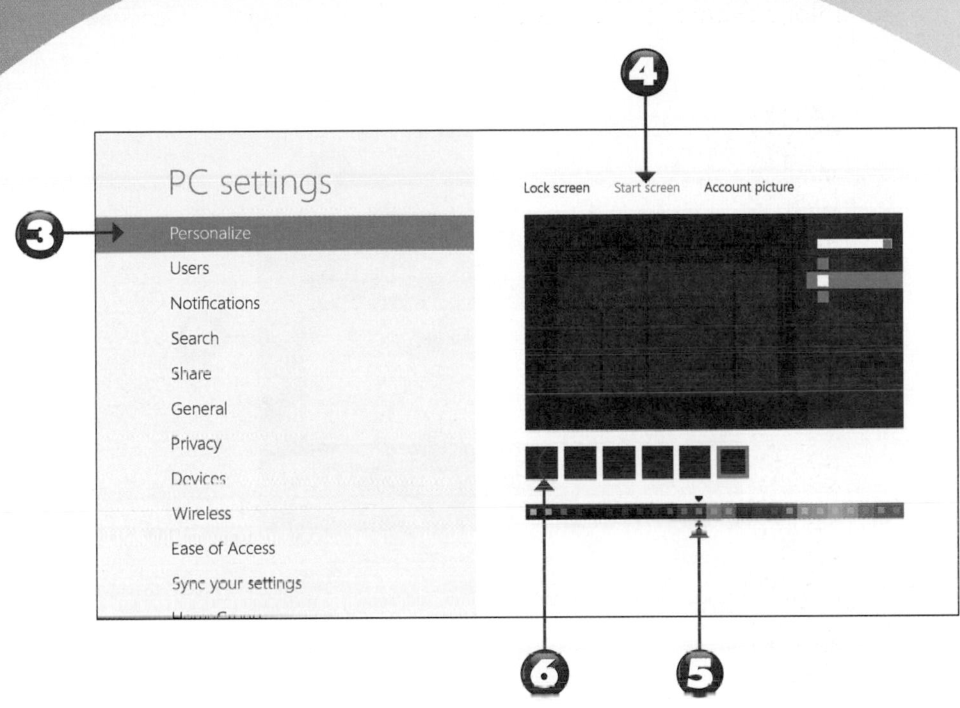

3. Click or tap **Personalize** in the left column.
4. Click or tap **Start Screen** in the right panel.
5. Drag the **Change Background Color** slider to the color you want.
6. Click or tap the desired background pattern.

End

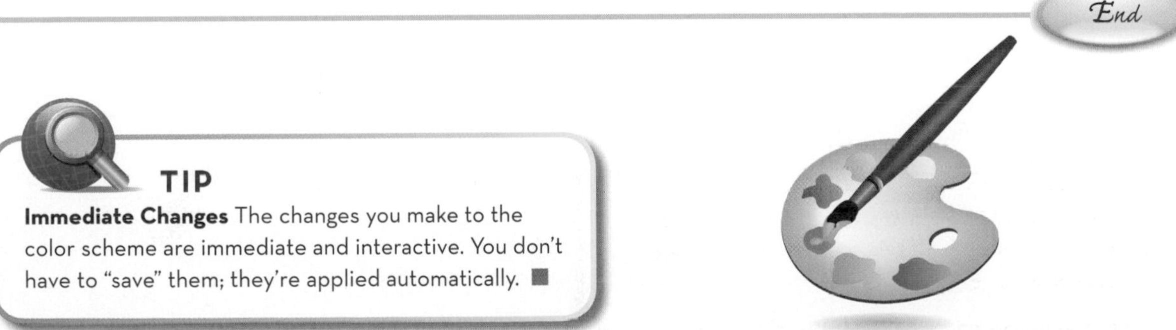

TIP

Immediate Changes The changes you make to the color scheme are immediate and interactive. You don't have to "save" them; they're applied automatically. ■

CHANGING YOUR PROFILE PICTURE

When you first configured Windows, you picked a default image to use as your profile picture. You can, at any time, change this picture to something more to your liking.

1. From the Start screen, click or tap your account name.
2. From the pop-up menu, click or tap **Change Account Picture**.

Continued

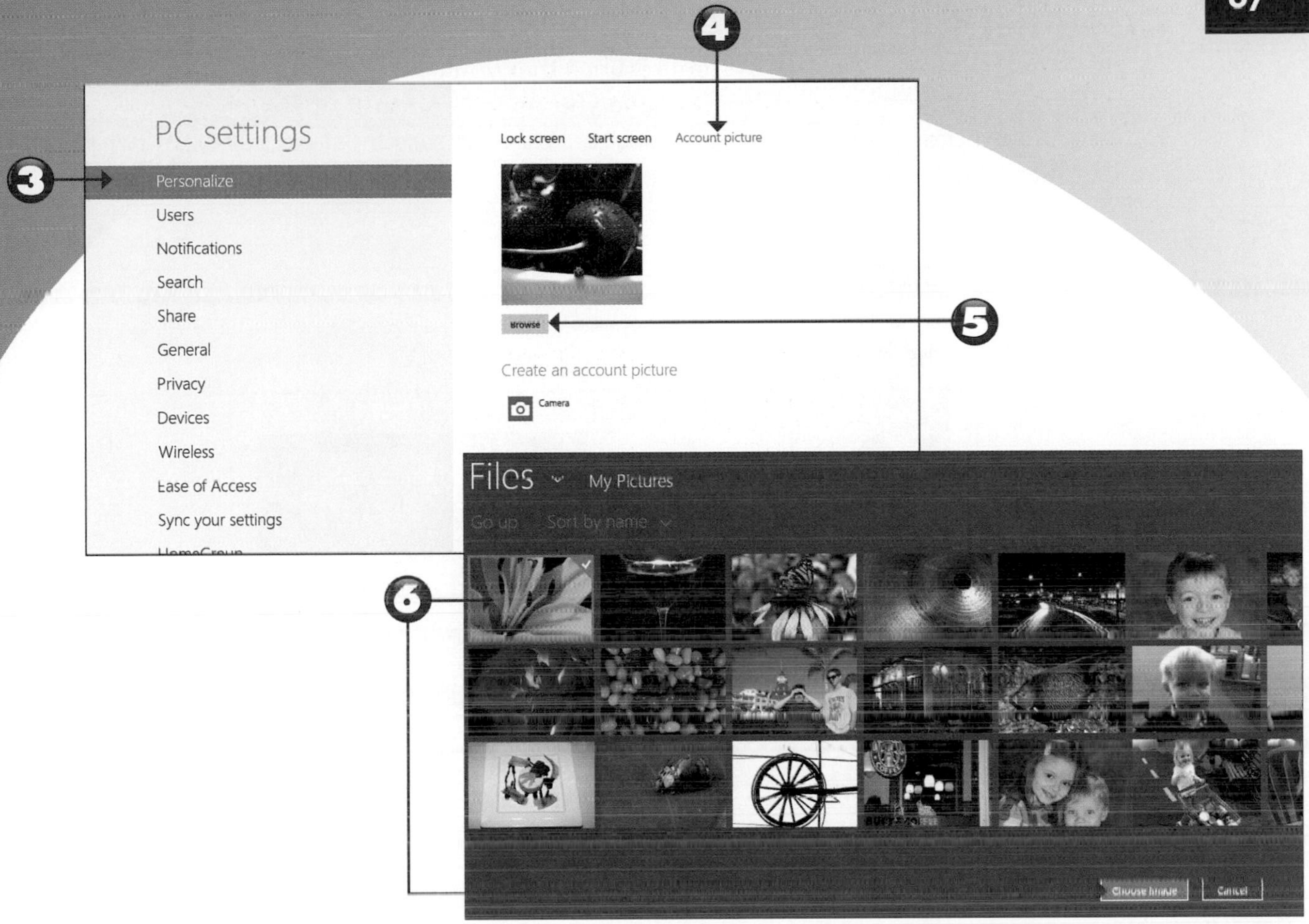

3. When the PC Settings page appears, select **Personalize** in the left column.

4. Select **Account Picture** in the right panel.

5. Click the **Browse** button.

6. When the Files screen appears, navigate to and click or tap the picture you want, and then tap or click the **Choose Image** button.

End

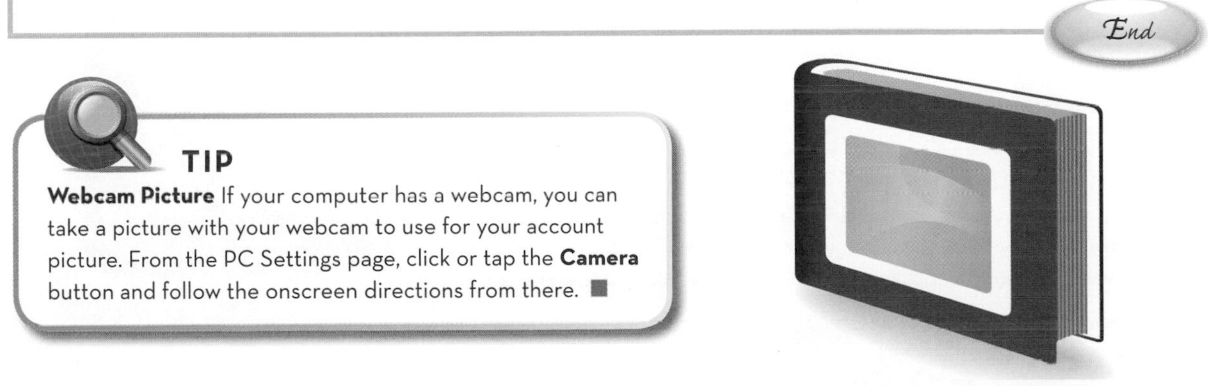

TIP

Webcam Picture If your computer has a webcam, you can take a picture with your webcam to use for your account picture. From the PC Settings page, click or tap the **Camera** button and follow the onscreen directions from there. ■

CONFIGURING WINDOWS SETTINGS

There are many other Windows system settings that you can configure, if you want. In most cases, the default settings work just find and you don't need to change a thing. However, you can change these settings, if you so desire. You configure most of these settings from the PC Settings screen.

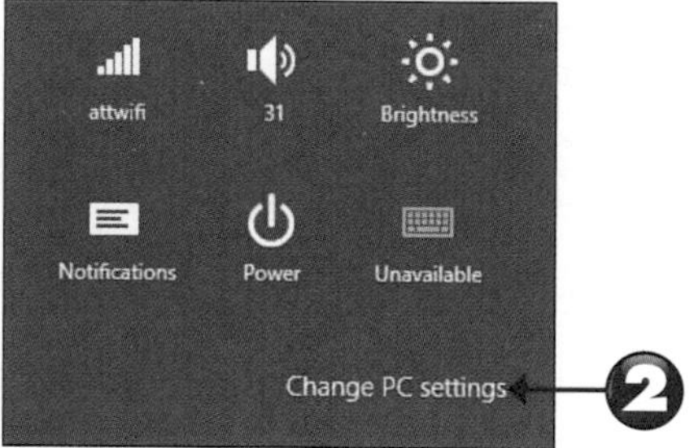

1. Display the charms bar and click or tap **Settings** to display the Settings panel.
2. Click or tap **Change PC Settings**.

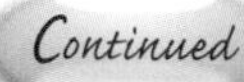

TIP

Windows Settings The following tabs are available on the PC Settings page: Personalize, Users, Notifications, Search, Share, General, Privacy, Devices, Wireless, Ease of Access, Sync Your Settings, HomeGroup, and Windows Update. ■

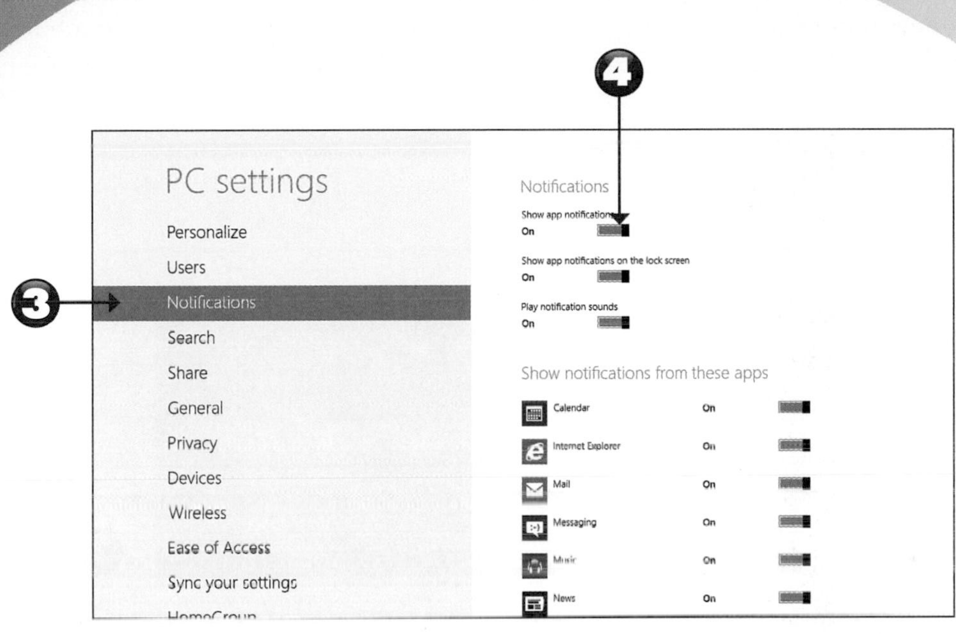

3 Select a tab on the left to display the associated settings on the right.

4 Configure the settings as necessary.

End

TIP

Control Panel You can find even more configuration settings in the Windows Control Panel, which is a holdover from older versions of Windows. To open the Control Panel, open the desktop, display the charms bar, click **Settings**, and then click or tap **Control Panel**. ■

SETTING UP ADDITIONAL USERS

Chances are you're not the only person using your computer; it's likely that you'll be sharing your PC with your spouse and kids, at least to some degree. Fortunately, you can configure Windows so that different people using your computer sign on with their own custom settings—and access to their own personal files. You do this by assigning each user in your household his own password-protected user account.

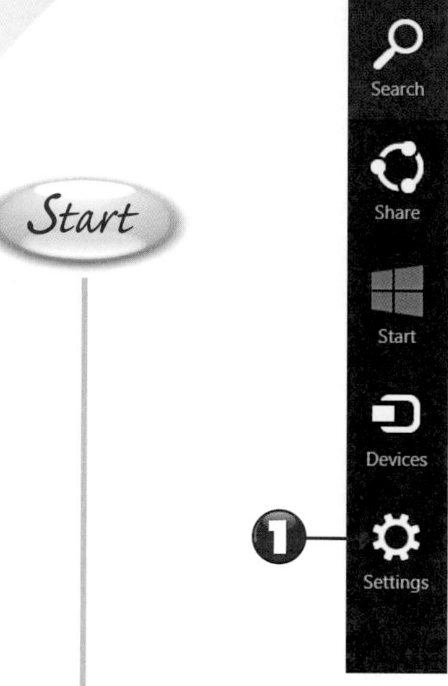

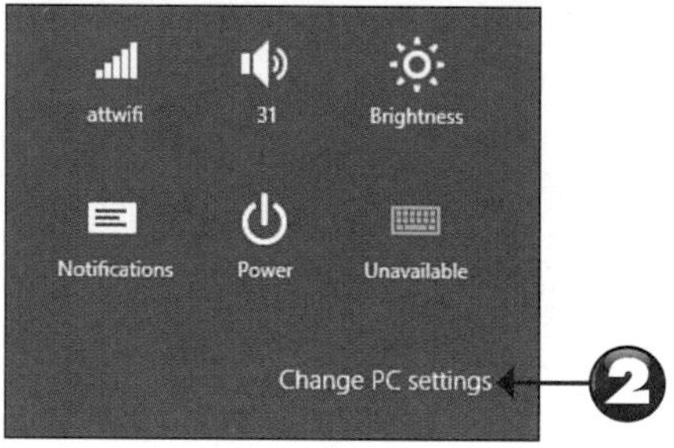

1. Display the charms bar and click or tap **Settings** to display the Settings panel.
2. Click or tap **Change PC Settings** to display the PC Settings page.

TIP

Two Types of Accounts Windows 8 lets you create two different types of user accounts: online and local. An *online account* is linked to a new or existing Microsoft Account and lets you synchronize your account settings between multiple computers. A *local account* is exclusive to your current computer; with a local account, you don't have to be connected to the Internet to log on to your computer. ■

NOTE

Microsoft Account By default, Windows creates new accounts using existing or new Microsoft Accounts. You need a Microsoft Account login to use many of the interactive features of Windows 8, such as linking your account to Facebook or Microsoft's SkyDrive; a Microsoft Account is also necessary to access features with live updates, such as the Weather and News apps. ■

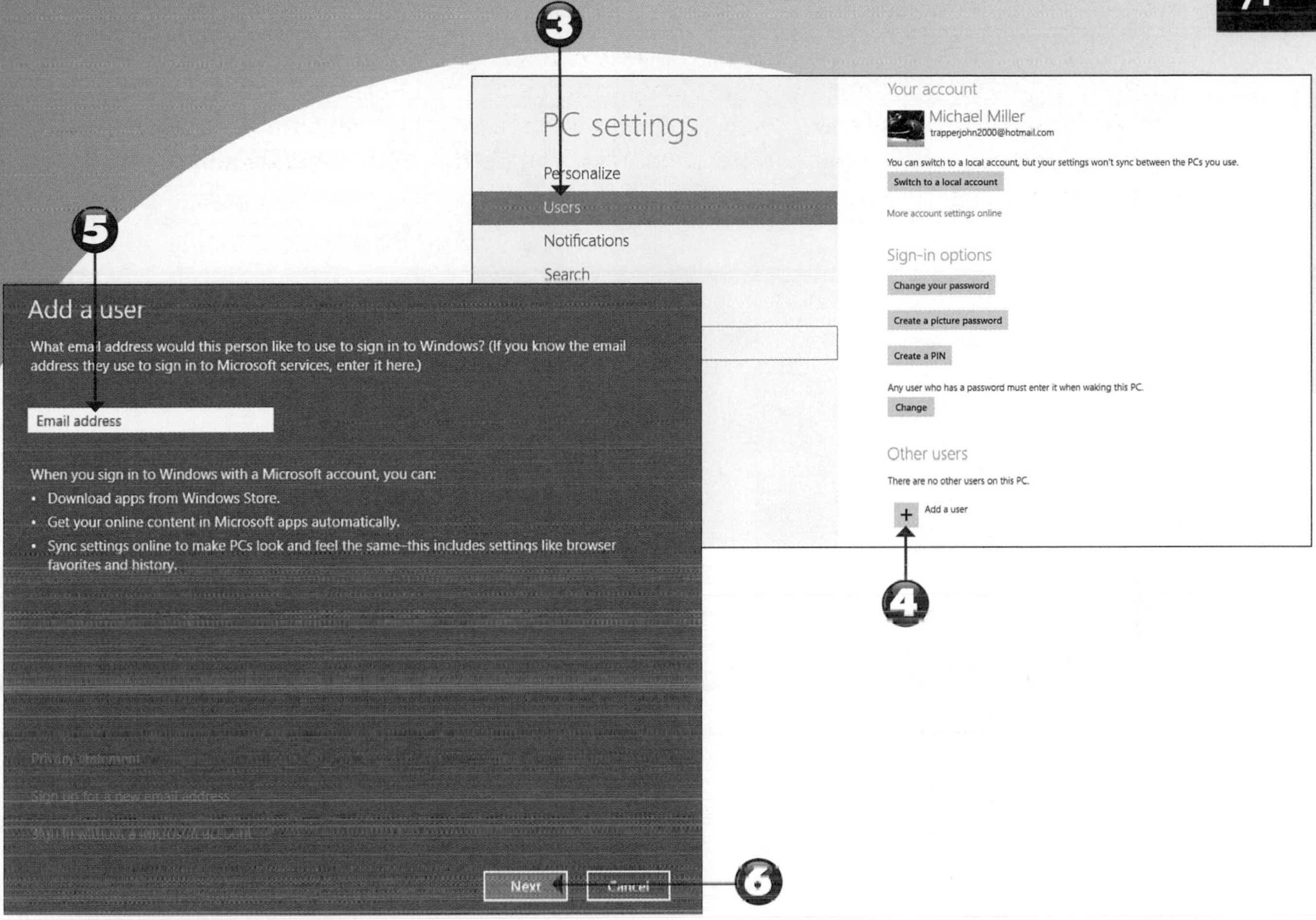

3. Click or tap **Users** in the left column.

4. Click or tap the **Add a User** button.

5. When the Add a User screen appears, enter the person's email address into the Email Address box. (If this person currently has a Microsoft Account, such as a Hotmail account, use the email address for that account.)

6. Click or tap the **Next** button.

Continued

TIP

Creating a New Microsoft Account If you have an existing Microsoft Account, such as for Hotmail or Xbox Live, you can use that as your Windows account. If you don't yet have a Microsoft Account, you can create one at any time—it's free. ■

TIP

Three Ways to Log In When you set up an account, you can choose from three different ways to log in. You can log in to an account with a traditional password, a PIN code, or a picture password. ■

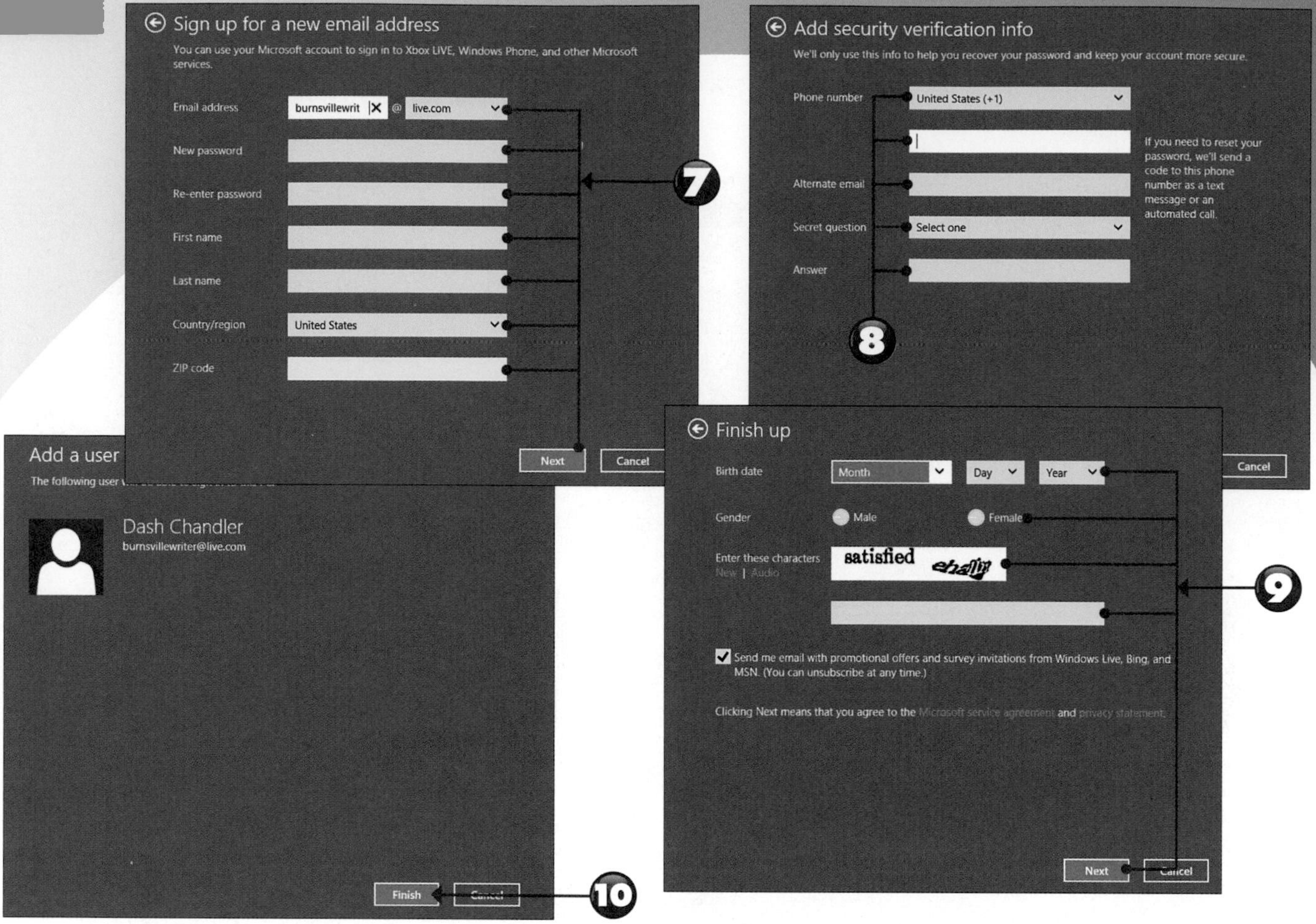

7 If you enter an email address that is not associated with an existing Microsoft Account, you are prompted to enter additional information (first name, last name, ZIP code, and so forth) to create a new account. Do so, and then click the **Next** button.

8 When prompted to add security verification info (phone number, alternate email, or secret question), do so, and then click the **Next** button.

9 When the Finish Up screen appears, enter your birth date and gender, enter the CAPTCHA characters, and then click the **Next** button.

10 When the final screen appears, click the **Finish** button.

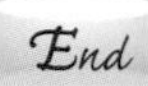

TIP

Setting Up a Local Account To set up a local account instead of a Microsoft Account, follow the previous steps until you get to the Add a User screen, and then click **Sign In Without a Microsoft Account**. When the next screen appears, click the **Local Account** button and follow the onscreen directions from there. ■

TIP

Switching to a Local Account If you created your initial Windows user account as one linked to a Microsoft Account, you may later decide that you'd rather have a local account, instead. To do this, display the PC Settings page, select **Users**, and then click the **Switch to a Local Account** button. Follow the onscreen instructions from there. ■

When the Finish Up screen appears, enter your birth date and gender, enter the CAPTCHA characters, and then click the **Next** button.
When the final screen appears, click the **Finish** button.

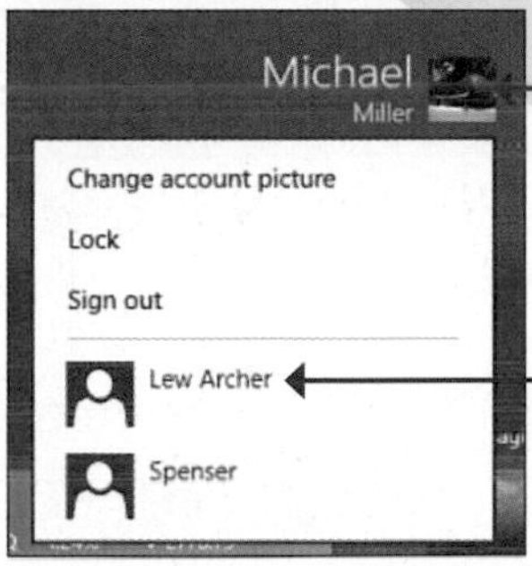

Start

1 SWITCHING BETWEEN USERS

2 If other people are using your computer, they may want to log on with their own accounts.

3 To do this, you'll need to change users—which you can do without shutting off your PC.

4 Press the Windows key to return to the Start screen.
Click or tap your username and picture in the top-right corner.

End

TIP

Signing Out When you switch users, both accounts remain active; the original user account is just suspended in the background. If you would rather log off completely from a given account, and return to the Windows Lock screen, click your username or picture on the Start screen, and then click **Sign Out**. ■

WORKING WITH WINDOWS 8 APPS

Most of the productive and fun things you do on your computer are done with *applications*, sometimes called *apps*. An app is a software program that performs one or more functions.

Some apps are work related, others provide useful information, and still others are more entertaining in nature. For example, the Windows Weather app lets you check current weather conditions and forecasts; the Microsoft Word app is a word processor that lets you write letters, reports, and other documents.

There are actually two kinds of apps in Windows 8. Apps newly developed for Windows 8 run full screen from the Windows Start screen. Older software apps run in individual windows on the traditional desktop—which itself runs as an app within Windows 8. Most people will use a mix of traditional and Metro-style apps in their day-to-day use.

APPS ON THE START SCREEN

LAUNCHING AN APP

You can launch an app wherever you find it. Many apps are "pinned" to the Start screen, in the form of tiles. Clicking the tile launches the app.

Start

1. Click or tap a tile to launch the associated app.

End

TIP

Other Places to Find Apps Not all apps are pinned to the Start screen. You can find additional apps on the Apps page, or you can search for apps—both of which are discussed later in this section. ■

CLOSING AN APP

In earlier versions of Windows you needed to close open apps when you were done with them. That's not the case in Windows 8; you can leave any newer app running as long as you like without using valuable system resources. You can still, however, close open apps, if you want.

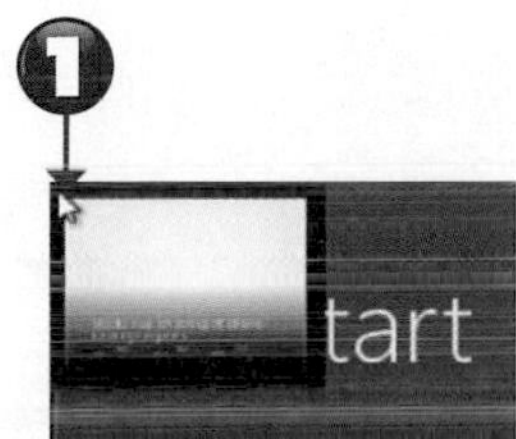

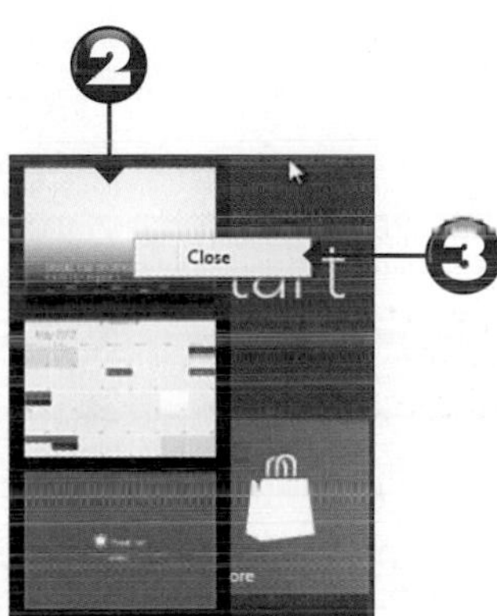

1. "Bump" the mouse cursor against the top-left corner of an open app to display a small app thumbnail, and then move the mouse cursor directly downward to display all running apps.
2. Right-click the app you want to close.
3. Select **Close** from the pop-up menu.

End

NOTE

Paused An open but unused app is essentially paused until you return to it, and consumes minimal system resources. ■

TIP

Swipe to Close To close an open app on a touch-screen device, swipe down from the top of the screen toward the center. This reduces the app to a small window and then closes it. ■

DISPLAYING ALL APPS

All the apps and utilities installed on your computer system are displayed on the Apps screen. Items on the Apps screen are organized by Apps, Windows Accessories, Windows Ease of Access, and Windows System. There may also be sections specific to your personal computer.

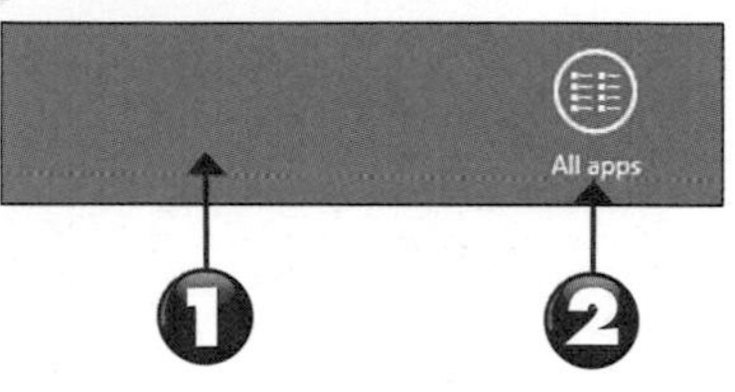

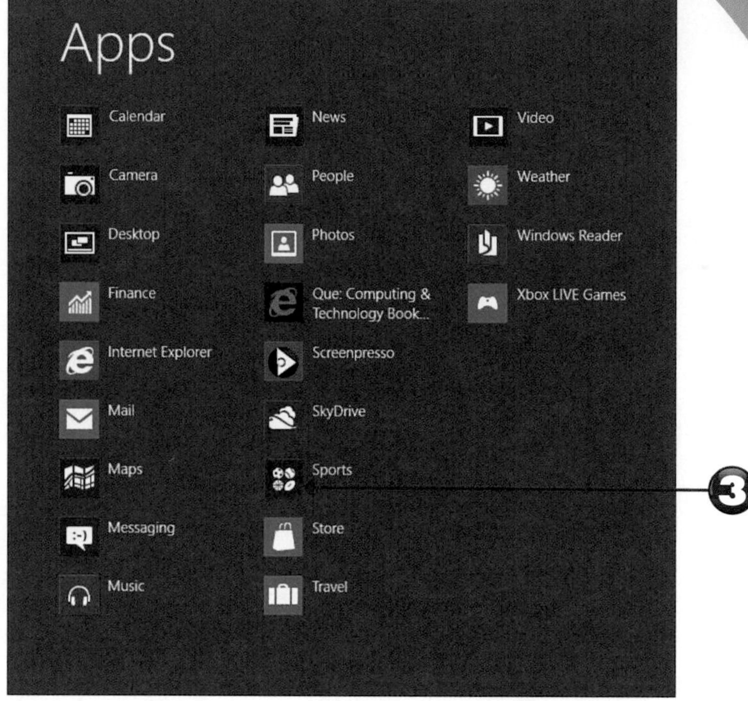

Start

1. Right-click in any open area of the Start screen to display the options bar.
2. Click the **All Apps** icon.
3. You now see the Apps screen. Click or tap an app to open it.

End

TIP

More Apps Scroll to the right on the Apps screen to view additional apps and utilities. ■

TIP

Swipe on a Touchscreen If you're using a touch-screen device, swipe your finger up from the bottom of the screen to display the options bar. ■

SEARCHING FOR APPS ON YOUR COMPUTER

If you have a lot of apps installed on the Apps screen or pinned to the Start screen, it may be challenging to find that one app you want. To that end, Windows lets you search for individual apps just by entering the name of the app.

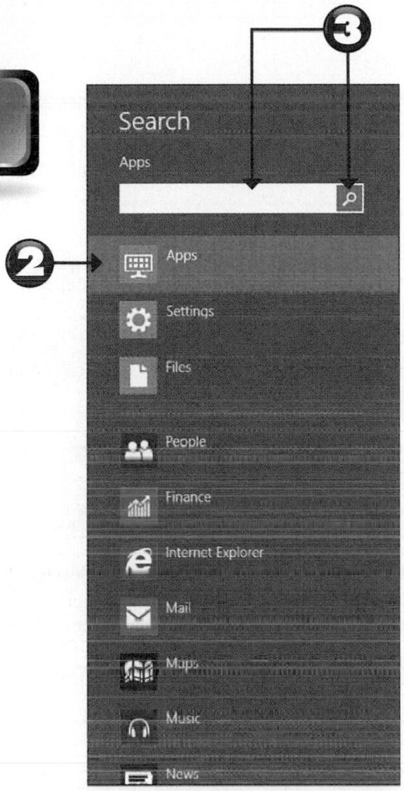

1. From the Start screen, press **Windows+Q** to display the Search panel.
2. If **Apps** is not selected from the search list, click or tap it now.
3. Enter the name of the app you're looking for into the Search box, then press the **Enter** key or click the **magnifying glass** button to start the search.
4. Windows now displays all apps that match your query. Click or tap an app to launch it.

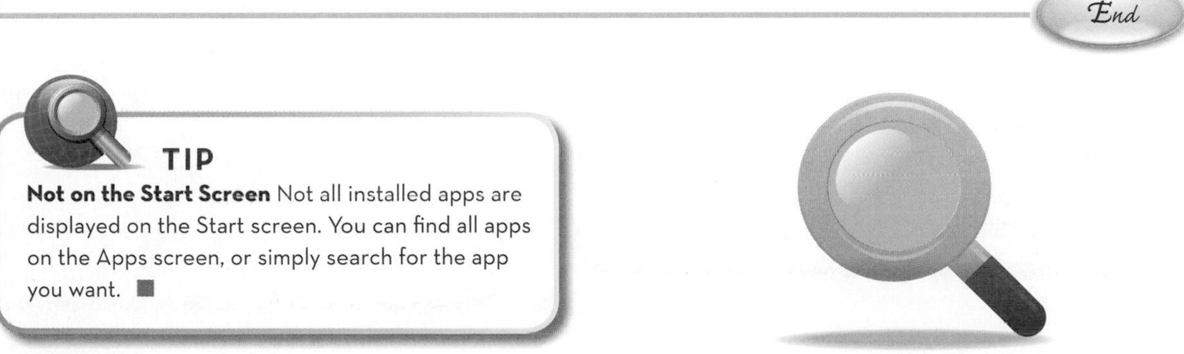

TIP

Not on the Start Screen Not all installed apps are displayed on the Start screen. You can find all apps on the Apps screen, or simply search for the app you want. ■

PINNING AN APP TO THE START SCREEN

You might find that it's easier to launch a frequently used app by adding it to the Windows Start screen. This is called *pinning* the app, and creates a tile for the app; click or tap the tile to launch the app.

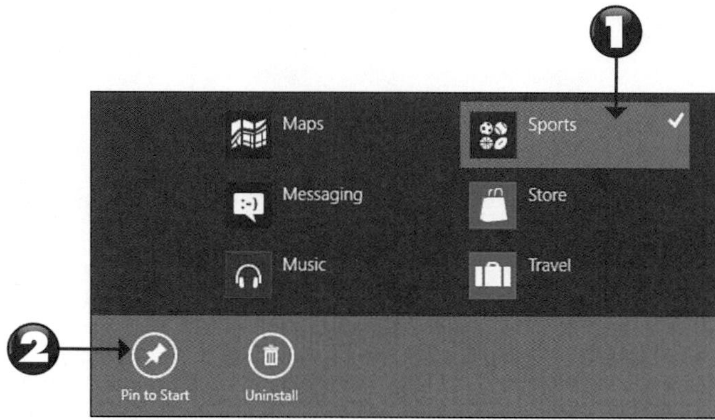

1. From the Apps screen or the search results screen, right-click the app you want to pin.
2. This displays the App Option bar at the bottom of the screen; click or tap **Pin to Start**.

End

TIP

Remove a Tile To remove an app's tile from the Start screen, right-click the tile to display the App Option bar, and then click or tap **Unpin from Start**. ■

SWITCHING BETWEEN OPEN APPS

If you have more than one open app, it's easy to switch between them. In fact, there are several ways to do this.

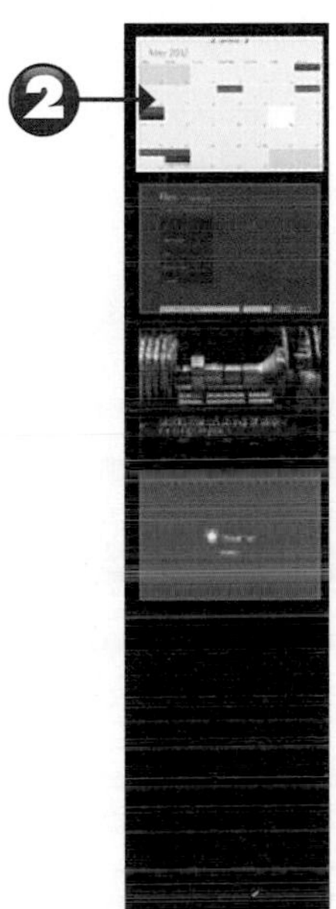

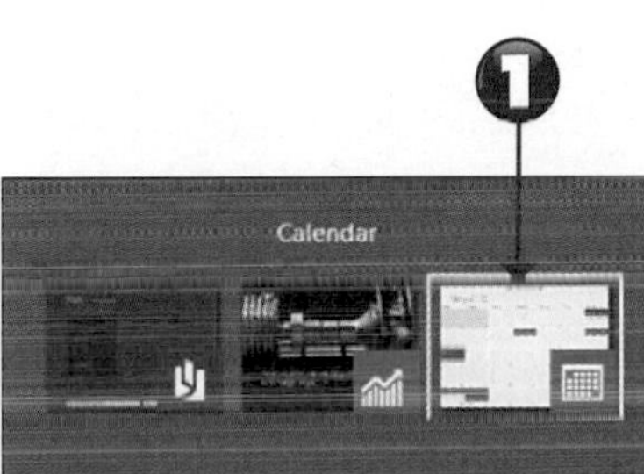

1. Press **Alt+Tab** to display the app box in the center of the screen, with the current app highlighted. Continue pressing **Tab** (while holding down the **Alt** button) to cycle through all open apps.

OR

2. Press **Windows+Tab** to display the Switcher panel at the left side of the screen, with the current app highlighted. Continue pressing **Tab** (while holding down the **Alt** button) to cycle through all open apps.

End

TIP

Display the Switcher Panel You can also display the Switcher panel by "bumping" your mouse against the top-left corner of the screen. This displays a small thumbnail of the open app; move your mouse downward to display the full Switcher panel. ■

TIP

Touchscreen Switching If you have a touchscreen computer or tablet, press and drag your finger from the left edge of the screen inward toward the center. The next open app appears on top of the previous app. ■

USING THE MAPS APP

Windows 8 ships with a number of useful apps built in to the operating system. For example, the Maps app lets you view street maps and generate driving directions. You launch the Maps app by clicking or tapping the **Maps** tile on the Windows Start screen.

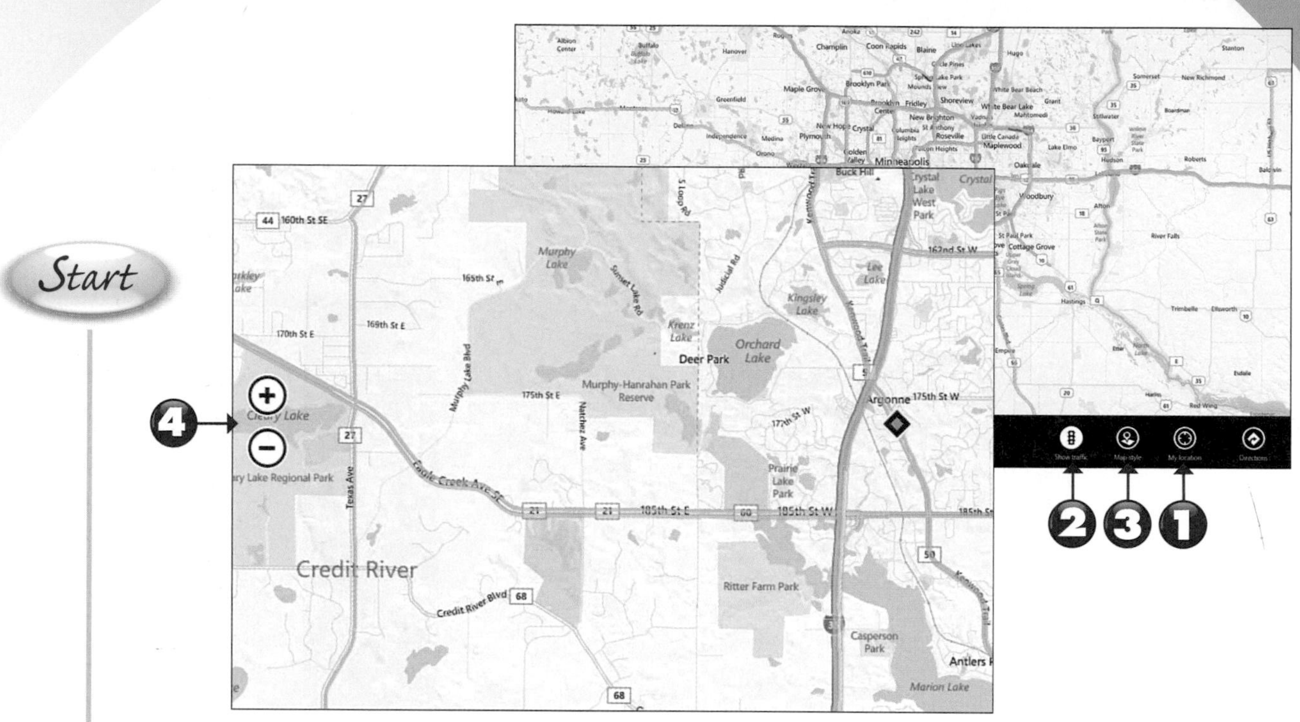

1. To display a street map of your current location, right-click to display the options bar, then click or tap **My Location**.
2. To show current traffic conditions (green is smooth flowing; yellow and red, less so), click or tap **Show Traffic** on the options bar.
3. To change from a traditional street map to a satellite map, click or tap **Map Style** on the options bar and select **Aerial View**. To switch back to the traditional map, select **Road View**.
4. Use your mouse or finger (on a touchscreen device) to drag the map in any direction. Zoom in or out of the map by using the zoom controls at the lower left.

Continued

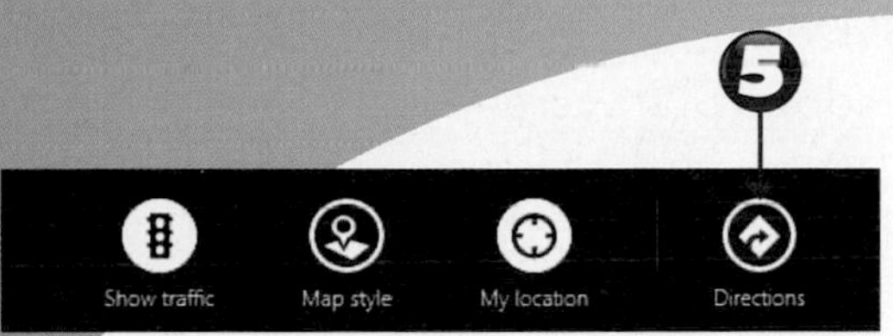

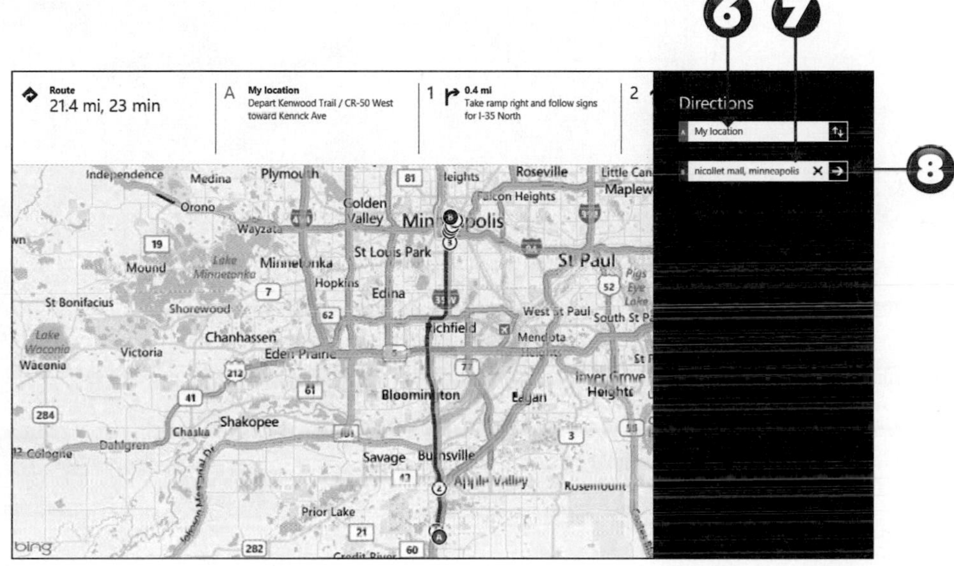

5 To generate driving directions, click or tap **Directions** on the options bar.

6 Enter your starting address into the Current Location box, or accept your current location.

7 Enter the ending address into the To box.

8 Click the right arrow button to display turn-by-turn directions onscreen.

End

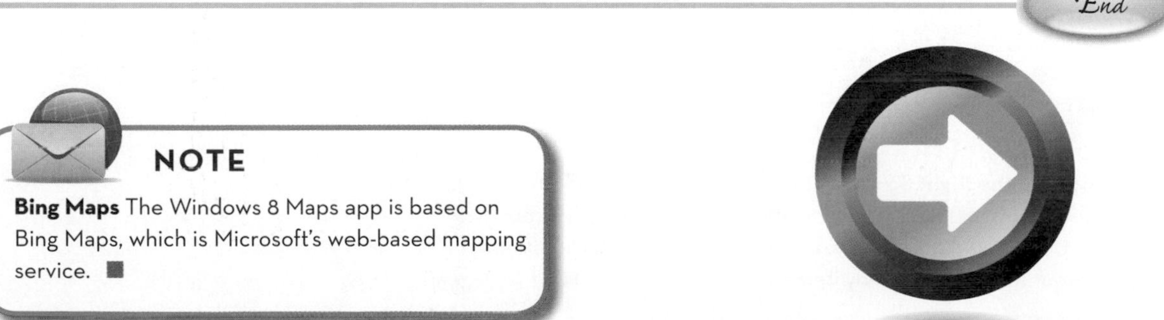

NOTE

Bing Maps The Windows 8 Maps app is based on Bing Maps, which is Microsoft's web-based mapping service. ■

USING THE WEATHER APP

The Windows 8 Weather app is useful before you even launch it. The Weather tile displays current weather conditions, "live," right on the Windows Start screen. Click or tap the app to view more detailed information.

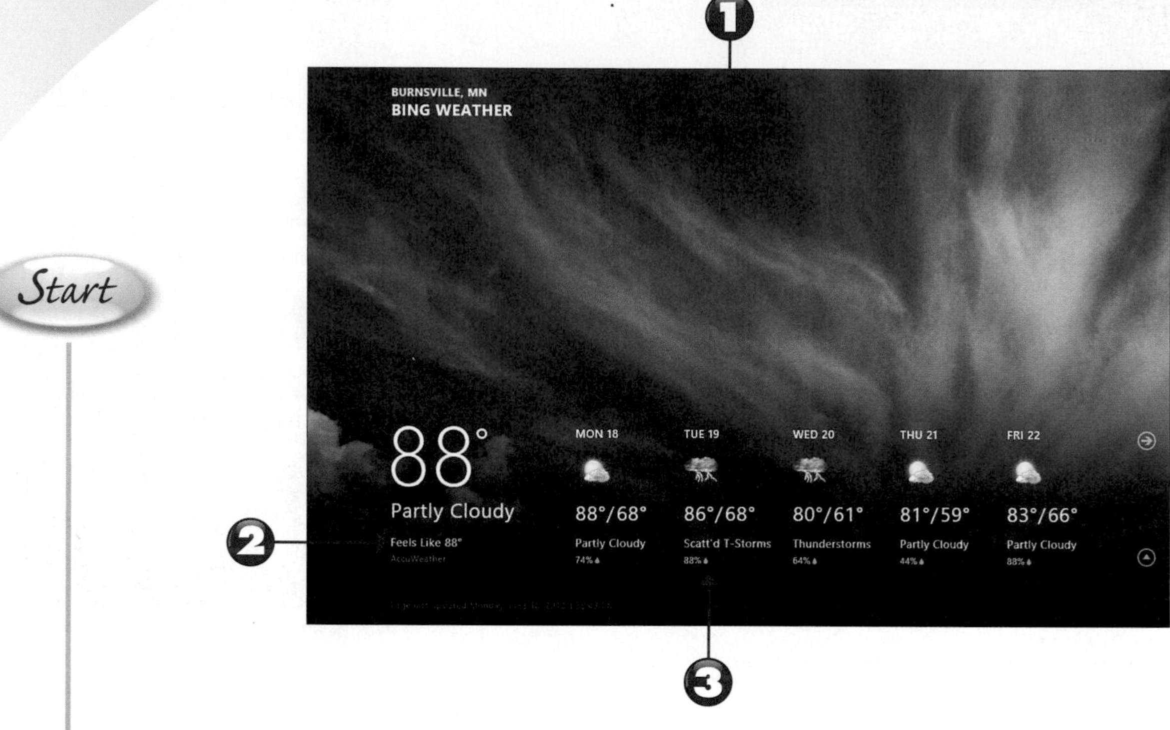

1. The background of the weather app represents current conditions; for example, a sunny spring day is represented by beautiful image of fresh leaves in the sunlight.
2. The current weather conditions are in the left corner; click this to display more detailed conditions, including wind, humidity, visibility, and barometric pressure.
3. The rest of the screen is devoted to a five-day forecast.

Continued

TIP

More to the Right Scroll right through the Weather app to view additional weather information, including an hourly forecast, various weather maps, and a graph for historical weather in your location. Click any item to view more detail. ■

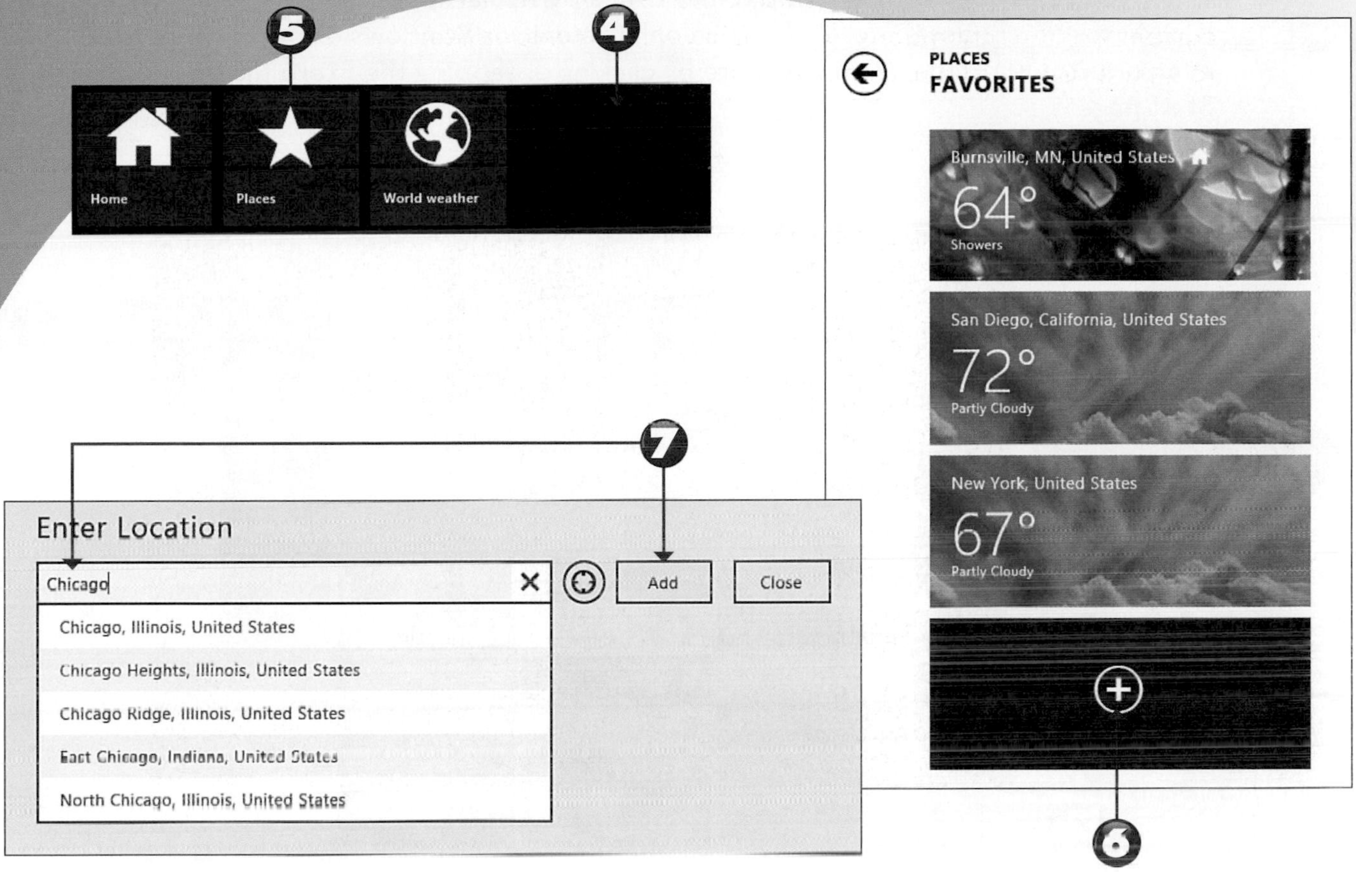

4. To configure the Weather app for your current location, right click anywhere on the screen to display the top and bottom options bars.

5. Click **Places** in the top bar to see a list of places already added.

6. Click or tap the + tile.

7. Enter a new location, either as the name of a city/state or ZIP code, and then click the **Add** button.

End

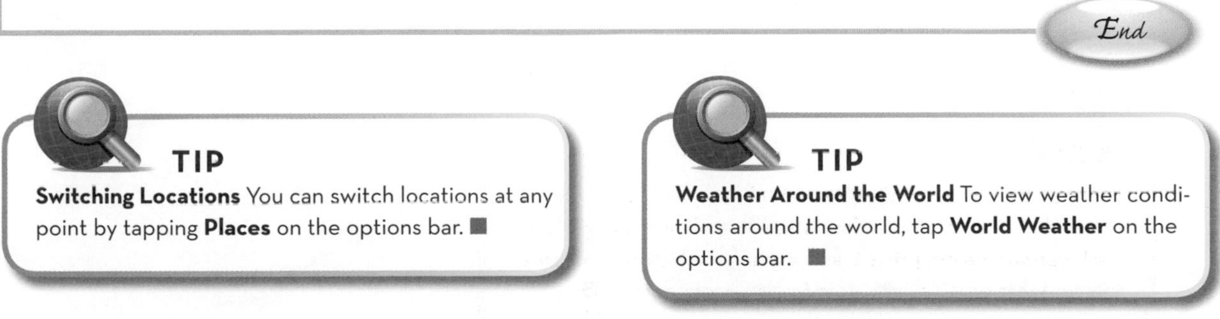

TIP

Switching Locations You can switch locations at any point by tapping **Places** on the options bar. ■

TIP

Weather Around the World To view weather conditions around the world, tap **World Weather** on the options bar. ■

FINDING NEW APPS IN THE WINDOWS STORE

When you're in need of a new app to perform a particular task, the first place to look is in the Microsoft Windows Store. This is an online store for Windows 8 specific apps, both free and paid. You shop the Windows Store by clicking or tapping the **Store** tile on the Windows Start page.

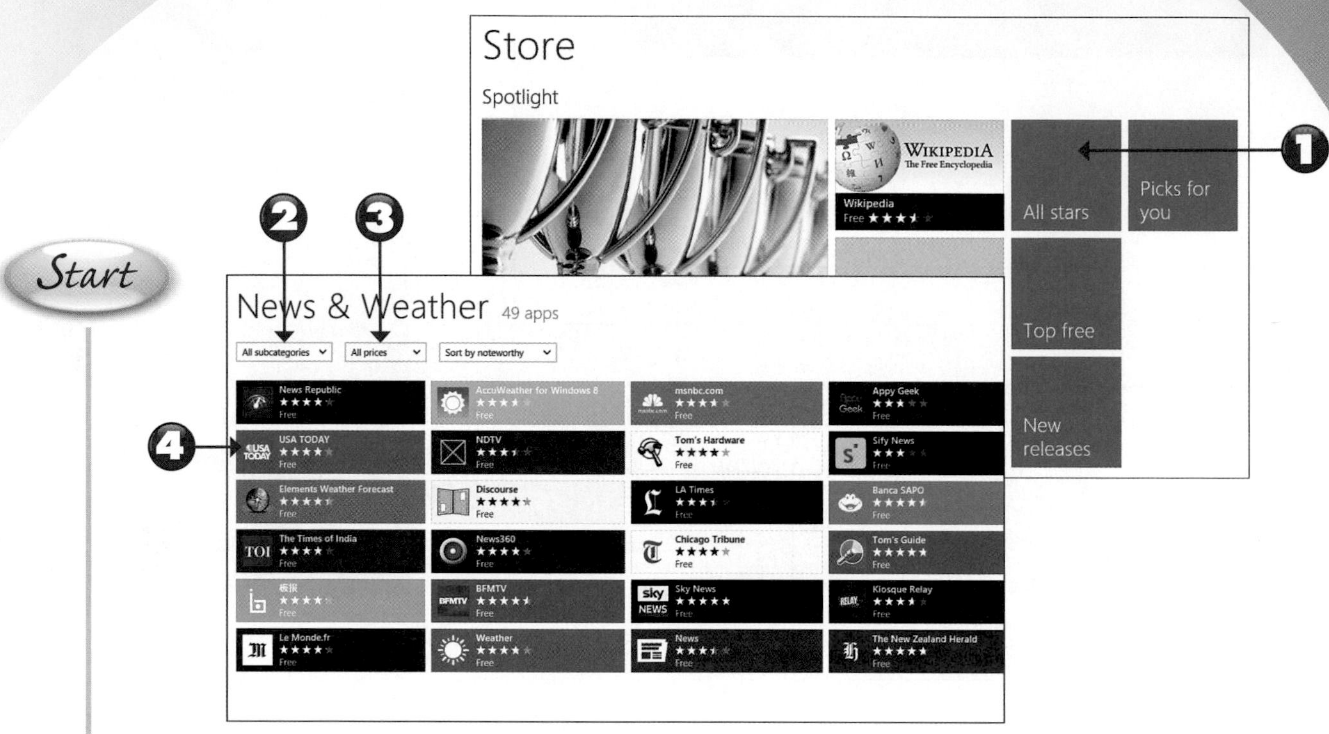

1. The Windows Store organizes apps by category. Scroll right to view more categories; tap a category to view all apps in that category.
2. To sort the apps within a category by free or paid, pull down the second list and select from Free, Free and Trail, or Paid.
3. To sort the apps within a category by another criteria (Noteworthy, Newest, Highest Rating, Lowest Price, or Highest Price), pull down the second list and make a selection.
4. Click or tap an app you want to purchase or download.

Continued

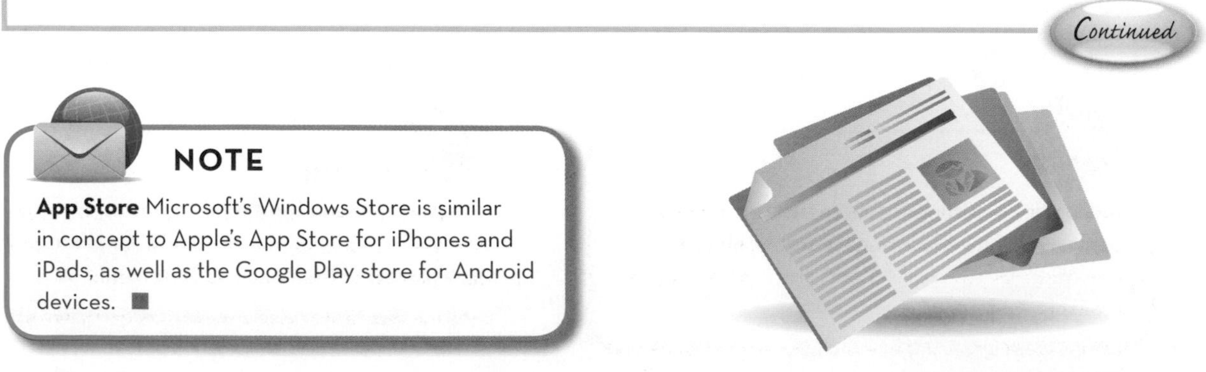

NOTE

App Store Microsoft's Windows Store is similar in concept to Apple's App Store for iPhones and iPads, as well as the Google Play store for Android devices. ■

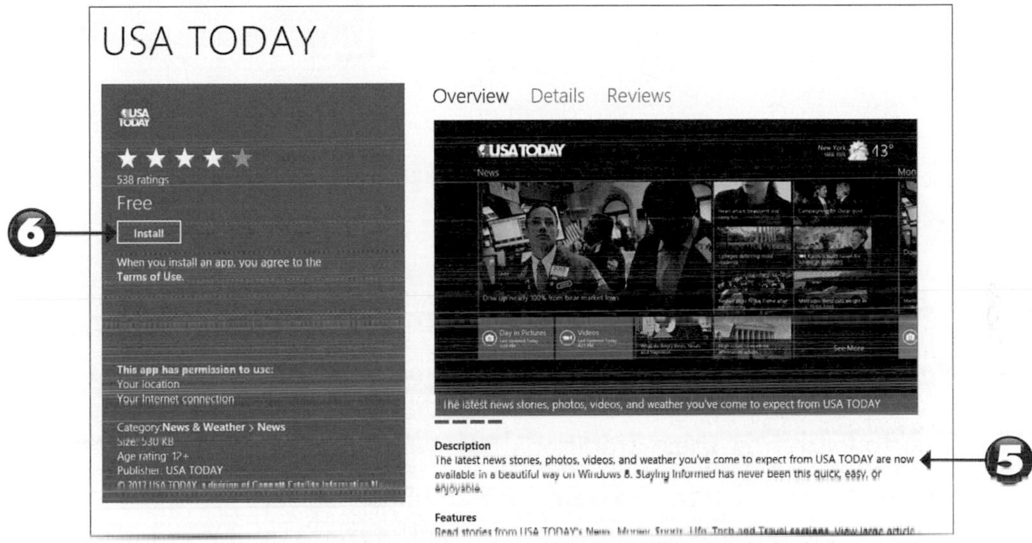
USA TODAY
Overview Details Reviews
538 ratings
Free
Install
When you install an app, you agree to the Terms of Use.
This app has permission to use:
Your location
Your Internet connection
Category News & Weather > News
Size: 530 KB
Age rating: 12+
Publisher: USA TODAY
The latest news stories, photos, videos, and weather you've come to expect from USA TODAY
Description
The latest news stories, photos, videos, and weather you've come to expect from USA TODAY are now available in a beautiful way on Windows 8. Staying informed has never been this quick, easy, or enjoyable.
Features
6
5

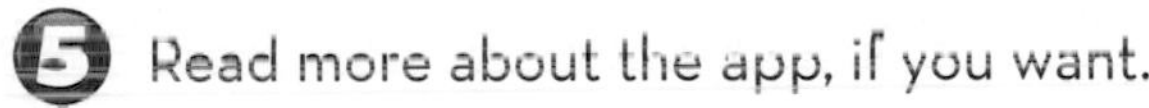

5 Read more about the app, if you want.

6 Click **Purchase** to purchase and install a paid app, or click **Install** to download and install a free app.

End

NOTE

Pricing Whereas a traditional computer software program can cost hundreds of dollars, most apps in the Windows Store cost $10 or less—and many are available for free. ■

TIP

Installing an App Installation of a Windows Store app is automatic. All downloaded apps are automatically pinned to the Windows Start menu. ■

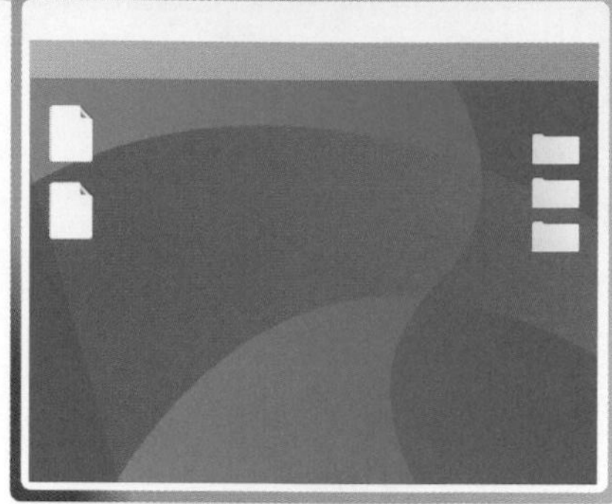

WORKING WITH TRADITIONAL DESKTOP APPS

As you learned in Chapter 6, "Working with Windows 8 Apps," there are lots of newer apps designed to work specifically with the Windows 8's new interface. But lots of older software programs that you might find useful are still available, such as Microsoft Word, Adobe Photoshop Elements, and even Apple's iTunes. You need to learn how these traditional software programs work.

You launch traditional software apps from the Start screen, the same as Metro-style apps. These older apps, however, run on the traditional Windows desktop, within their own windows. Therefore, you can have multiple open apps onscreen at the same time, with the windows stacked on top of or tiled next to each other.

EXPLORING THE WINDOWS 8 DESKTOP

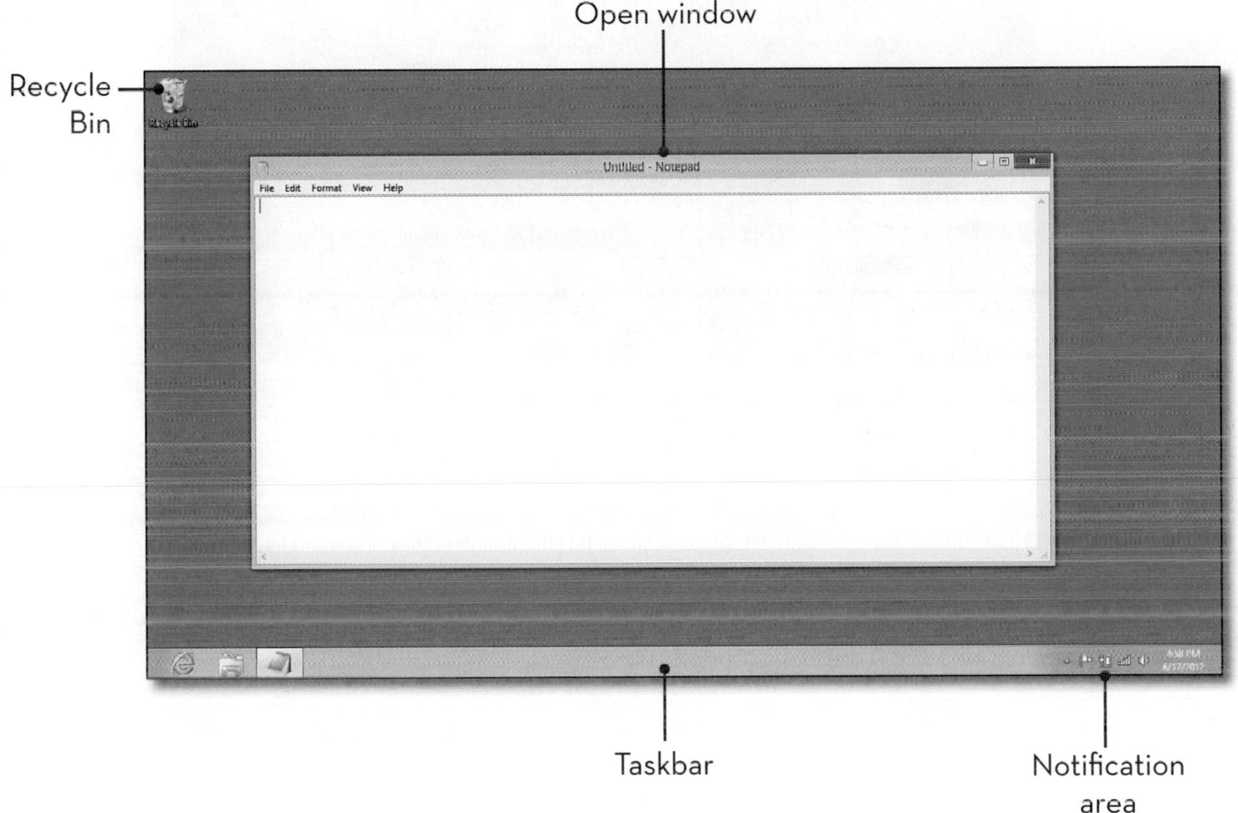

DISPLAYING THE TRADITIONAL DESKTOP

To display the traditional Windows desktop, all you have to do is tap or click the Desktop tile on the Start screen. This opens the desktop operating environment, from which you can use traditional software apps.

1. Click or tap the **Desktop** tile on the Start screen.

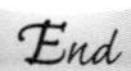

NOTE

Launching Automatically The traditional desktop launches automatically when you open a traditional app. ■

TIP

Windows 8 Desktop In earlier versions of Windows, all you had was the desktop; there wasn't a tiled Start screen. The older desktop featured a Start button and Start menu where all apps were listed. In Windows 8, there is no Start button or Start menu on the desktop; instead, you launch programs from the Start screen. ■

SCROLLING A WINDOW

Many windows contain more information than can be displayed in the window at once. When you have a long document or web page, for example, only the first part of the document or page is displayed in the window. To view the rest of the document or page, you have to scroll down through the window, using the various parts of the scrollbar.

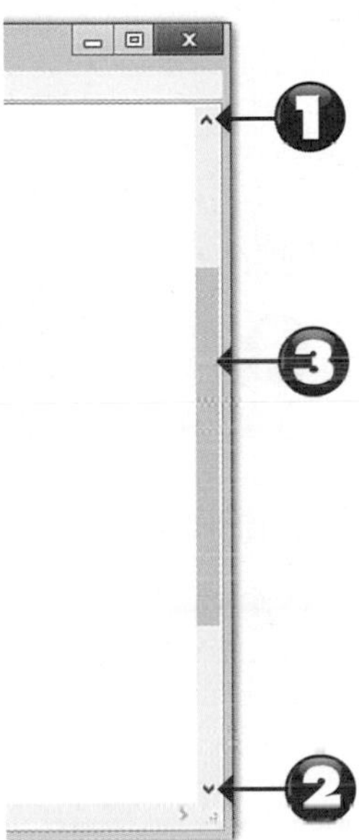

1. Click the up arrow on the window's scrollbar to scroll up one line at a time.
2. Click the down arrow on the window's scrollbar to scroll down one line at a time.
3. Click and drag the scroll box (slider) to scroll up or down in a smooth motion.

End

TIP

Full-Screen Scroll To scroll an entire screen at a time, click the scrollbar between the scroll box and the end arrow. ■

MAXIMIZING, MINIMIZING, AND CLOSING A WINDOW

After you've opened a window, you can maximize it to display full screen. You can also minimize it so that it disappears from the desktop and resides as a button on the Windows taskbar, and you can close it completely.

Start

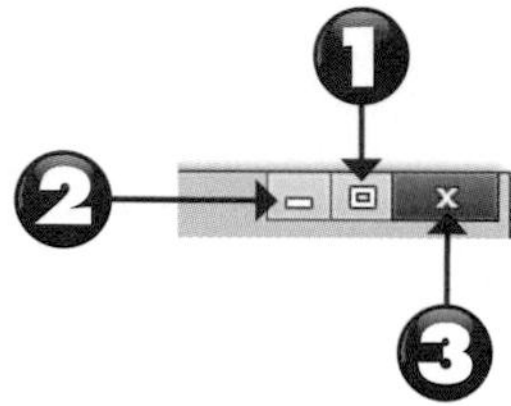

1. To maximize the window, click the **Maximize** button.
2. To minimize the window, click the **Minimize** button.
3. To close the window completely, click the **Close** button.

End

TIP

Restoring a Window If a window is already maximized, the Maximize button changes to a Restore Down button. When you click the Restore Down button, the window resumes its previous (pre-maximized) dimensions. ■

SNAPPING A WINDOW

You can automatically organize the open windows on the desktop in several ways. You can easily maximize windows and stack multiple windows side by side with just a few drags of the mouse.

Start

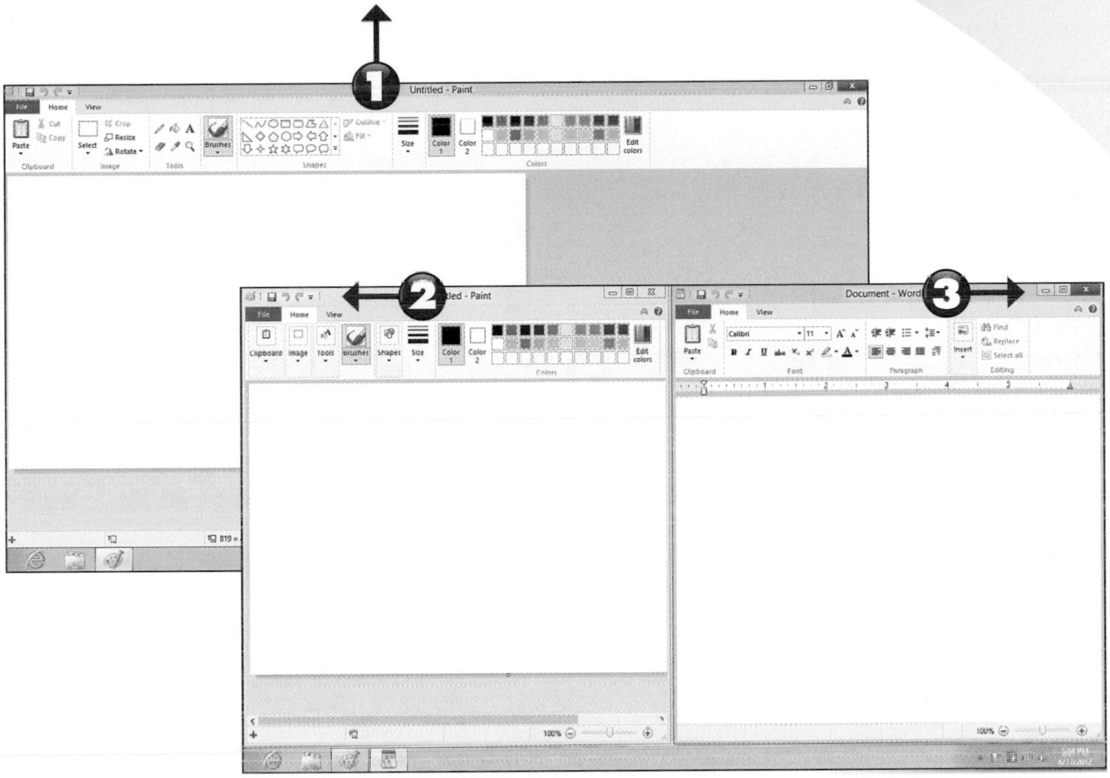

1. To maximize a window, click the window's title bar and drag it to the top edge of the screen, or press **Windows + up arrow**.
2. To snap a window to the left side of the screen, click the window's title bar and drag it to the left edge of the screen, or press **Windows + left arrow**.
3. To snap a window to the right side of the screen, click the window's title bar and drag it to the right edge of the screen, or press **Windows + right arrow**.

End

TIP

Restoring a Maximized Window To restore a maximized window, click the window's title bar and drag it down from the top of the screen, or press **Windows + down arrow**. ■

USING MENUS

Many older Windows programs use a set of pull-down menus to store all the commands and operations you can perform. The menus are aligned across the top of the window, just below the title bar, in what is called a *menu bar*. You open (or pull down) a menu by clicking the menu's name; you select a menu item by clicking it with your mouse.

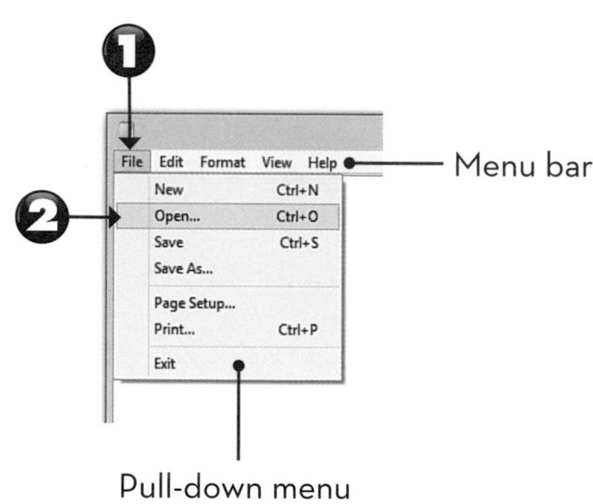

1. Click the menu's name to pull down the menu.
2. Click the menu item to select it.

End

TIP

Not All Items Are Available If an item in a menu, toolbar, or dialog box is dimmed (or grayed), that means it isn't available for the current task. ■

USING TOOLBARS AND RIBBONS

Some Windows programs put the most frequently used operations on one or more *toolbars* or *ribbons*, usually located just below the menu bar. A toolbar looks like a row of buttons, each with a small picture (called an *icon*) and maybe a bit of text. You activate the associated command or operation by clicking the button with your mouse.

Start

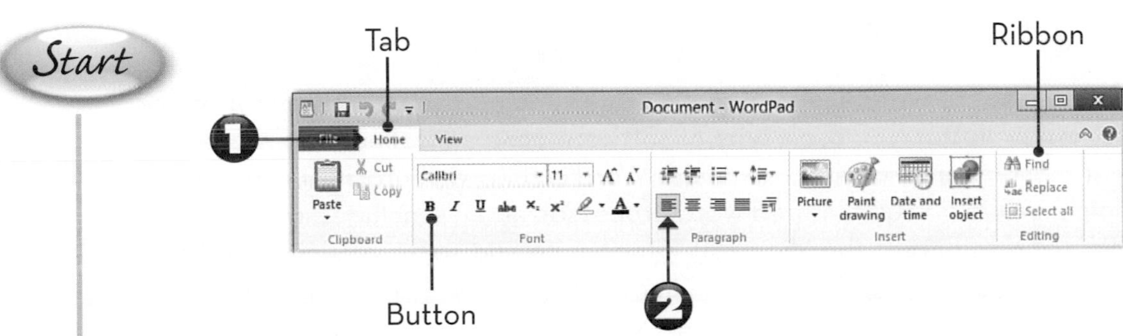

1. Click a tab to select that particular ribbon.
2. Click a ribbon/toolbar button to select that operation.

End

TIP

Long Toolbars If the toolbar is too long to display fully on your screen, you'll see a right arrow at the far-right side of the toolbar. Click this arrow to display the buttons that aren't currently visible. ■

NOTE

Ribbons The ribbon interface is found in many newer applications. Most older applications use toolbars instead. ■

USING MICROSOFT WORD

When you want to write a letter, fire off a quick memo, create a fancy report, or publish a newsletter, you use a type of software program called a *word processor*. For most computer users, Microsoft Word is the word processing program of choice. Word is a full-featured word processor, and it's included on many new PCs and as part of the Microsoft Office suite and some versions of Microsoft Works. You can use Word for all your writing needs—from basic letters to fancy newsletters and everything in between.

Two versions of Word are available. Microsoft Word Web App is a free web-based version you access using Internet Explorer or another web browser. There's also the traditional desktop software version of Word, which can be purchased from any consumer electronics store or downloaded from Internet retailers.

For many users, the Word Web App is sufficient, even though it lacks some of the advanced features of the more expensive desktop version. If you want to do sophisticated page layouts, mail merges, and similar functions, you'll need to purchase the desktop software version of Word. Otherwise, use the free online version—it's fine for writing memos, letters, and the like.

COMPARING DESKTOP AND WEB VERSIONS OF WORD

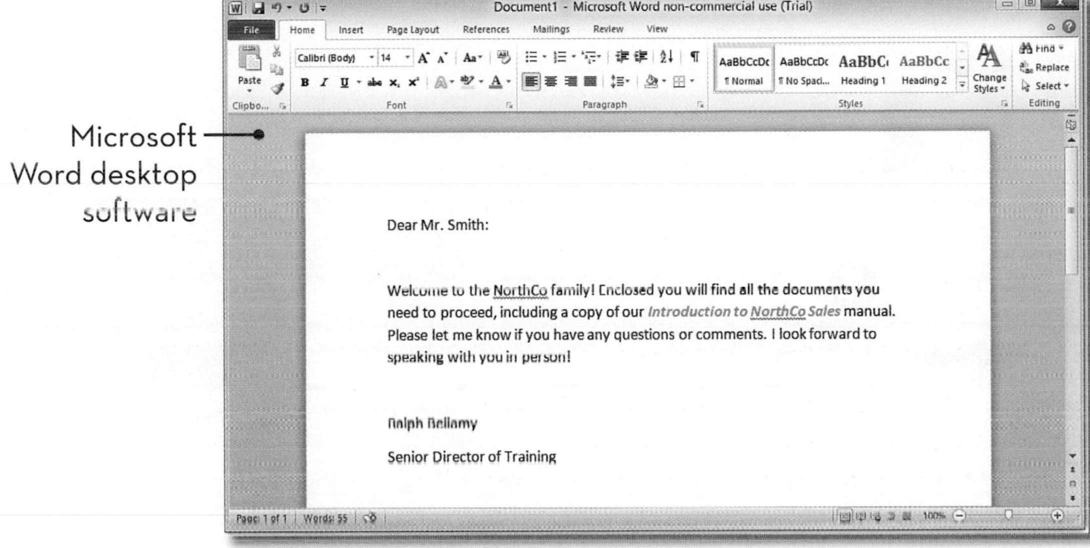

Microsoft Word desktop software

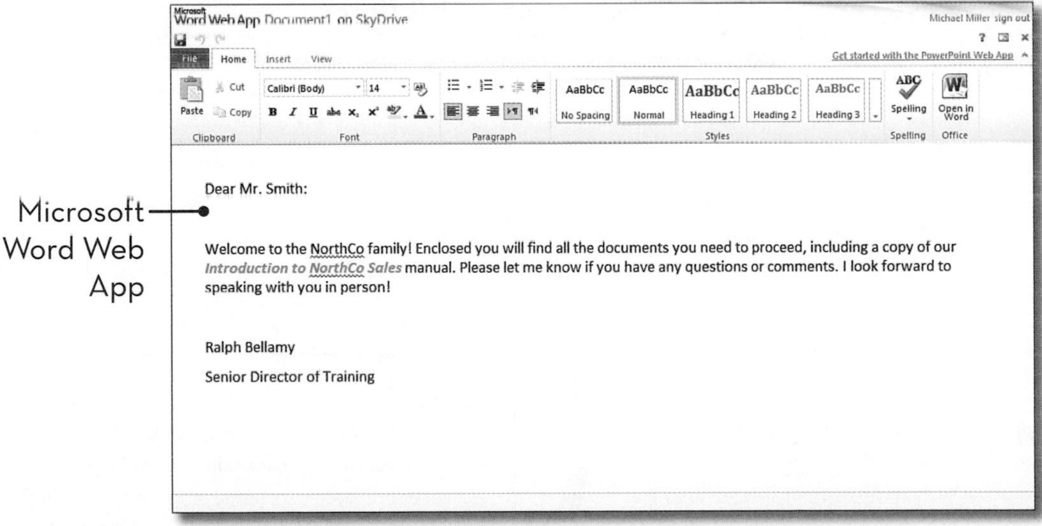

Microsoft Word Web App

LAUNCHING THE WORD WEB APP

If you don't want to go to all the trouble of purchasing and installing an expensive piece of software, you can use the free Microsoft Word Web App from your web browser. You access Word Web App (and all the free Office Web Apps) from Microsoft's SkyDrive web-based storage system.

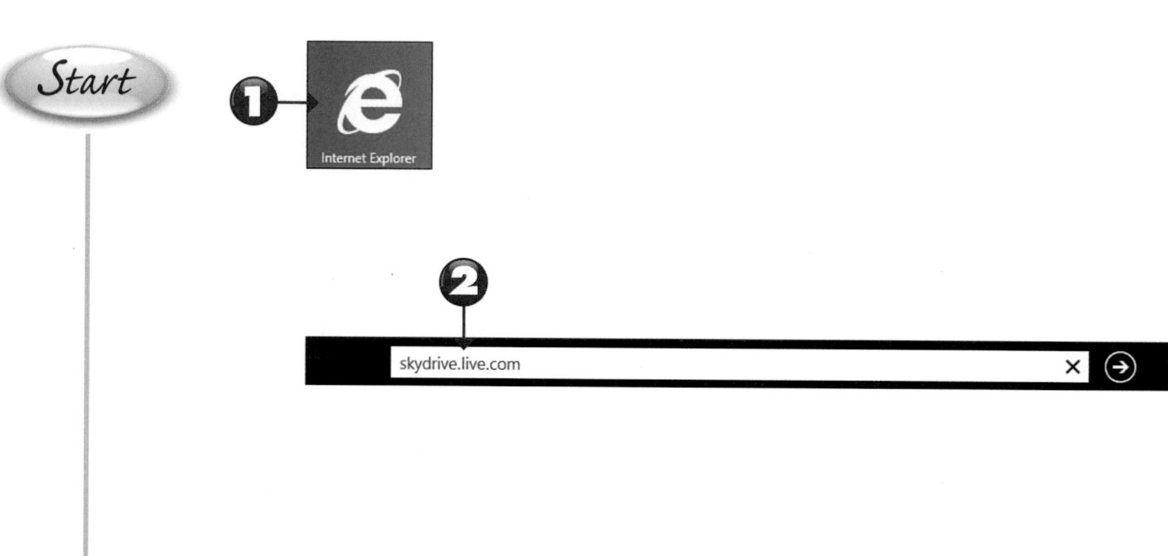

1. From the Windows Start screen, click or tap the **Internet Explorer** tile.
2. Enter **skydrive.live.com** into the Address box and press **Enter**.

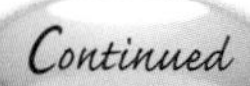

NOTE

SkyDrive App You can also open and edit existing Word documents using the SkyDrive app found on the Windows 8 Start screen. However, at this writing, you can't use the SkyDrive app to create new documents; you have to do this from within Internet Explorer. ■

NOTE

Office Web Apps Microsoft's Office Web Apps include Word (word processing), Excel (spreadsheets), PowerPoint (presentations), and OneNote (notes and planning). Learn more about Office Web Apps online at office.microsoft.com/en-us/web-apps/. ■

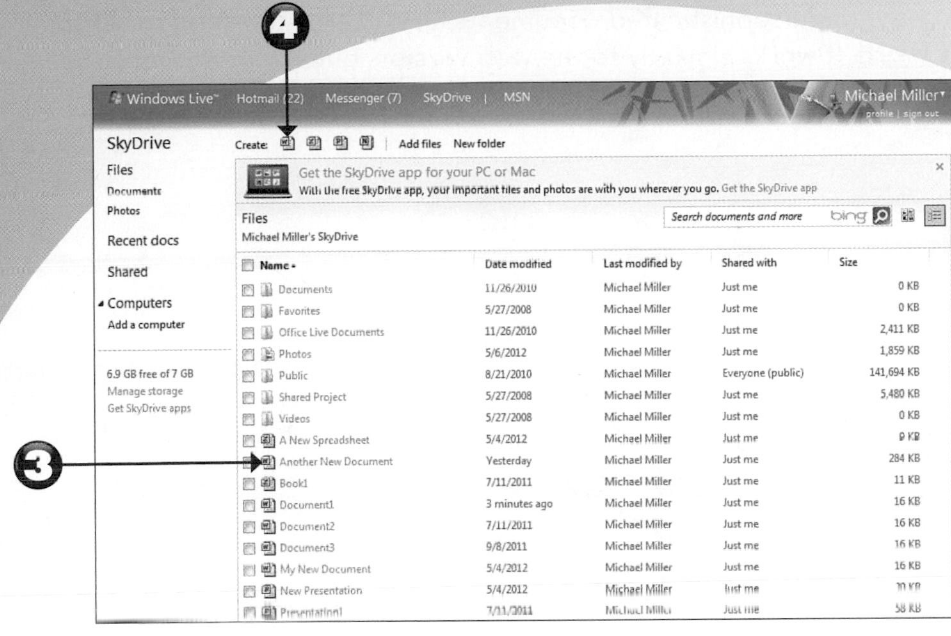

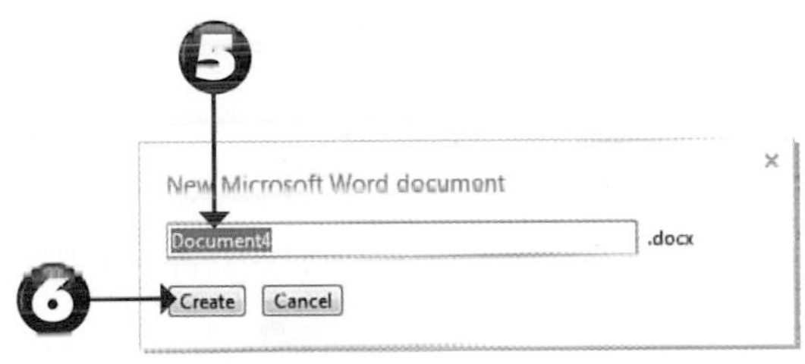

3 You now see all the files you've previously uploaded to SkyDrive, organized in the folders you created. To open an existing document, double-click it.

4 To open a new Word document, click the **Word** icon in the Create bar at the top of the screen.

5 Enter a name for this new document into the New Microsoft Word Document dialog box.

6 Click the **Create** button.

End

NOTE

Icons Word, Excel, and PowerPoint files are displayed with icons that include the app logos, so you can quickly see what kind of file you're looking at. ■

LAUNCHING THE WORD DESKTOP APP

When you need to create more sophisticated documents, use the full-featured desktop version of Microsoft Word. It works similarly to the web version, but with more formatting options.

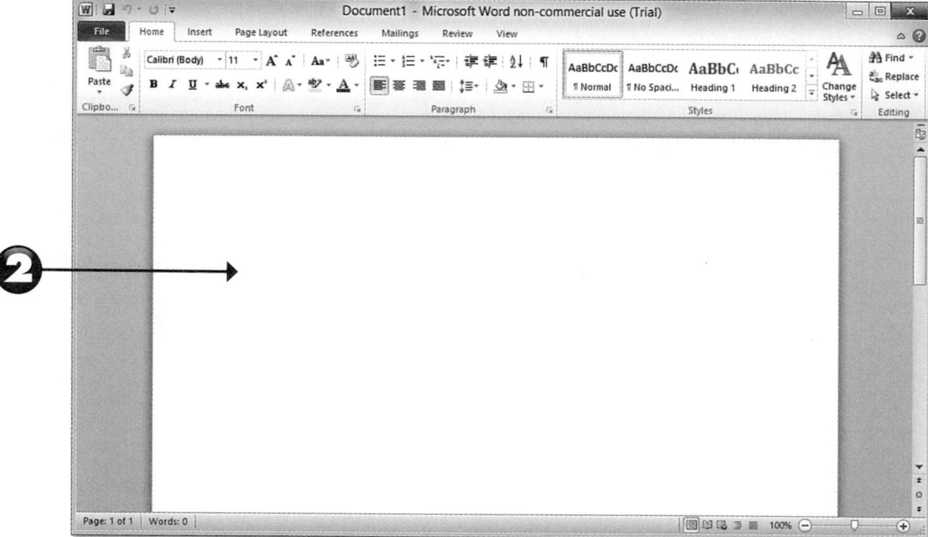

1. From the Windows Start screen, click or tap the **Microsoft Word** tile.
2. Word now launches with a blank document onscreen.

End

NOTE

Word in Office You usually purchase Microsoft Word as part of the Microsoft Office suite of programs. There are several editions of Microsoft Office. For most home users, the Home and Student Edition is the right fit; it includes Word, Excel, and PowerPoint, and costs just $119.99. ■

NOTE

Trial Version Many PC manufacturers include a trial version of Word on their new machines. You can typically use this trial version for 90 days before you decide whether to purchase it. ■

NAVIGATING THE WORD WEB APP

The Word Web App, like the desktop version of Word, uses a ribbon-based interface with different ribbons for different types of operations. Each ribbon contains buttons and controls for specific operations. For example, the Home ribbon contains controls for formatting fonts, paragraphs, and the like; the Insert ribbon includes controls for inserting tables, pictures, clip art, and such.

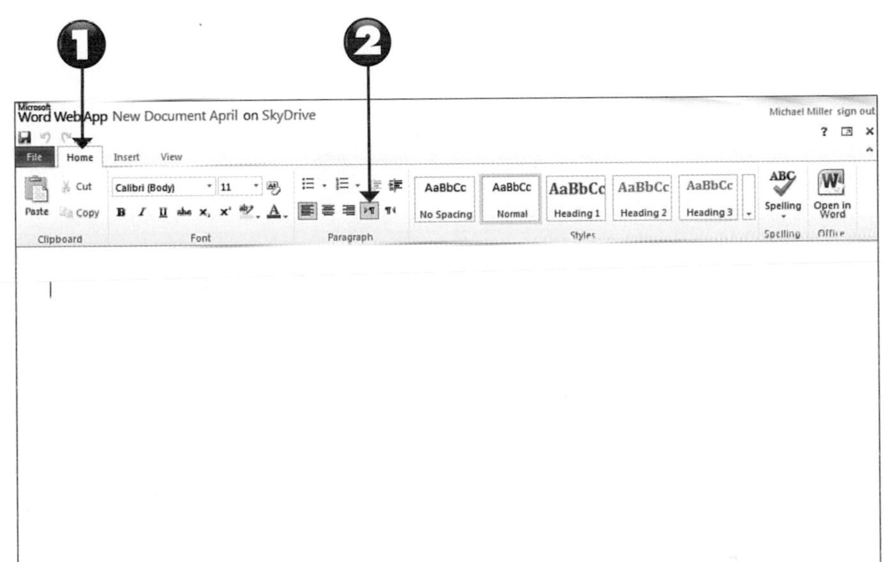

1. Click any tab to display the related ribbon.
2. Click a button or control on the ribbon to perform the given operation.

End

TIP

Context-Sensitive Ribbons Some ribbons appear automatically when you perform a specific task. For example, if you insert a picture and then select that picture, a new Format ribbon tab (not otherwise visible) will appear, with controls for formatting the selected picture. ■

TIP

Different Ribbons The desktop software version of Microsoft Word contains additional ribbons (such as Page Layout, References, and Mailings) not found in the Word Web App. ■

ENTERING TEXT

You enter text in a Word document at the *insertion point*, which appears onscreen as a blinking cursor. When you start typing on your keyboard, the new text is added at the insertion point.

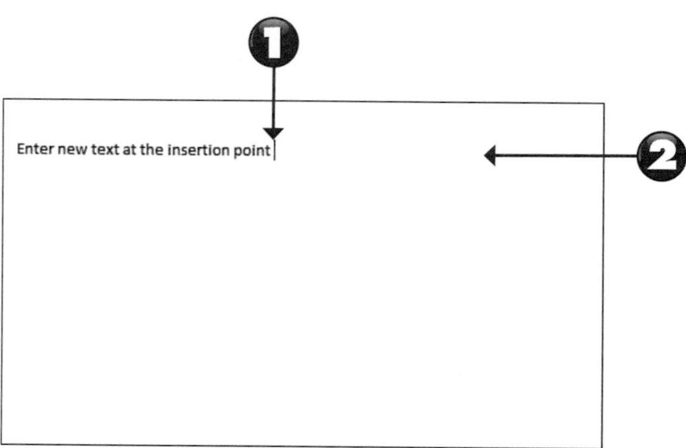

1. Within your document, click where you want to enter the new text.

2. Type the text.

End

TIP

Move the Insertion Point You move the insertion point with your mouse by clicking a new position in your text. You move the insertion point with your keyboard by using your keyboard's arrow keys. ■

NOTE

Working with Documents Anything you create with Word—a letter, memo, newsletter, and so on—is called a *document*. A document is nothing more than a computer file that can be copied, moved, deleted, or edited from within Word. ■

CUTTING/COPYING AND PASTING TEXT

Word lets you cut, copy, and paste text—or graphics—to and from anywhere in your document or between documents. Use your mouse to select the text you want to edit, and then select the appropriate command from the Home ribbon.

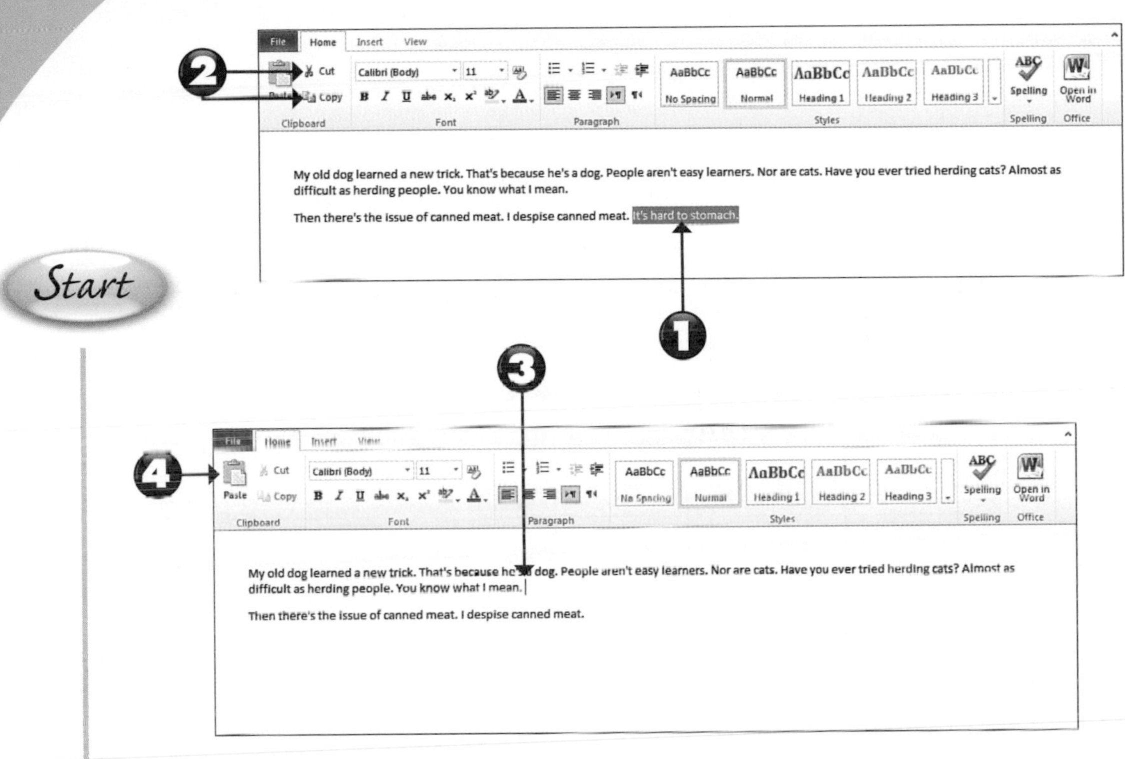

1. Click and drag the cursor to select the text you want to copy or cut.
2. From the Home ribbon, click **Copy** to copy the text or **Cut** to cut the text.
3. Within the document, click where you want to paste the cut or copied text.
4. From the Home ribbon, click **Paste**.

End

TIP

Keyboard Shortcuts You also can select text using your keyboard; use the Shift key—in combination with other keys—to highlight blocks of text. For example, Shift + left arrow selects one character to the left. ■

NOTE

Cut Versus Copy Cutting text removes the text from the original location and then pastes it into a new location. Copying text leaves the text in the original location and pastes a copy of it into a new location—essentially duplicating the text. ■

FORMATTING TEXT

After your text is entered and edited, you can use Word's numerous formatting options to add some pizzazz to your document.

Start

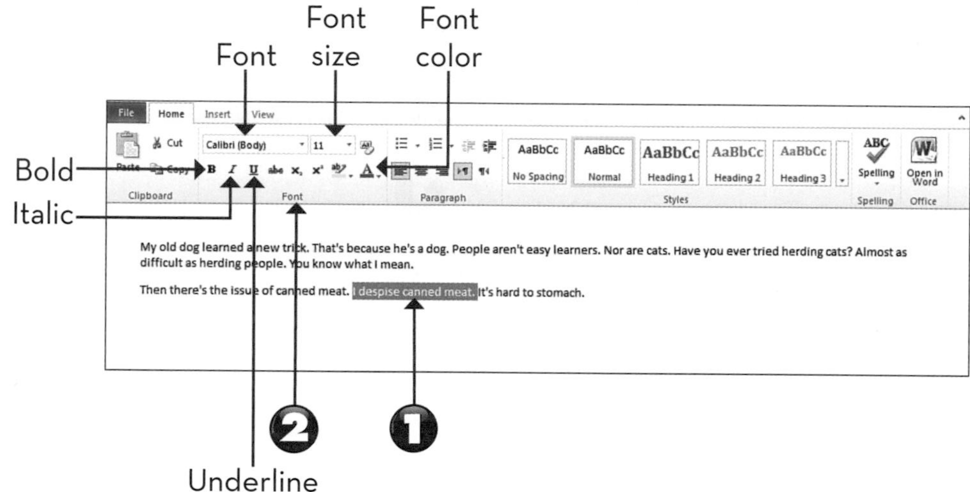

1. Click and drag the cursor over the text you want to edit.

2. Click the desired button in the Font section of the Home ribbon—**Font**, **Font Size**, **Bold**, **Italic**, **Underline**, or **Font Color**.

End

FORMATTING PARAGRAPHS

When you're creating a more complex document, you need to format more than just a few words here and there. To format complete paragraphs, use Word's Paragraph formatting options on the Home ribbon.

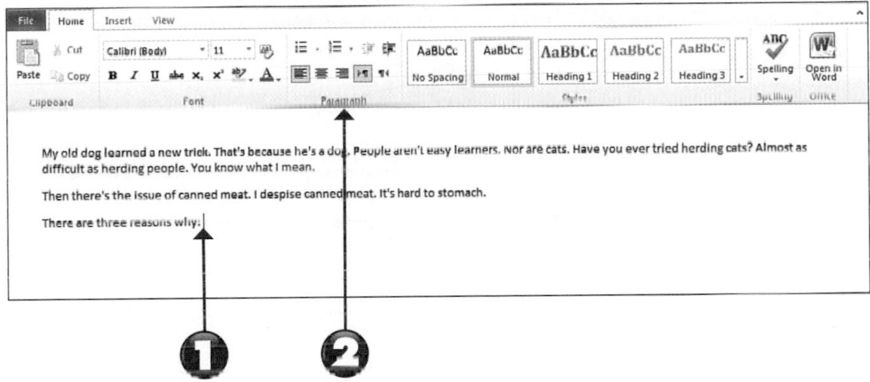

1. Click anywhere within the paragraph you want to format.
2. Click the desired button in the Paragraph section of the Home ribbon—including **Bullets**, **Numbering**, **Decrease Indent**, **Increase Indent, Line Spacing**, or any of the **Align Text** options.

End

TIP

Spell Checking If you misspell a word, it appears onscreen with a squiggly red underline. Right-click the misspelled word and select the correct spelling from the list. ■

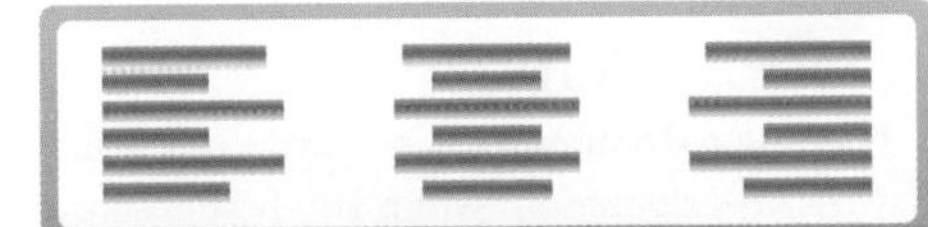

SAVING YOUR WORK

As you work on a file, you need to save your edits periodically. This is an easy process.

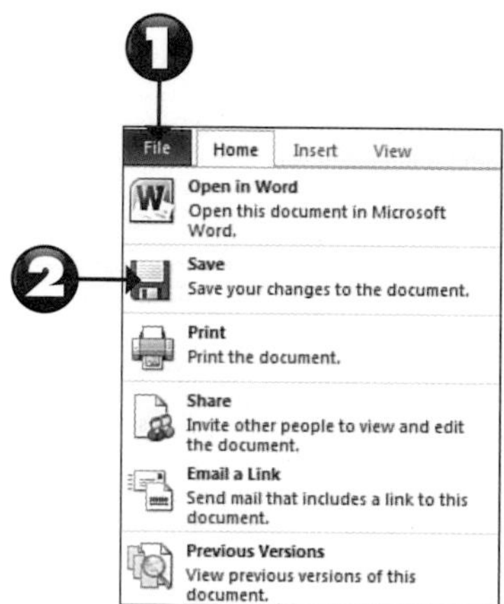

1. Select the **File** ribbon.
2. Click **Save**.

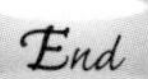

TIP

Naming a Document The Word Web App named your new document when you first created it. The desktop version of Word prompts you to name a document the first time you save it. ■

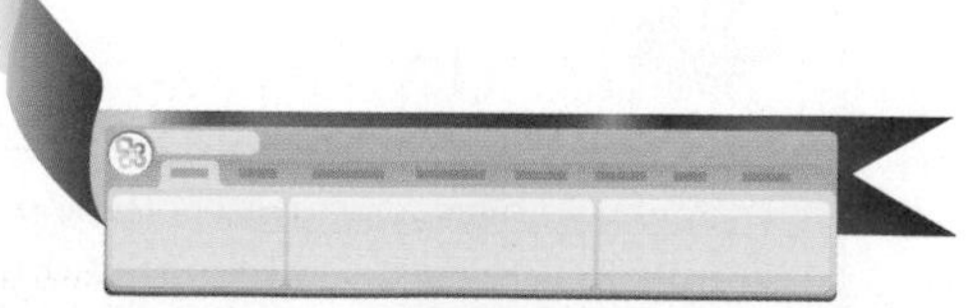

PRINTING A DOCUMENT

When you've finished editing your document, you can instruct Word to send a copy to printer. With the Word Web App, this involves creating a PDF-format copy of your doc ment, opening that document with a PDF viewer app (such as Adobe Reader), and the using that app's print function to print the document.

Start

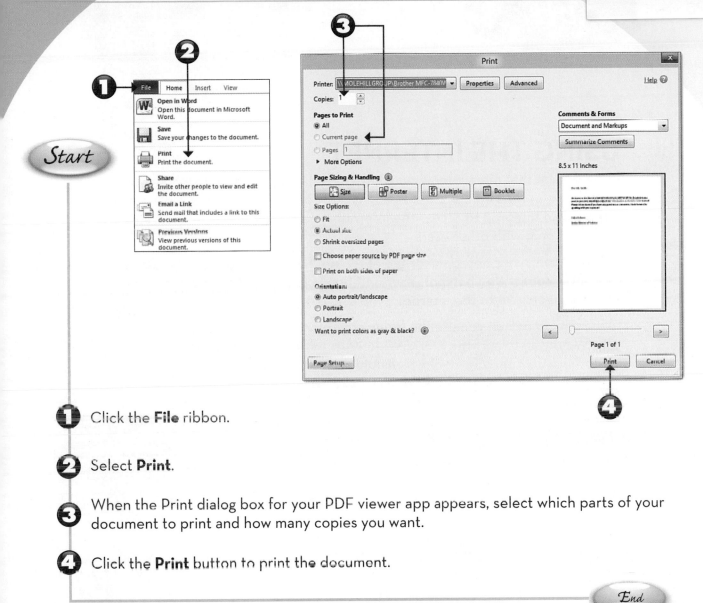

1. Click the **File** ribbon.
2. Select **Print**.
3. When the Print dialog box for your PDF viewer app appears, select which parts of your document to print and how many copies you want.
4. Click the **Print** button to print the document.

End

TIP

PDF Printing The Word Web App uses your computer's default PDF viewer to print your documents. If you don't have a PDF viewer installed on your system, you can download Adobe Reader for free from get.adobe.com/reader/. ■

TIP

Open or Save? If you're prompted to open or save the PDF document when printing from the Word Web App, select **Open**. This should open the Print dialog box for your PDF viewer app. ■

USING THE INTERNET

It used to be that most people bought personal computers to do work—word processing, spreadsheets, databases, that sort of thing. But today, most many people also buy PCs to access the Internet—to send and receive email, surf the Web, and chat with other users.

If you're using your notebook or tablet PC on the road, all you have to do is look for a public WiFi hotspot. Your notebook connects to the hotspot, which then connects you to the Internet, simple as pie.

Once you go online, you use the Internet Explorer (IE) *web browser* (included with Windows) to surf the World Wide Web. Information on the Web is presented in *web pages*, each of which contains text, graphics, and links to other web pages. A web page resides at a *website*, which is nothing more than a collection of web pages. The main page of a website is called the *home page*, which serves as an opening screen that provides a brief overview and a sort of menu of everything you can find at that site.

COMPARING THE WINDOWS 8 AND DESKTOP VERSIONS OF IE

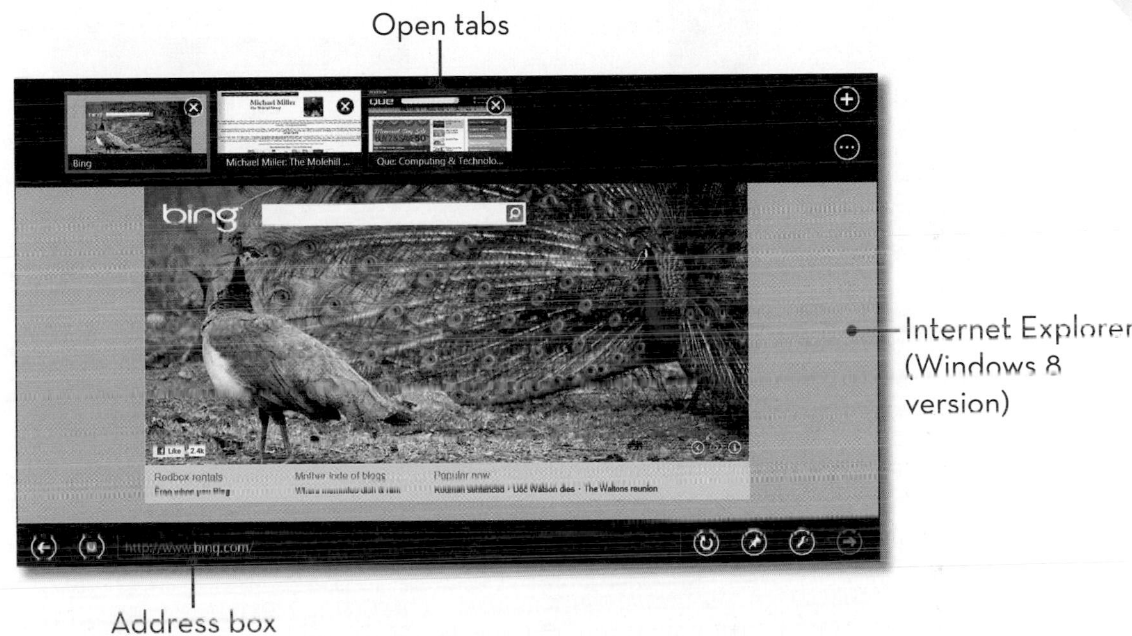

CONNECTING TO AN INTERNET WIFI HOTSPOT

If you have a notebook or tablet PC, you have the option to connect to the Internet when you're out and about. Many coffeehouses, libraries, hotels, and public spaces offer wireless WiFi Internet service, either free or for an hourly or daily fee.

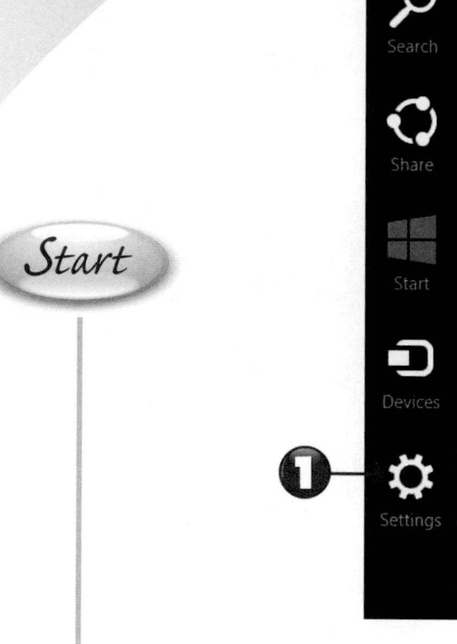

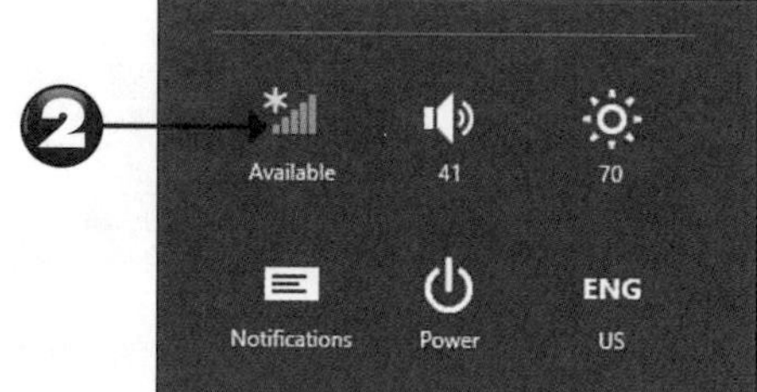

1. From the Start screen, display the charms bar, and then click or tap **Settings** to display the Settings panel.
2. Click or tap the **WiFi** icon. (If there are WiFi networks nearby, the icon should be labeled Available.)

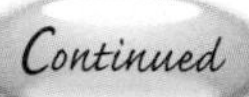

NOTE

Wireless Hotspots A *hotspot* is a public place that offers wireless access to the Internet using WiFi technology. Some hotspots are free for all to access; others require some sort of payment. ■

NOTE

Finding the WiFi Signal When you're near a WiFi hotspot, your PC should automatically pick up the WiFi signal. Just make sure that your WiFi adapter is turned on (some notebooks have a switch for this, either on the front or on the side of the unit), and then follow these directions to find and connect to the nearest hotspot. ■

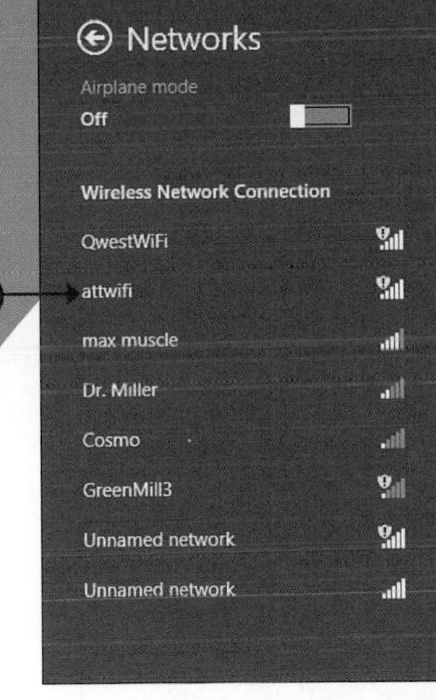

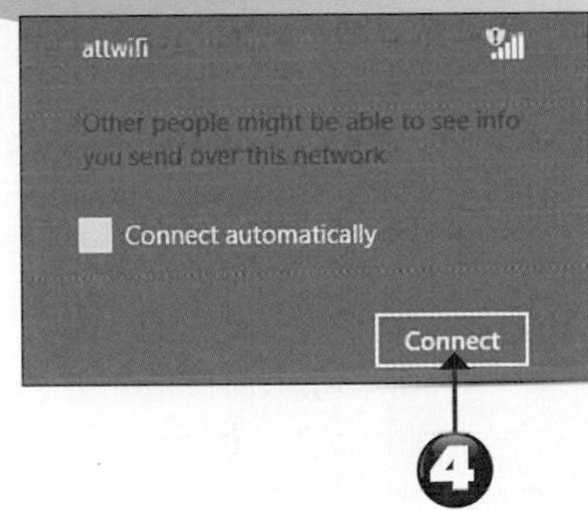

3 You now see a list of available wireless networks. Click or tap the network to which you want to connect.

4 This expands the panel; click **Connect** to connect to the selected hotspot.

5 If the hotspot has free public access, you can now open IE (from the Start screen) and surf normally. If the hotspot requires a password, payment, or other logon procedure, Windows should open IE and display the hotspot's login page. Enter the appropriate information to begin surfing.

End

TIP

Mobile Broadband If your notebook or tablet is configured to connect to your mobile phone carrier's data network, you'll see additional mobile broadband connection options within Windows. By default, Windows connects to available free or low-cost WiFi networks first. If no WiFi networks are available, it will connect to the data network you select. ■

TIP

Airplane Mode If you're using your notebook or tablet on an airplane, you can switch to Window's special Airplane mode so that you can use your computer while in the air. To switch into Airplane mode, go to the Start screen and display the charms bar, click **Settings**, and then click **Change PC Settings**. On the next page, select **Wireless** from the left column, and then click "on" the **Airplane Mode** option. You can switch off Airplane mode when your plane lands. ■

BROWSING THE WEB WITH IE

Internet Explorer is a web browser that lets you quickly and easily browse the World Wide Web. Windows 8 includes two versions of IE: a Windows 8 version optimized for full-screen use, and the traditional version found on the Windows desktop. Most users will find the Windows 8 version, accessed from the Start screen, the most convenient to use.

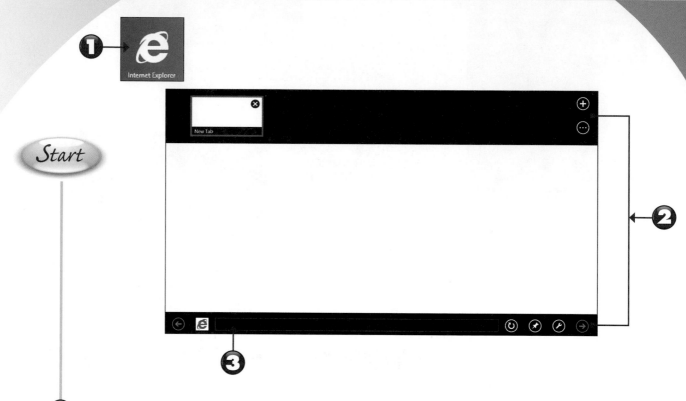

1. Launch IE by clicking or tapping the **Internet Explorer** tile on the Windows Start screen.
2. Right-click anywhere on the screen to display the options bars at the top and bottom of the screen.
3. Let's find out what's happening out in the real world by visiting one of the most popular news sites on the Web. Enter **www.cnn.com** in the Address box, and then press **Enter**.

Continued

NOTE

Other Browsers Internet Explorer isn't the only web browser you can use. Other browsers you can install and use with the traditional Windows desktop include Google Chrome (www.google.com/chrome/), Mozilla Firefox (www.mozilla.org/firefox/), and Apple Safari (www.apple.com/safari/). ■

4. Click any headline or link to read the complete story.

Continued

TIP

Home Page? The desktop version of IE lets you set a *home page* that automatically opens whenever you launch the browser. The Metro version of IE does not have a similar feature—although if you set a home page in the desktop version, it will display automatically in the Metro version, as well. ■

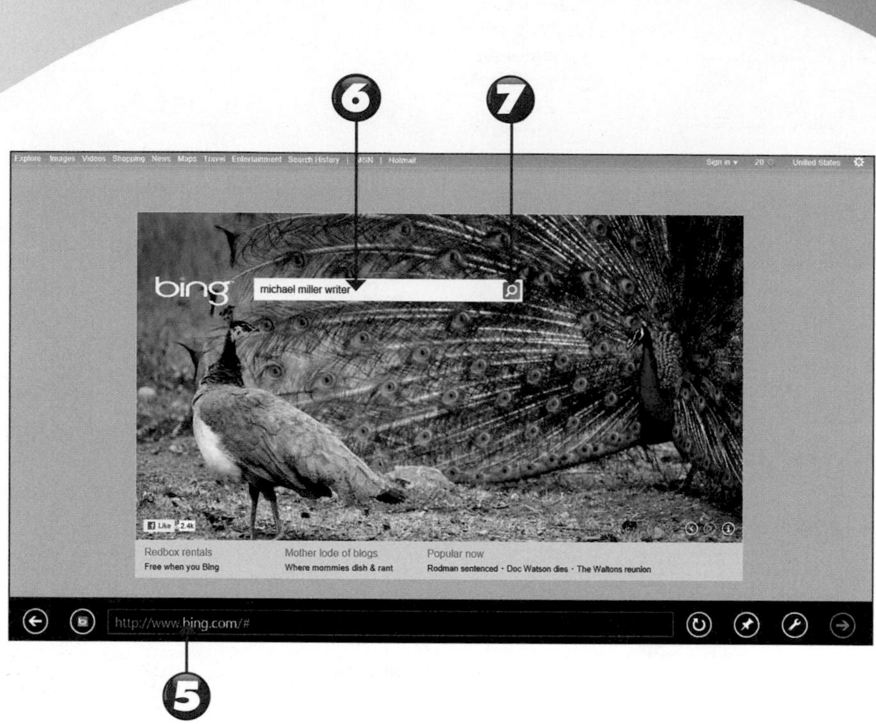

5. Now, let's do a little searching with Microsoft Bing. Enter **www.bing.com** in the Address box and press **Enter**.
6. Ready to search? Enter **michael miller writer** in the Search box.
7. Click the **Search** (magnifying glass) button to begin the search.

Continued

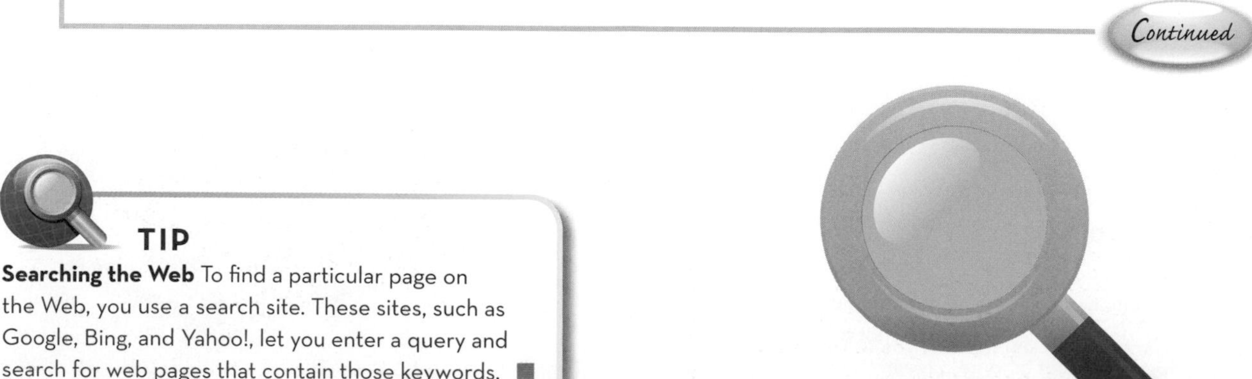

TIP

Searching the Web To find a particular page on the Web, you use a search site. These sites, such as Google, Bing, and Yahoo!, let you enter a query and search for web pages that contain those keywords. ■

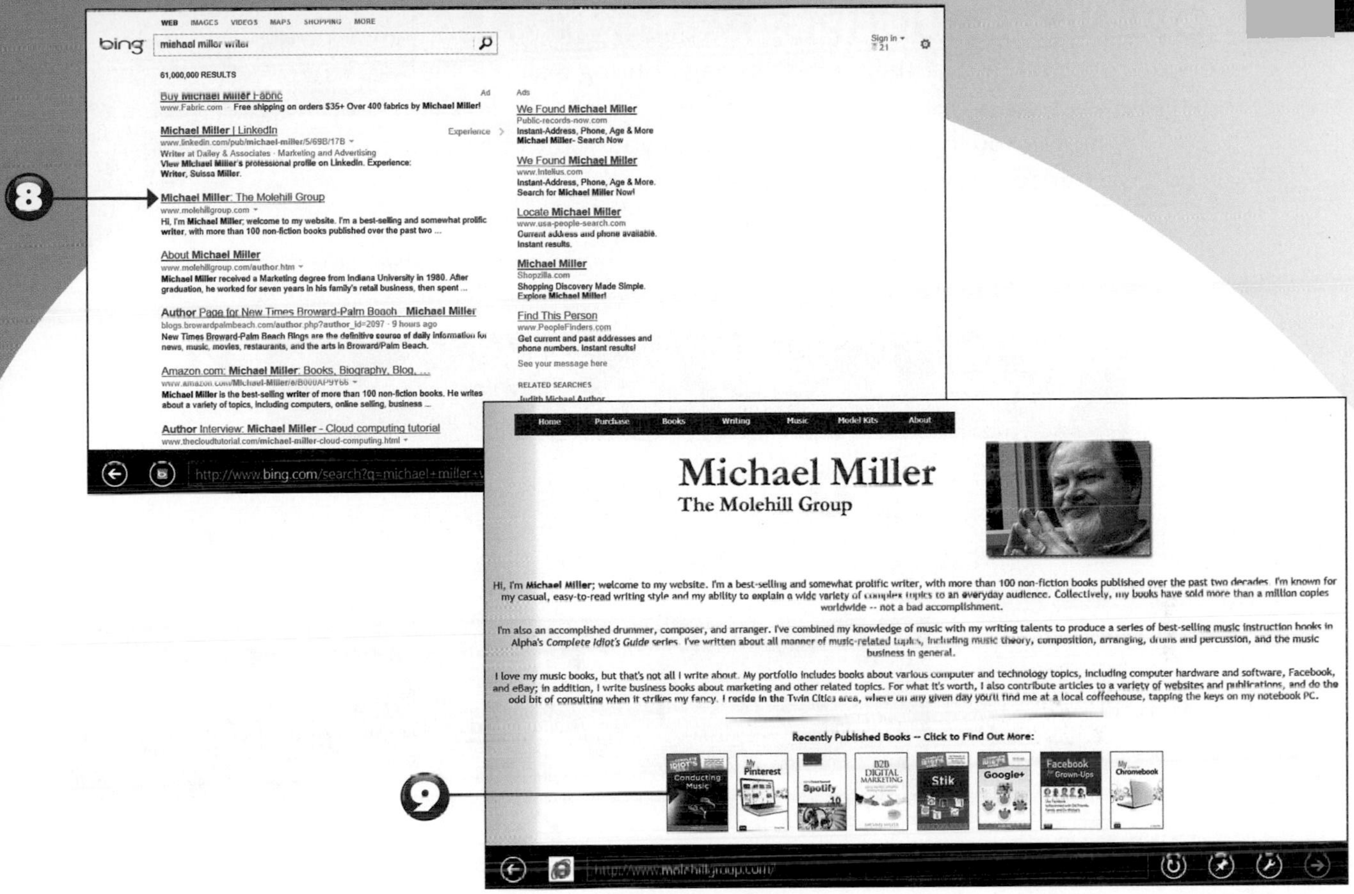

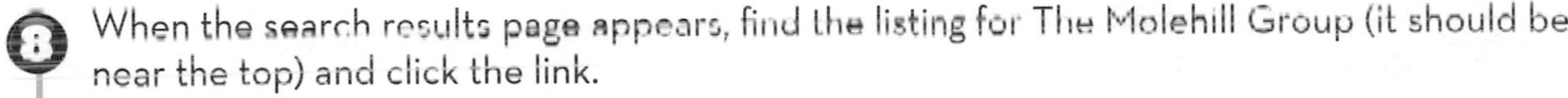

8. When the search results page appears, find the listing for The Molehill Group (it should be near the top) and click the link.

9. You're now taken to *my* website, The Molehill Group. Click one of the book pictures to read more about that book.

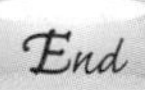

TIP

Going Back To return to the last-viewed web page, click the **Back** button on the bottom options bar, or press the **Backspace** key on your keyboard. If you've backed up several pages and want to return to the page you were on last, click the **Forward** button. ■

OPENING MULTIPLE PAGES IN TABS

If you're visiting more than one web page during a single session, you can display each page as a separate *tab* in the web browser. This use of tabs lets you keep multiple web pages open simultaneously—which is great when you want to reference different pages or want to run web-based applications in the background.

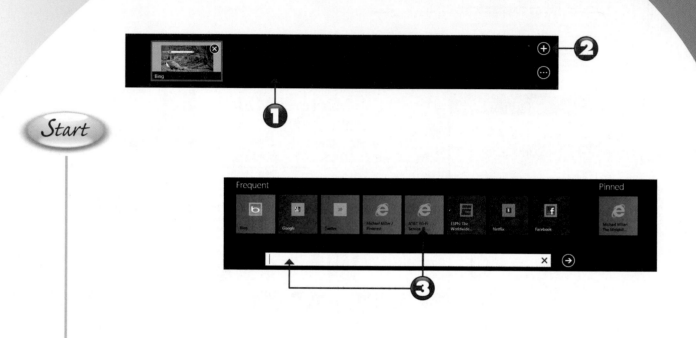

1. To open a new tab, right-click within the browser to display the tab bar at the top of the screen.
2. Click or tap the **New Tab (+)** button to display the Frequent and Pinned bar at the bottom of the screen.
3. Either click a tile on this screen or enter a new web page address in the Address box.

End

TIP

InPrivate Browsing If you want to browse anonymously, without any traces of your history recorded, activate IE's InPrivate Browsing mode on a new tab. Display the tab bar and click the "three dot" (**...**) button, and then click **New InPrivate Tab** from the pop-up menu. ■

SWITCHING BETWEEN TABS

Switching between open web pages is as easy as clicking different tabs. IE displays a small thumbnail of each open page/tab on the tab bar.

Start

1. Right-click within the browser to display the tab bar.
2. Click or tap the tab you want to view.

End

TIP

Closing a Tab To close any open tab, click or tap the **X** by the tab.

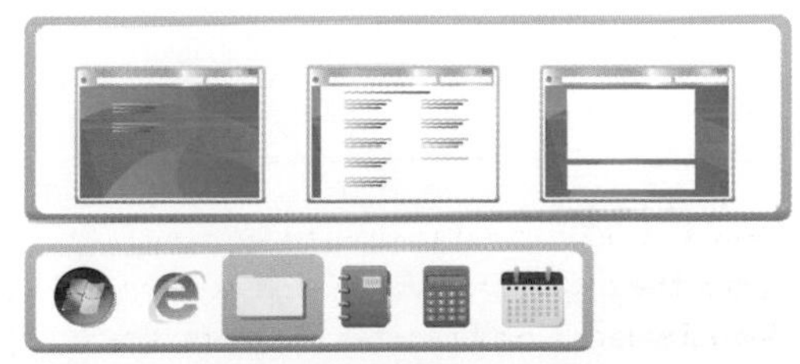

SAVING FAVORITE PAGES

When you find a web page you like, you can pin it as a tile to the Windows Start screen. This process also saves the web page to IE's Frequent and Pinned screen, which you can access from within IE. This way, you can easily access any of your favorite sites just by selecting them from the list.

Start

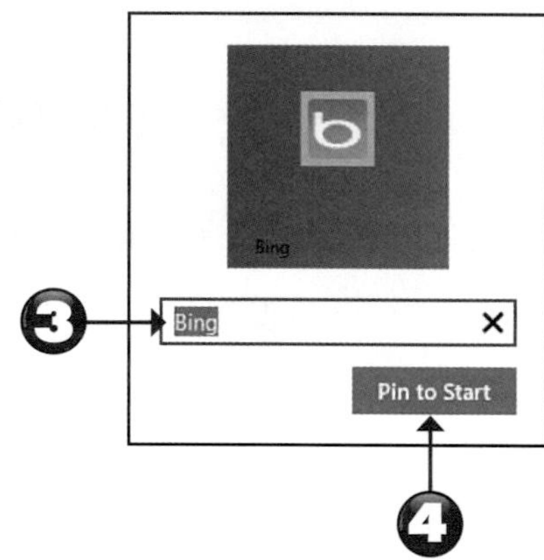

1. Navigate to the web page you want to pin, and then right-click the page to display the address bar.
2. Click or tap the **Pin to Start** button.
3. When the Pin panel appears, confirm or edit the name of the page.
4. Click or tap the **Pin to Start** button.

End

NOTE

Favorite Pages The desktop version of IE lets you save your favorite pages in a Favorites list. Metro IE lets you pin favorite pages to the Start screen, but does not offer a Favorites list. ■

RETURNING TO A FAVORITE PAGE

To return to a page you've saved as a favorite, you can click or tap that page's tile on the Start screen, or select that page from the Frequent and Pinned Screen in IE.

Start

1. Right-click the current page to display the address bar.
2. Click or tab within the Address box to display the Frequent and Pinned page.
3. Click or tap the page you want to revisit.

End

NOTE

Frequent and Pinned The Frequent column displays those pages you've visited most often. The Pinned column displays those pages you've pinned to the Start menu. ■

LAUNCHING THE DESKTOP VERSION OF IE

The Windows 8 version of Internet Explorer is easy to use and more than sufficient for most users. More experienced users, however, might prefer the additional functionality found in the traditional version of IE, which runs on the Windows 8 desktop.

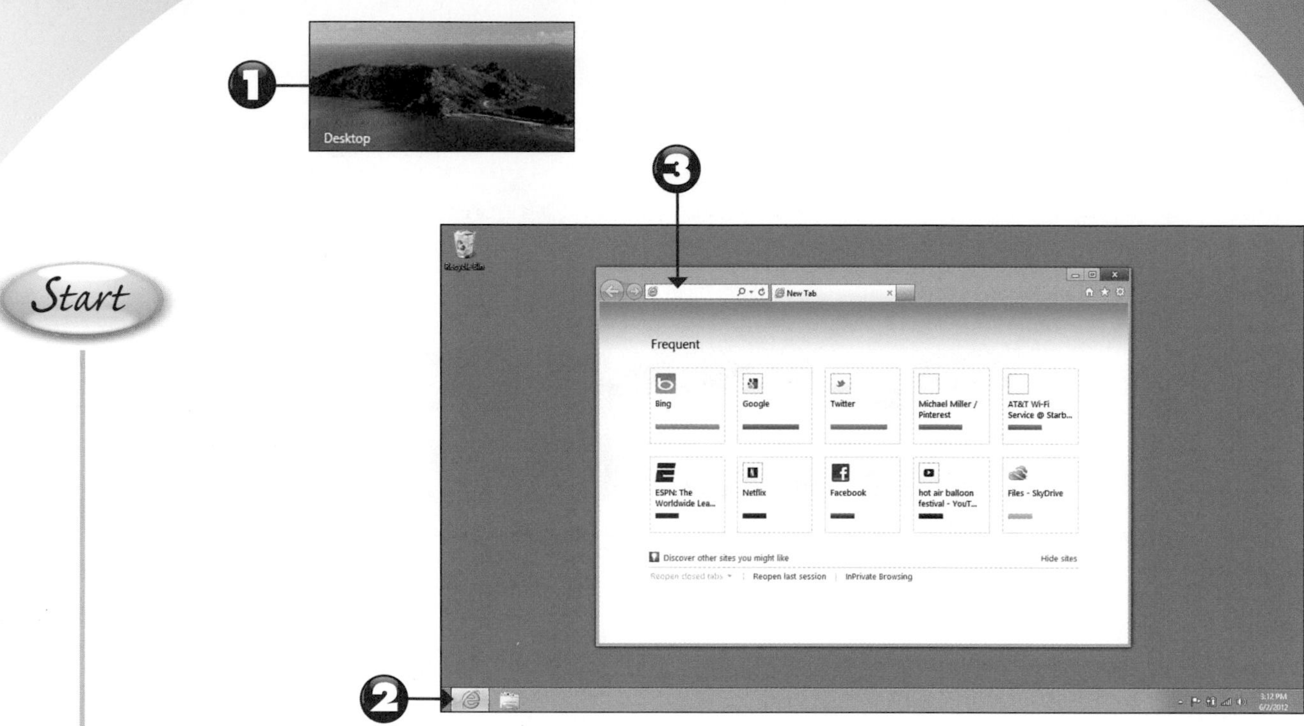

1. From the Windows Start screen, click or tap the **Desktop** icon.
2. When the Windows Desktop appears, click the **Internet Explorer** icon on the taskbar at the bottom of the screen.
3. Internet Explorer now opens in its own window on the desktop. Enter a new web address into the Address box.

NOTE

IE on the Desktop The desktop version of IE looks and acts more like a traditional web browser and features additional functionality. Use the desktop version of IE when you need to keep large lists of favorite pages, print pages, manage downloaded files, and perform other advanced operations. ■

SEARCHING THE WEB WITH GOOGLE

A web search engine lets you search for nearly anything online. The most popular search engine today is Google (www.google.com), which indexes billions of individual web pages. Google is very easy to use and returns extremely accurate results.

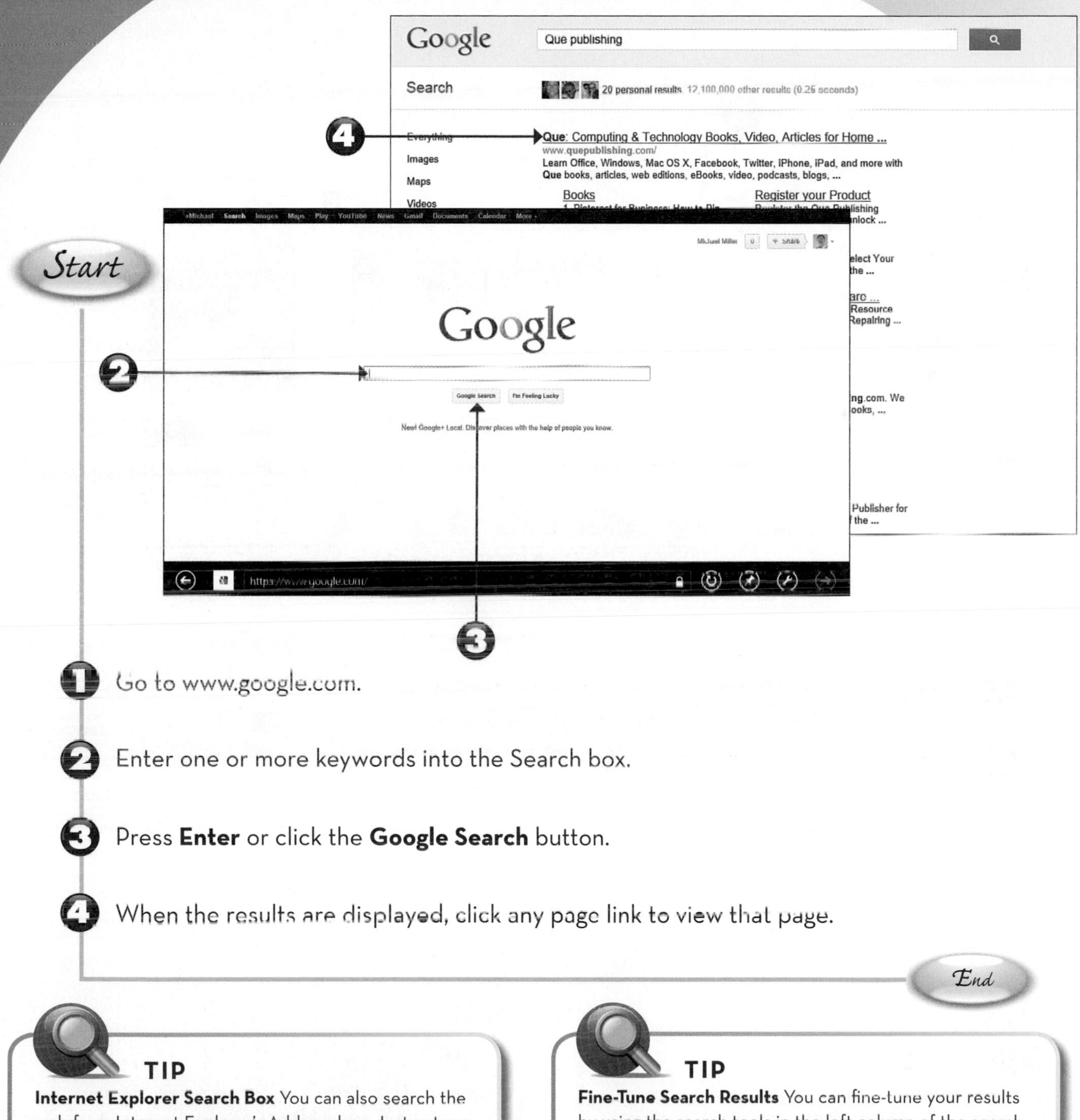

1. Go to www.google.com.
2. Enter one or more keywords into the Search box.
3. Press **Enter** or click the **Google Search** button.
4. When the results are displayed, click any page link to view that page.

End

TIP

Internet Explorer Search Box You can also search the web from Internet Explorer's Address box. Just enter a query instead of a web page address, and IE will search your default search engine for matching pages. ■

TIP

Fine-Tune Search Results You can fine-tune your results by using the search tools in the left column of the search results page. Click **More Search Tools** and select to filter by date/time, images, visited pages, reading level, location, and other criteria. ■

SHOPPING ONLINE

The Internet is a great place to buy things, from books to clothing to household items to cars. Online shopping is safe and convenient—all you need is your computer and a credit card.

Start

1. Find an online store that sells the item you're shopping for.

2. Search or browse for the product you like.

Continued

TIP

Traditional Retailers Online Most bricks-and-mortar retailers have equivalent online stores. For example, you can shop at Target online at www.target.com, or Macy's online at www.macys.com. Most catalog merchants also have their own websites where you can order online. ■

TIP

Online-Only Retailers Many big online-only retailers sell a variety of merchandise. The most popular of these include Amazon.com (www.amazon.com) and Overstock.com (www.overstock.com). ■

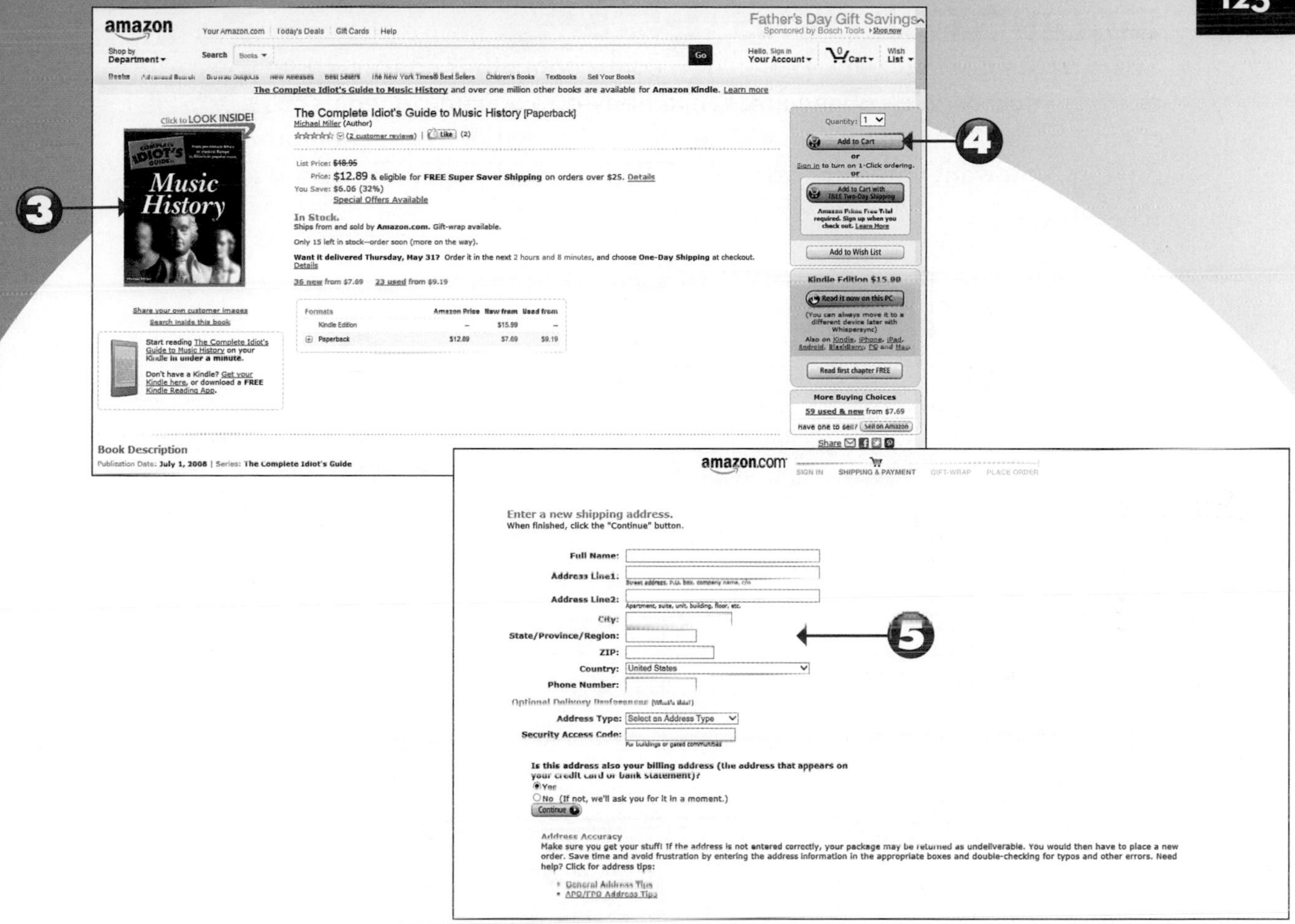

Examine the product by viewing the photos and information on the product listing page.

Order the product by clicking a **Buy It Now** or **Add to Cart** button on the product listing page. This puts the item in your online shopping cart.

Check out by entering your shipping and payment (credit card) information.

End

TIP

In-Stock Items The better online retailers tell you either on the product description page or during the checkout process whether an item is in stock. Look for this information to help you decide how to group your items for shipment. ■

TIP

Shop Safely The safest way to shop online is to pay via credit card, as your credit card company offers various consumer protections. (Smaller merchants might accept credit cards via PayPal or a similar online payment service; this is also acceptable.) Also make sure the retailer you buy from offers an acceptable returns policy, just in case. ■

BIDDING FOR ITEMS ON EBAY

Some of the best bargains on the Web come from other consumers selling items via online auction at eBay (www.ebay.com). While eBay offers fixed-priced items, too (look for the Buy It Now button), many consumers like the excitement of the auction process. Once you find an item, you want you place your bid. Other users also place bids, and at the end of the auction the highest bidder wins.

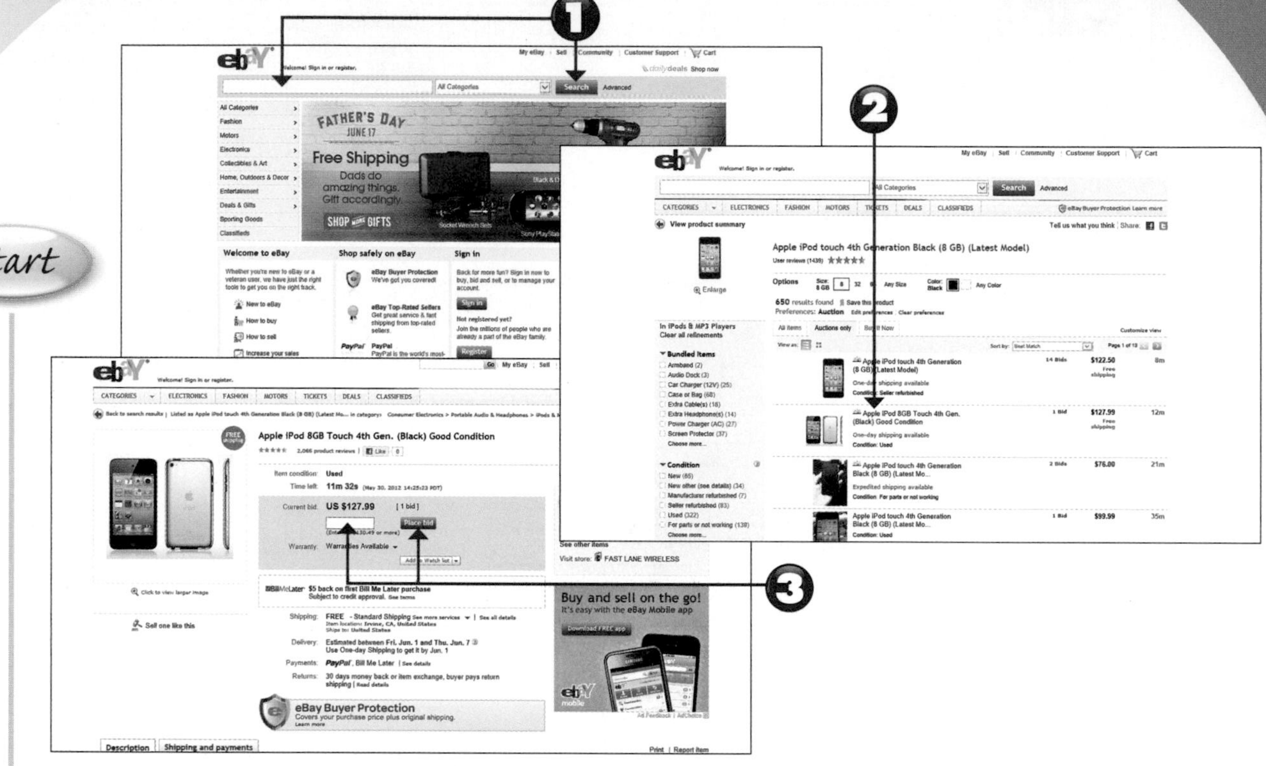

Start

1. On the eBay home page (www.ebay.com), enter keywords describing the item you're looking for into the Search box, and then click the **Search** button.

2. When the search results page appears, click the link for the item you're interested in.

3. Enter the maximum amount you're willing to pay into the empty bid box, and then click the **Place Bid** button.

End

TIP

Place Your Best Bid Always bid the highest amount you're willing to pay. eBay's proxy software enters only the minimum bid necessary, without revealing your maximum bid amount. Your bid will be raised automatically when other users bid until the bid amount reaches your maximum. ■

TIP

You Win! If you're the high bidder at the end of the auction period, you win! When you receive the end-of-auction notification email from eBay, click the **Pay For It** button and follow the onscreen instructions from there. ■

BUYING ITEMS ON CRAIGSLIST

When you're looking to buy something locally, you can often find great bargains on Craigslist (www.craigslist.org), an online classified advertising site. Browse the ads until you find what you want, and then arrange with the seller to make the purchase.

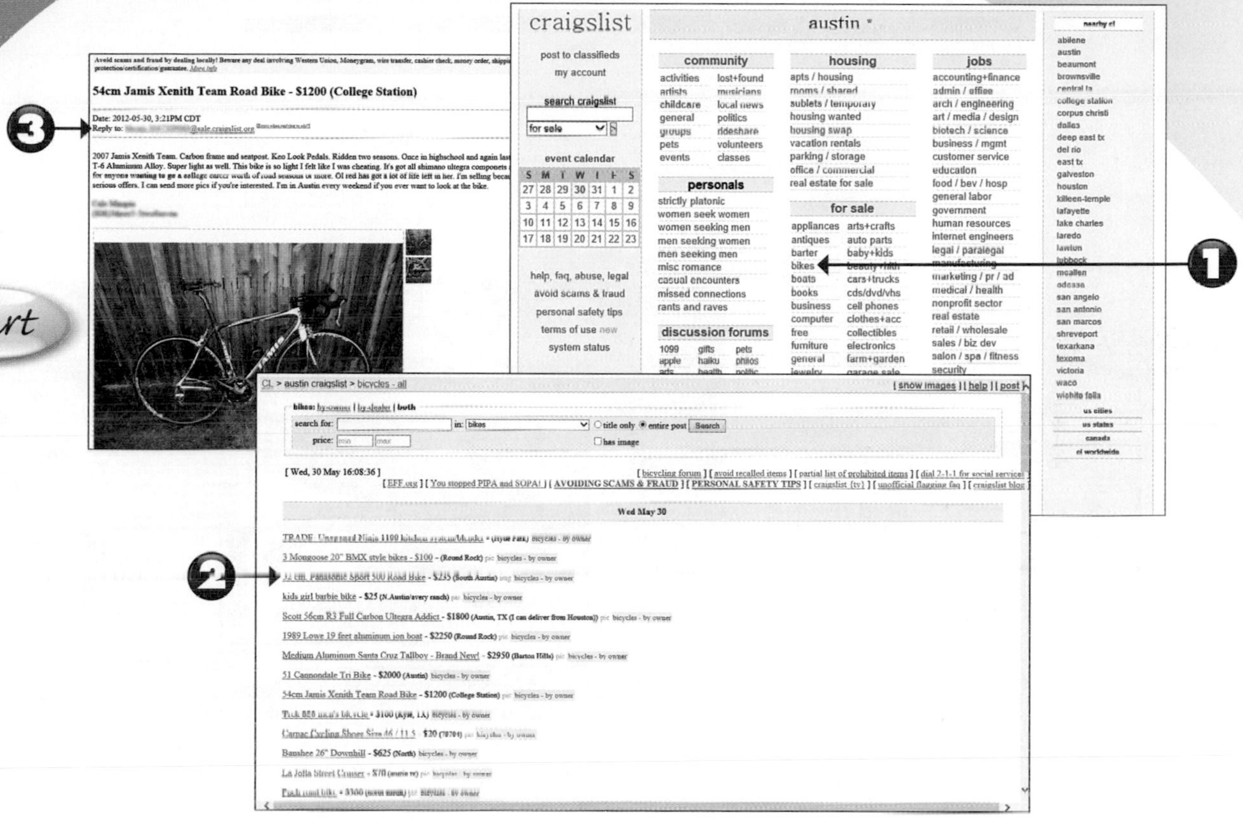

Start

1. On the Craigslist home page for your location and click the category you're looking for within the For Sale section.

2. Click the link for the item you're interested in.

3. Click the **Reply To** link to email the seller and express your interest.

End

NOTE

Classified Ads Listings on Craigslist are just like traditional newspaper classified ads. All transactions are between you and the seller; Craigslist is just the "middleman." ■

TIP

Contacting the Seller When you contact the seller via email, let him know you're interested in the item and would like to see it in person. The seller should reply with a suggested time and place to view and possibly purchase the item. ■

FINDING NEWS AND OTHER INFORMATION ONLINE

The Web is a terrific source for all sorts of news and information. Let's take a quick look at some of the most popular news, weather, and sports sites—the best way to stay informed online!

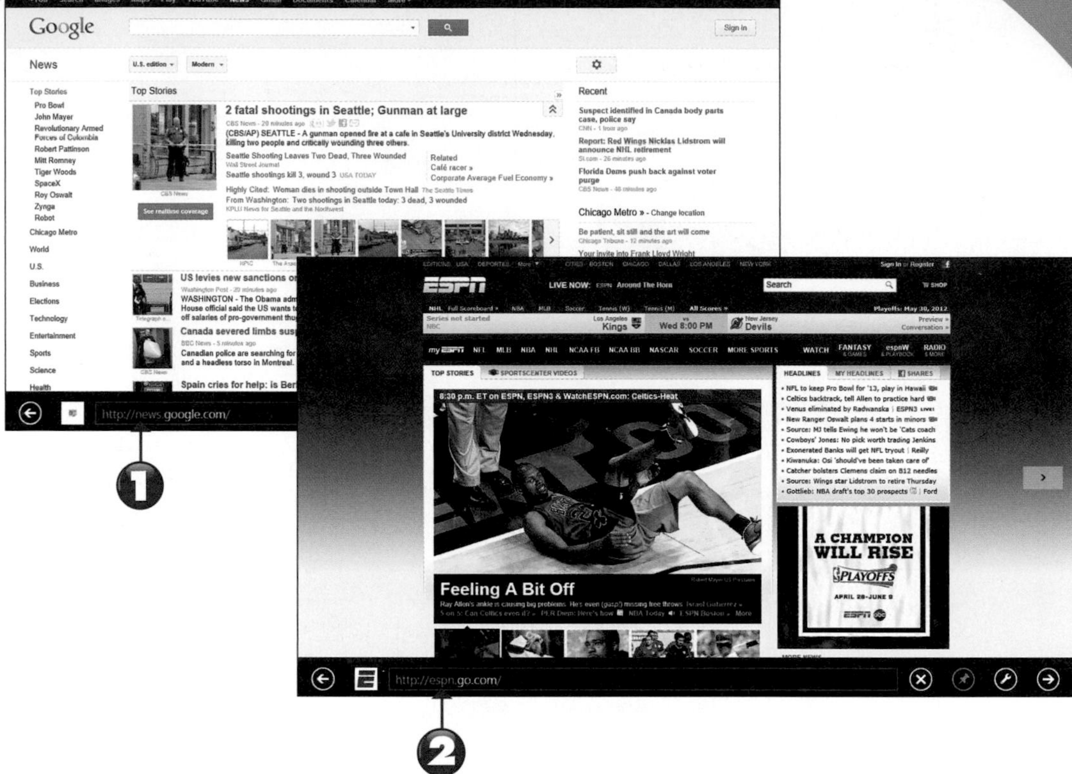

Start

1. For the top headlines from a variety of sources, go to Google News (news.google.com).

2. For comprehensive sports coverage, go to ESPN.com (espn.go.com).

Continued

TIP

More News Other full-service news sites include ABC News (abcnews.go.com), CBSNews.com (www.cbsnews.com), CNN.com (www.cnn.com), and MSNBC (www.msnbc.msn.com). ■

NOTE

More Sports Other popular sports sites include FOX Sports on MSN (msn.foxsports.com), *Sports Illustrated* Online (sportsillustrated.cnn.com), and SportingNews (aol.sportingnews.com). ■

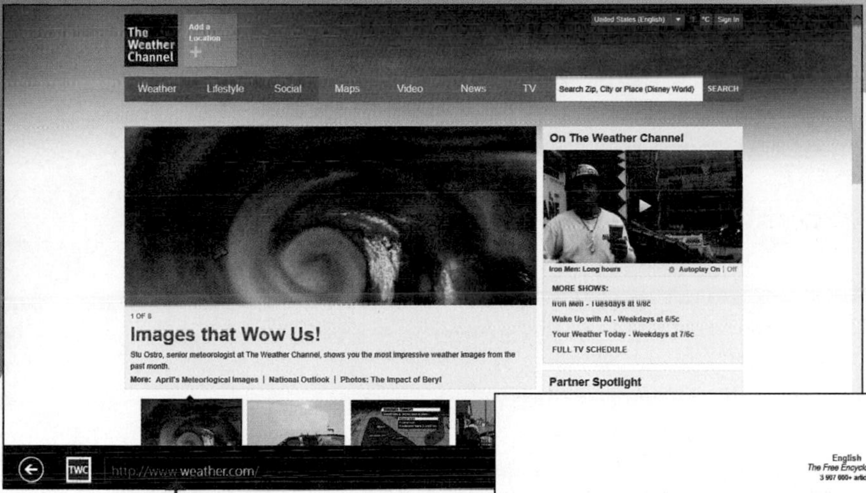

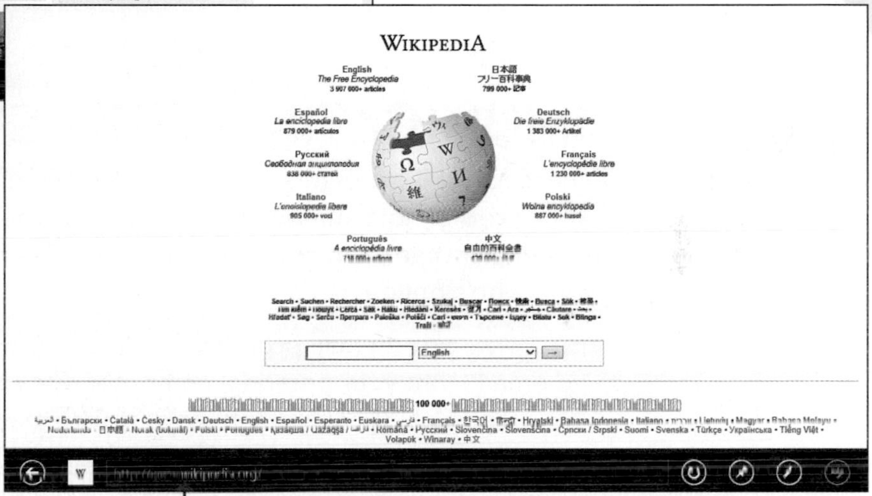

3 The online site for The Weather Channel is found at www.weather.com.

4 Search for a variety of useful and interesting information on Wikipedia (www.wikipedia.org).

End

TIP

More Weather Other popular weather sites include AccuWeather (www.accuweather.com), Weather Underground (www.wunderground.com), and WeatherNation (www.weathernationtv.com). ■

NOTE

Wikipedia Wikipedia is like a traditional encyclopedia, but online with articles written and edited by actual users. (You can even write your own articles, if you're expert in a given topic!) ■

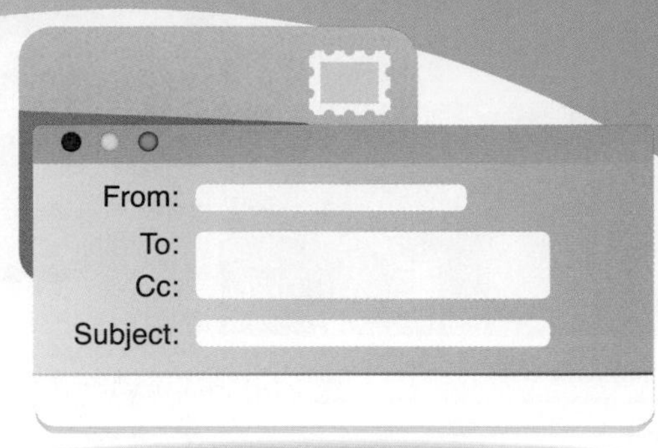

COMMUNICATING WITH EMAIL

An email message is like a regular letter, except that it's composed electronically and delivered almost immediately via the Internet. You can use email to send both text messages and computer files (such as digital photos) to pretty much anyone who's online.

You can use a dedicated email program, such as Windows 8's Mail app, to send and receive email from your personal computer. Or you can use a web mail service such as Gmail or Hotmail to manage all your email from any web browser on any computer. Either approach is good and lets you create, send, and read email messages from all your friends, family, and colleagues.

WINDOWS 8 MAIL APP

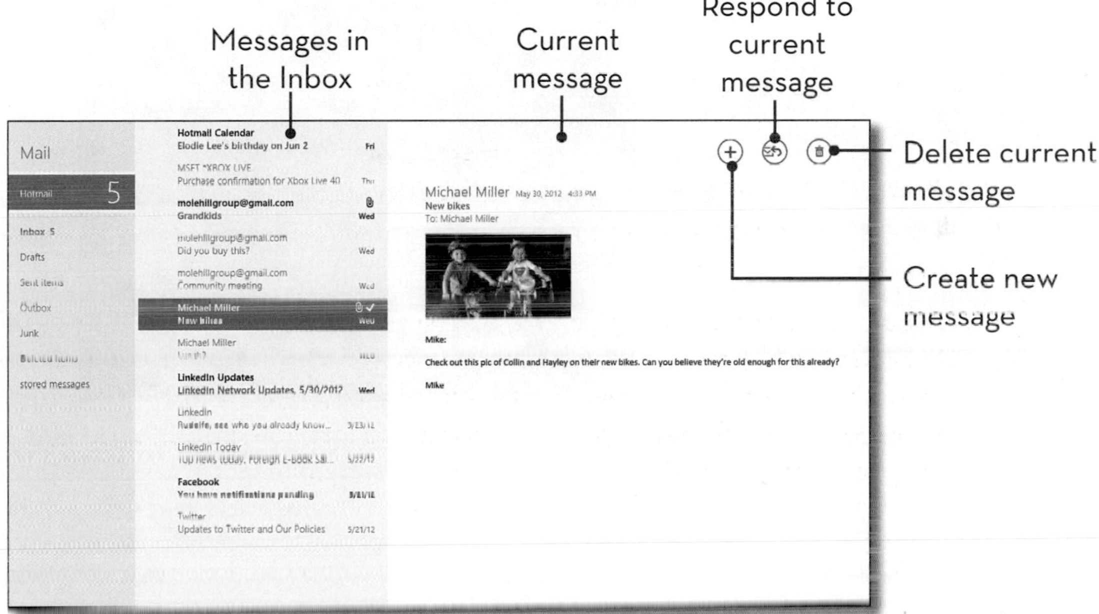

VIEWING YOUR INBOX AND READING MESSAGES

Windows 8 includes a built-in Mail app for sending and receiving email messages. By default, the Mail app manages email from the Windows Live Hotmail account linked to your Microsoft Account. This means you'll see Hotmail messages in your Mail Inbox and be able to easily send emails from your Hotmail account.

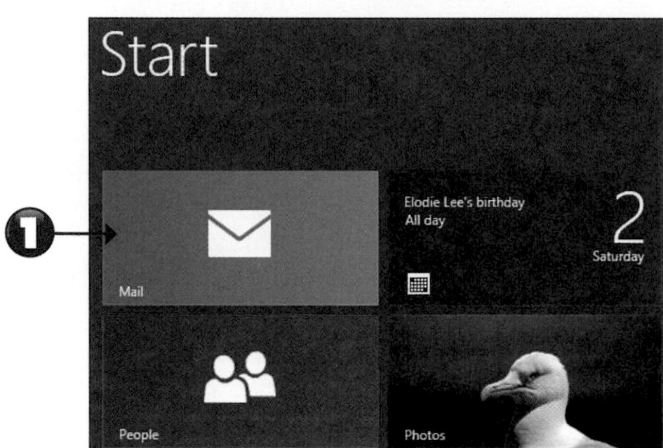

1. From the Windows Start screen, click or tap the **Mail** tile.

Continued

TIP

Tile Info On the Start screen, the Mail app is a "live" tile; your most recent unread messages scroll across the face of the tile, and the number at the bottom left indicates how many unread messages you have. ■

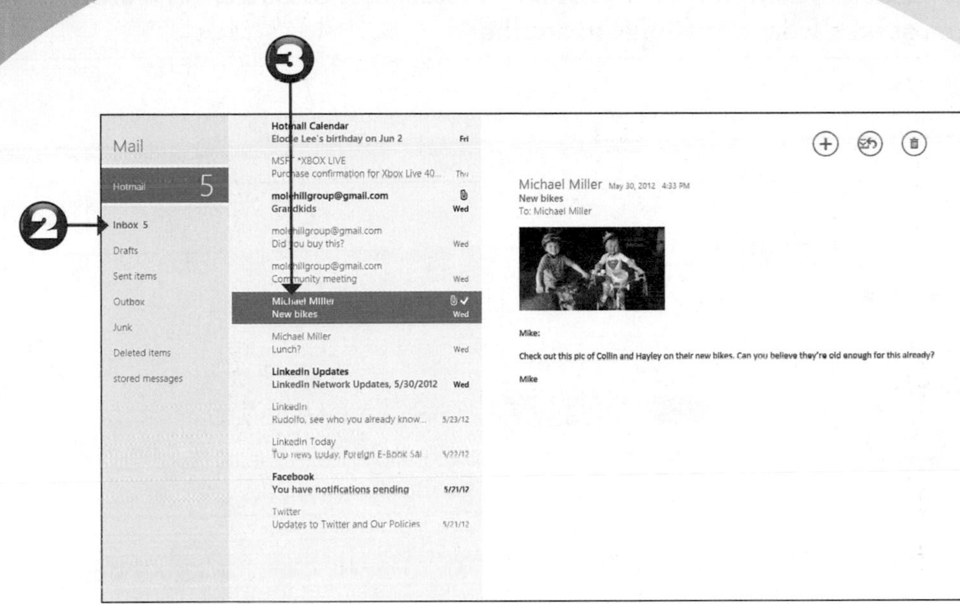

2. When the Mail app launches, select **Inbox** from the Mail pane on the left.

3. This displays a list of all your incoming email messages. Tap a message to view it in the content pane on the right.

End

CAUTION

Attached Viruses Beware of receiving unexpected email messages with file attachments. Opening the attachment may infect your computer with a virus or spyware! You should *never* open email attachments that you weren't expecting—or from senders you don't know. ■

MOVING A MESSAGE TO ANOTHER FOLDER

New messages are stored in the Mail app's Inbox, which is actually a folder. Mail uses other folders, too; there are folders for Drafts, Sent Items, Outbox (messages waiting to be sent), Junk (spam), Deleted Messages, and Stored Messages. For better organization, you can easily move messages from one folder to another.

Start

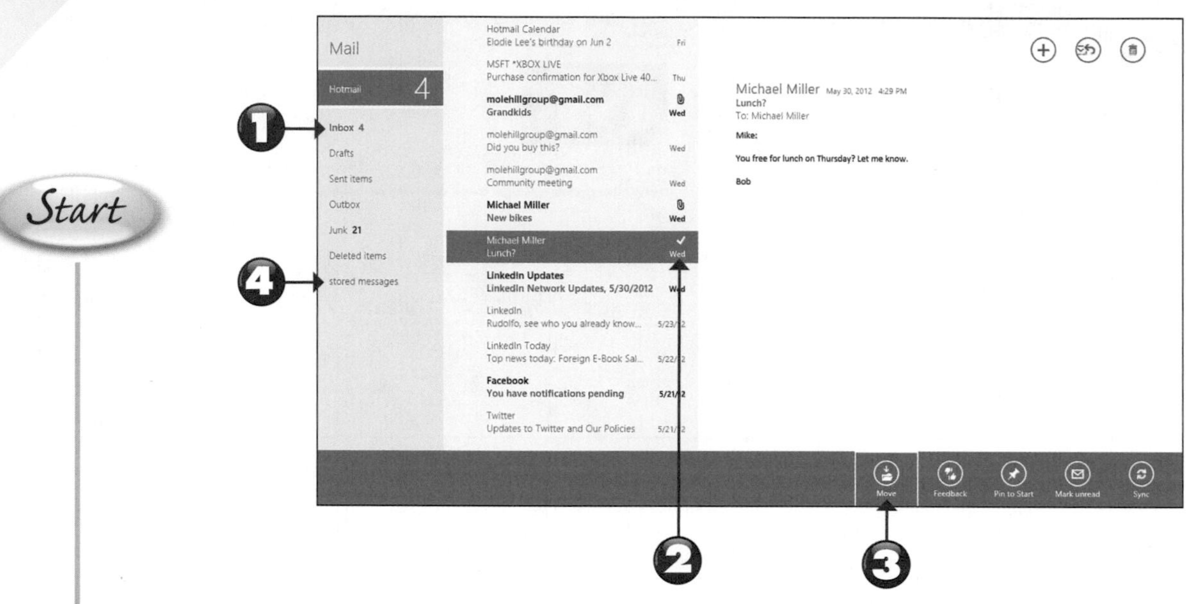

1. In the Mail app, all folders are displayed in the sidebar on the left. Click or tap any folder to view its contents.
2. Click the message you want to move.
3. Right-click anywhere onscreen to display the options bar, and then click **Move**.
4. Click the destination folder.

End

NOTE

Drafts A draft message is one you've started but not yet sent. ■

TIP

Organized Folders It's a good idea to clear excess messages from your Inbox by moving them to the Stored Messages folder. ■

REPLYING TO AN EMAIL MESSAGE

Replying to an email message is as easy as clicking a button and typing your reply. The bot tom of your reply "quotes" the text of the original message.

Start

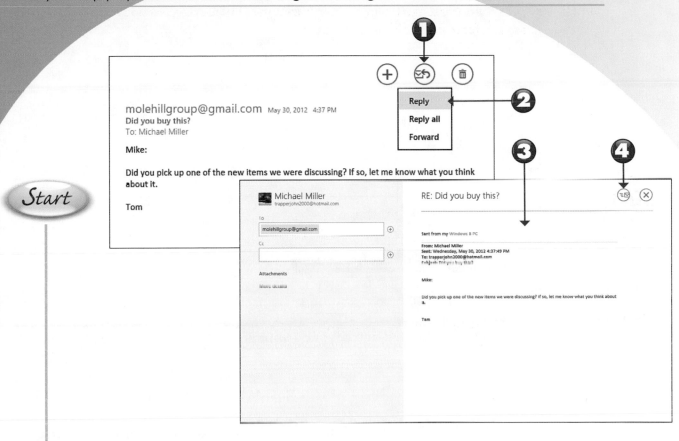

1. From an open message, click or tap the **Respond** button at the top of screen.
2. Select **Reply** from the pop-up menu to display the Reply screen.
3. Enter your reply at the top of the message; the bottom of the message "quotes" the original message.
4. Click or tap the **Send** button when you're ready to send the message.

End

TIP

Unread Messages In the Inbox, the subject lines of unread messages are displayed in colored bold type. The subject lines of messages you've read are displayed in normal type. ■

COMPOSING A NEW EMAIL MESSAGE

Composing a new message is similar to replying to a message. The big difference is that you have to manually enter the recipient's email address.

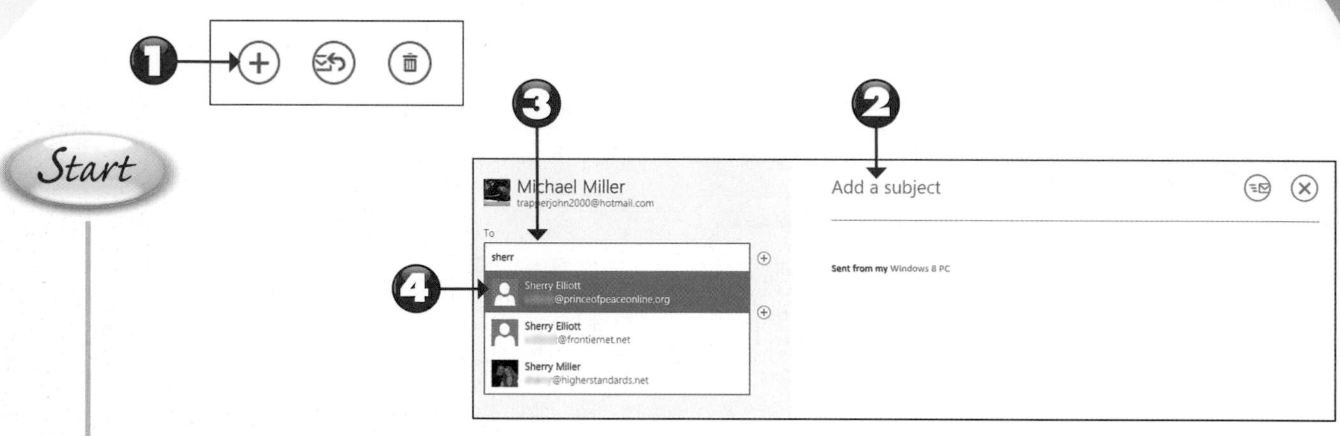

1. Click the **New** (+) button at the top of any Mail screen to display the new message screen.
2. Click or tap the **Add a Subject** area and type a subject for this message.
3. Click or tap within the **To** box and begin entering the name or email address of the message's recipient.
4. Mail will display a list of matching names from your contact list; select the person you want to email.

TIP

Formatting Your Message Use the Bold, Italic, Underline, Font, Font Color, and other buttons in the options bar to format your message. ■

TIP

Copying Other Recipients You can also carbon copies (Cc) to additional recipients. (A blind carbon copy is not visible to other recipients.) Just enter one or more email addresses into the Cc box. ■

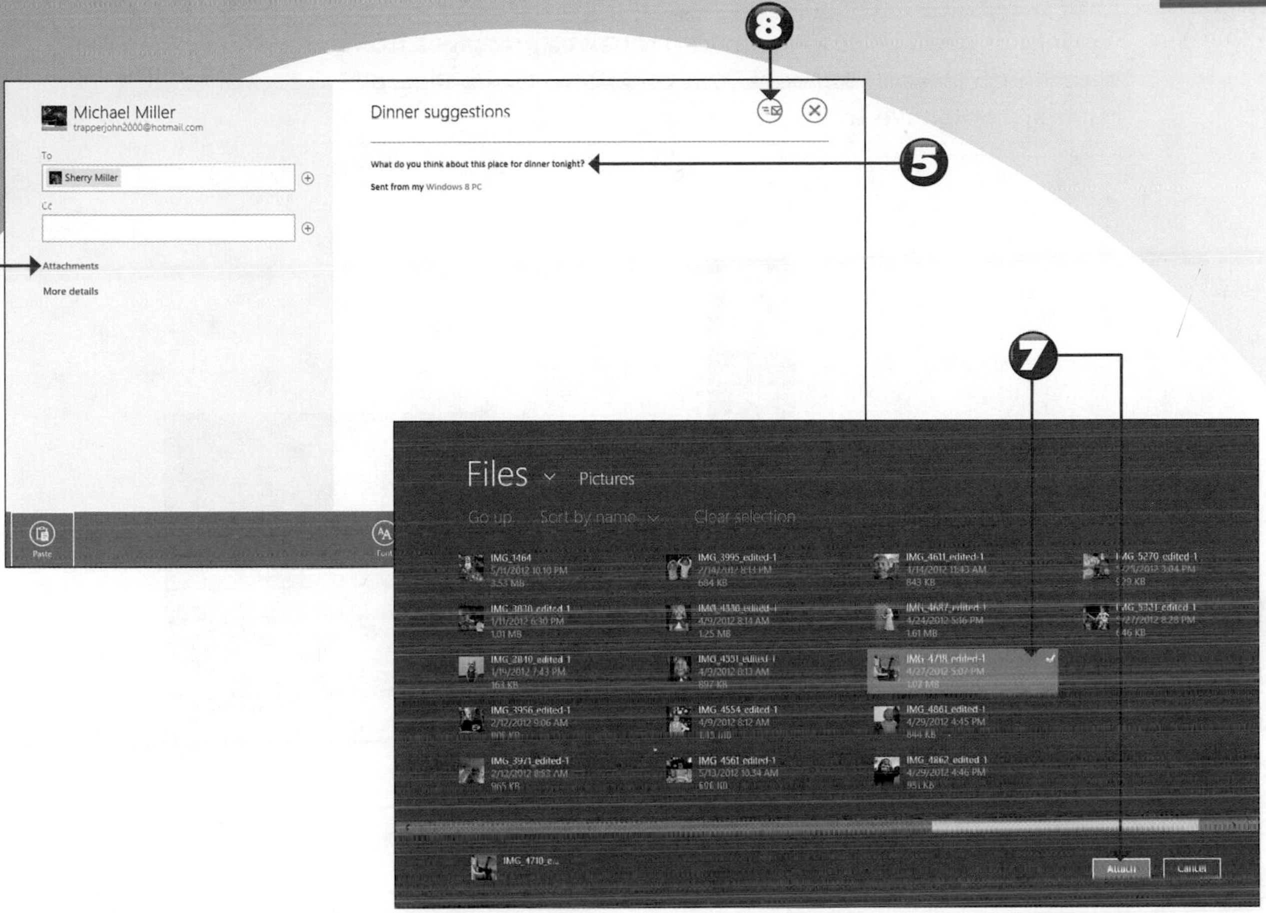

5 Click or tap within the main body of the message area and type your message.

6 To attach a file to this message, click **Attachments** under the address boxes.

7 When the Files screen appears, navigate to and select the file you want to attach, and then click the **Attach** button.

8 When you're ready to send the email, click the **Send** button at the top of the message.

End

TIP

Attaching Files One of the easiest ways to share a digital photo or other file with another user is via email, as an *attachment* to a standard email message. When the message is sent, the file travels along with it; when the message is received, the file is right there, waiting to be opened. ■

CAUTION

Large Files Be wary of sending extra-large files over the Internet. They can take a long time to upload—and just as long for the recipient to download when received. ■

ADDING OTHER ACCOUNTS TO THE MAIL APP

By default, the Mail app sends and receives messages from the email account associated with your Microsoft account. You can, however, configure Mail to work with other email accounts, if you have them.

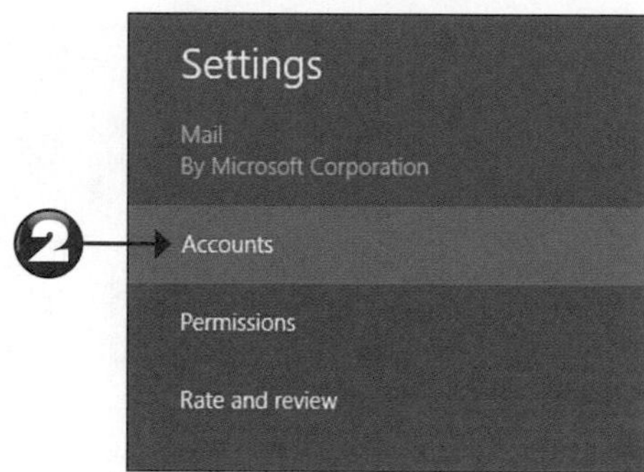

1. From within the Mail app, display the charms bar, and then click or tap **Settings**.
2. When the Settings pane appears, click or tap **Accounts**.

Continued

TIP

Switching Accounts To view the Inbox of another email account, right-click to display the options bar, and then click **Accounts**. When the Accounts pane appears, click or tap the name of the email account you want to view. ■

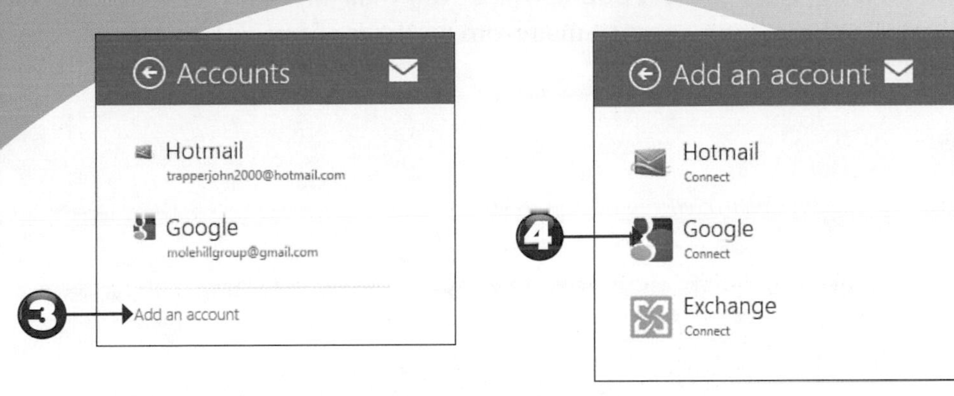

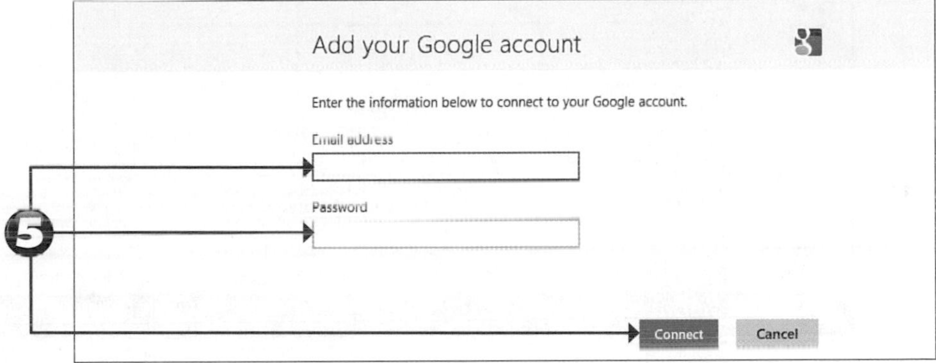

3. When the Accounts pane appears, click or tap **Add an Account**.

4. When the next pane appears, click the type of account you want to add.

5. When the Add Your Account pane appears, enter your email address and password, and then click the **Connect** button.

End

TIP

Account Types The Mail app lets you add Hotmail, Gmail, and Microsoft Exchange email accounts. ■

USING WEB-BASED GMAIL

Google's Gmail is one of the most popular free web mail services. Anyone can sign up for a free Gmail account and then access email from any computer with an Internet connection, using any web browser.

1. Launch Internet Explorer and go to mail.google.com.

2. Click the **Inbox** link to display all incoming messages.

3. Click the header for the message you want to view.

Continued

NOTE

Free Gmail Gmail is free to use. All you need to do is sign up for a Google account—which is also free. You can do this from the mail.google.com web page. ■

NOTE

Other Web Mail Services Other popular web mail services include Microsoft's Windows Live Hotmail (www.hotmail.com) and Yahoo! Mail (mail.yahoo.com). ■

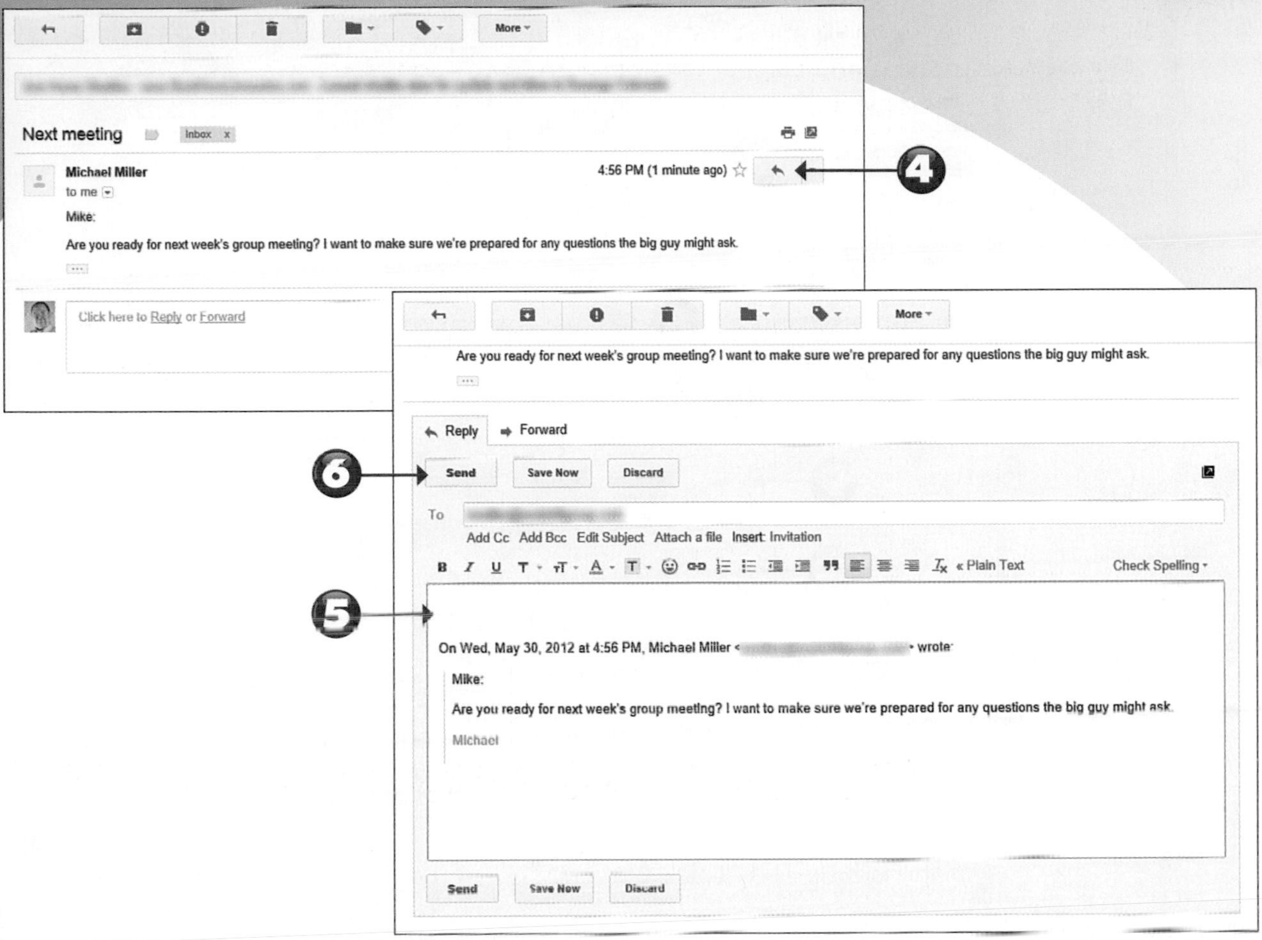

4 To reply to an open message, click **Reply**.

5 Enter your reply text in the message window.

6 Click the **Send** button to send your reply to the original sender.

Continued

NOTE

POP Email Post Office Protocol (POP) email is available from most Internet service providers (ISPs). It requires the use of a dedicated email program and the configuration of that program with information about the ISP's incoming and outgoing email servers. ■

NOTE

POP Versus Web Mail POP email, like web mail, is typically free. However, you can only access POP email from the email program installed on a single computer; you can't send or receive email from other computers, as you can with web mail. ■

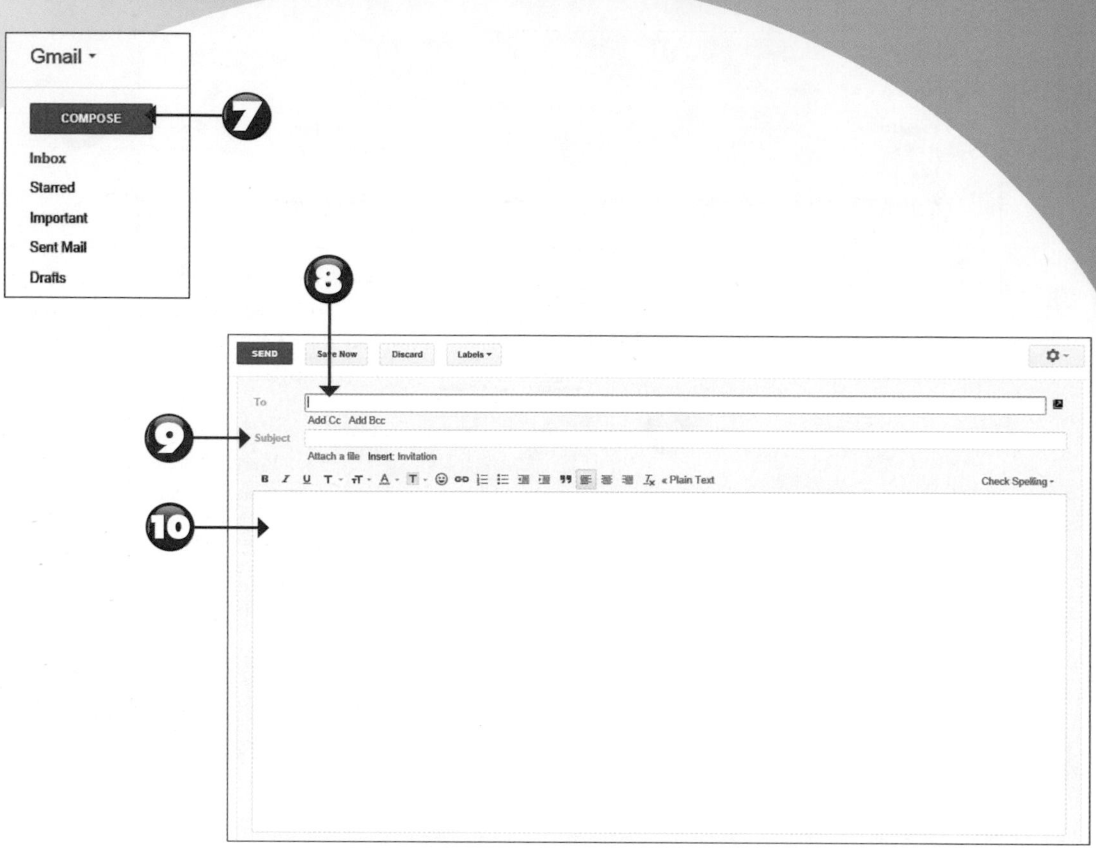

7. To send a new email message, click **Compose** from any Gmail page.

8. Enter the email address of the recipient(s) in the To box.

9. Enter a subject in the Subject box.

10. Move your cursor to the main message area and type your message.

TIP

Send to Multiple Recipients You can enter multiple addresses in the To box as long as you separate the addresses with a semicolon, like this: books@molehillgroup.com; gjetson@sprockets.com.

TIP

Cc and Bcc Gmail also lets you send carbon copies (Cc) and blind carbon copies (Bcc) to additional recipients. (A blind carbon copy is not visible to other recipients.) Just click the **Add Cc** or **Add Bcc** links to add these addresses.

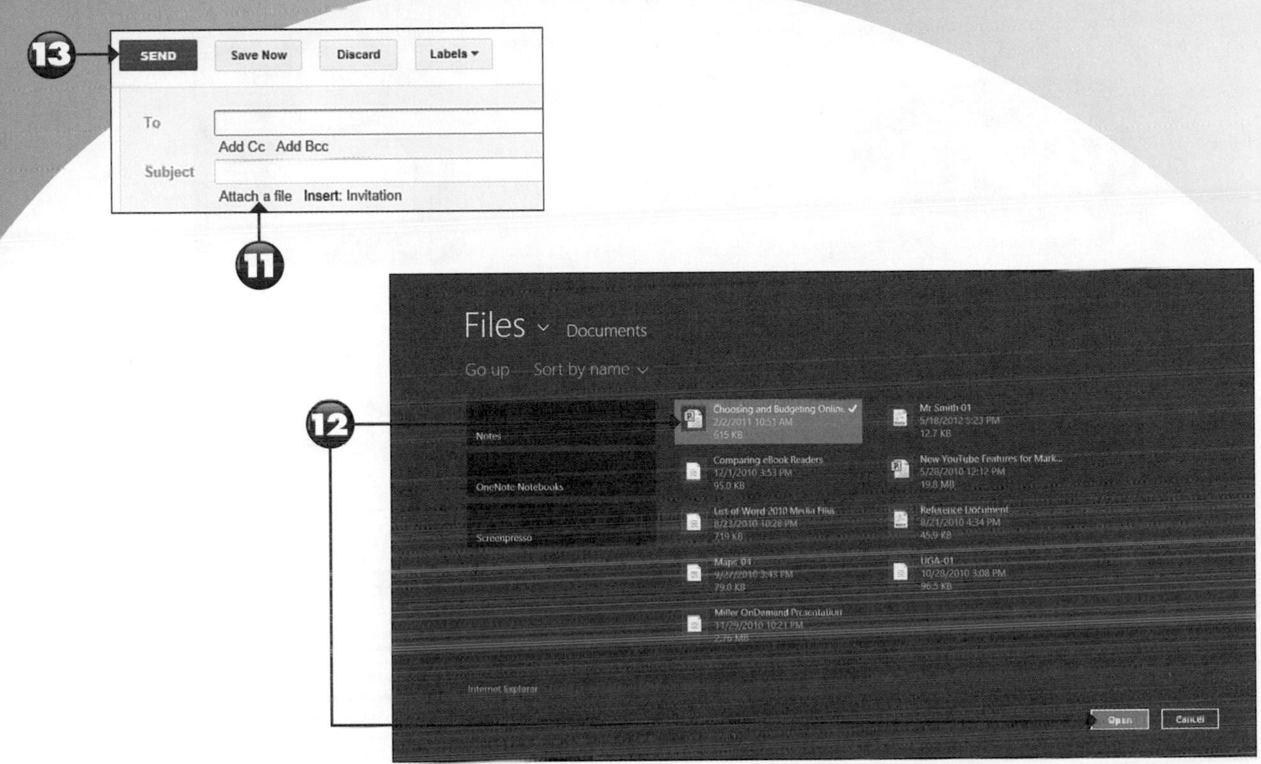

11. To attach a file to a message, click **Attach a File**.

12. When the Files screen appears, navigate to and select the file you want to attach, and then click the **Open** button.

13. Send the message by clicking the **Send** button.

End

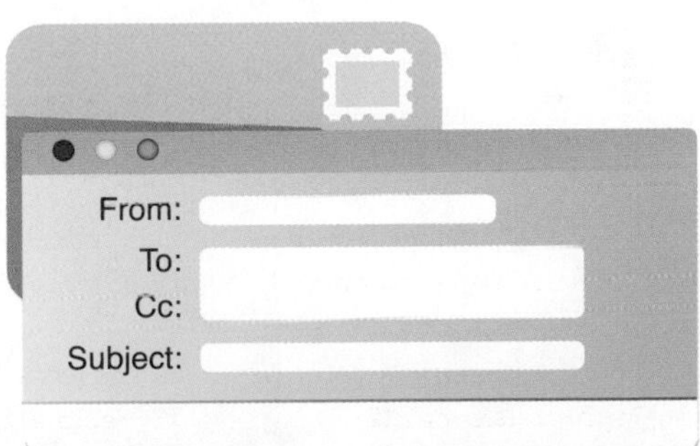

SHARING WITH FACEBOOK AND OTHER SOCIAL NETWORKS

Social networking enables people to share experiences and opinions with each other via community-based websites. It's a great way to keep up-to-date on what your friends and family are doing.

In practice, a social network is just a large website that aims to create a community of users. Each user of the community posts his or her own personal profile on the site. You use the information in these profiles to connect with other people you know on the network, or with those who share your interests.

The goal is to create a network of these online "friends," and then share your activities with them via a series of posts or status updates. All your online friends read your posts, as well as posts from other friends, in a continuously updated *news feed*. The news feed is the one place where you can read updates from all your online friends and family; it's where you find out what's really happening.

The biggest social network today is a site called Facebook; chances are all your friends are already using it. Other popular social networks include Pinterest and Twitter, both of which have their own unique characteristics.

COMPARING FACEBOOK, PINTEREST, AND TWITTER

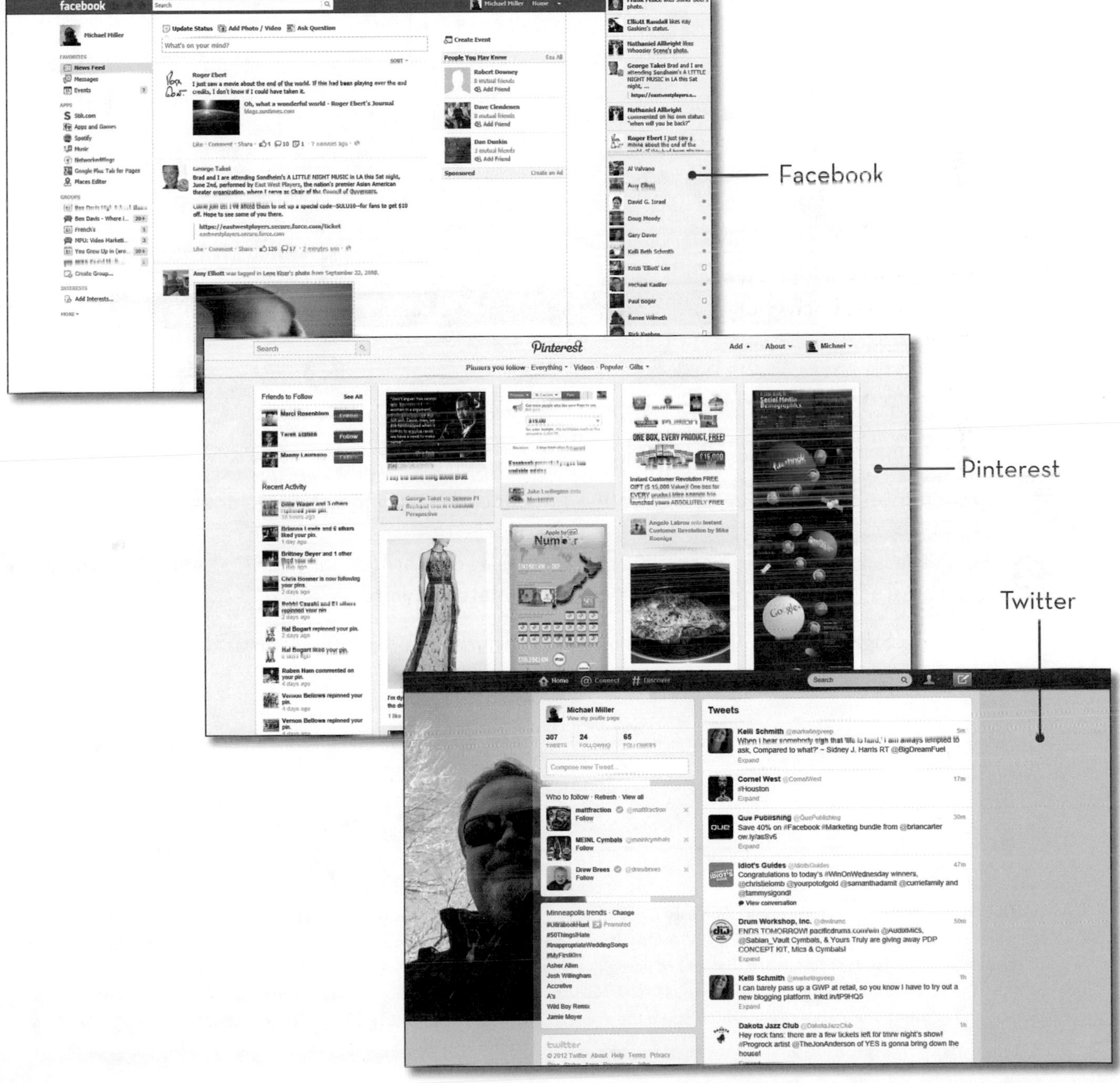

SETTING UP A FACEBOOK ACCOUNT

Facebook is the number-one social network today, with more than 800 million active users worldwide. To use Facebook, you have to sign up for an account and enter some personal information. Fortunately, signing up for an account is both easy and free.

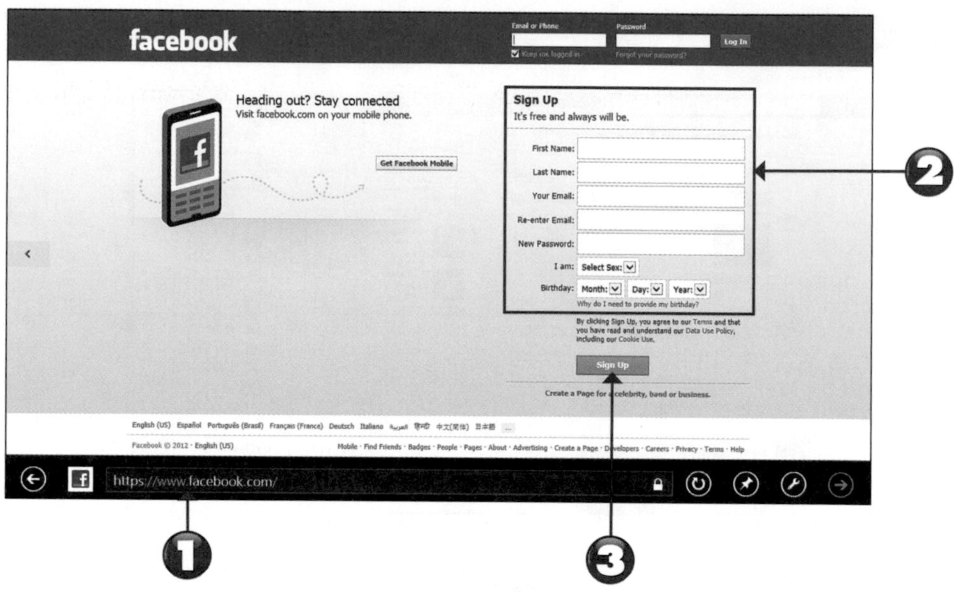

1. Launch Internet Explorer and go to the Facebook home page at www.facebook.com.
2. Go to the Sign Up section and enter the requested information: your first and last name, email address, desired password, gender, and date of birth.
3. Click the **Sign Up** button. Facebook now sends you an email message asking you to confirm your new Facebook account; when you receive this email, click the link to proceed.

End

NOTE

CAPTCHA When prompted on Facebook's Security Check page, enter the "secret words" from the onscreen CAPTCHA. A CAPTCHA is a type of challenge-response test to ensure that you're actually a human being, rather than a computer program. Websites use CAPTCHAs to cut down on the amount of computer-generated spam they receive. ■

NOTE

Additional Information After you've created your Facebook account, you'll be prompted to enter additional personal information and then search for friends. You can do both of these things now or later, as you want. ■

NAVIGATING FACEBOOK'S HOME PAGE

Once you sign into your account, you see Facebook's home page. You use the left column to click to various content on the site. The large column in the middle displays your *News Feed*, a stream of posts from all your Facebook friends. The next column displays various Facebook ads and messages. The rightmost column (visible on widescreen displays) hosts the hosts the *Ticker* (a scrolling list of your friends' activity) and the Chat panel, for messaging online friends in real time.

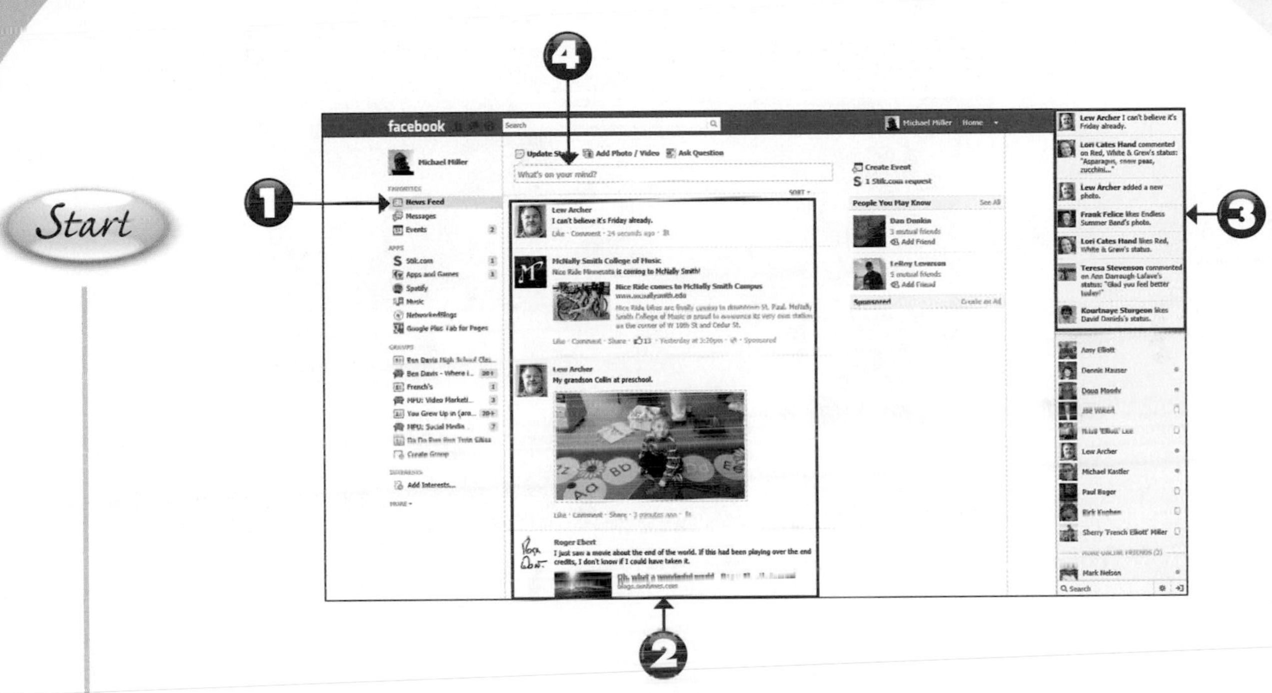

1. Sign in to your Facebook account and select **News Feed** in the left sidebar.
2. View status updates from your friends in the News Feed.
3. View real-time activity in the Ticker.
4. Post new status updates from the box at the top of the page.

End

TIP

Three or Four Columns Facebook displays four columns on certain widescreen displays, but only three columns on smaller displays or when in a desktop browser window. The three-column display combines the Ticker, Chat panel, and notifications/ads into a single column on the right. ■

TIP

Sorting the News Feed By default, the first items in the News Feed are your Top Stories, those updates that Facebook thinks you should be most interested in. Other updates (what Facebook calls Recent Stories) are just below the Top Stories section; scroll down to view them. ■

FINDING FACEBOOK FRIENDS

The easiest way to find friends on Facebook is to let Facebook find them for you—based on the information you provided for your personal profile. The more Facebook knows about you, especially in terms of where you've worked and gone to school, the more friends it can find.

1. Click your name on the toolbar to display your Profile page.
2. Click the **Friends** item near the top of the page.

Continued

NOTE

News Feed To see a person's status updates in your News Feed, he must be on your friends list. ■

NOTE

Suggested Friends The people Facebook suggests as friends are typically people who went to the same schools you did, worked at the same companies you did, or are friends of your current friends. ■

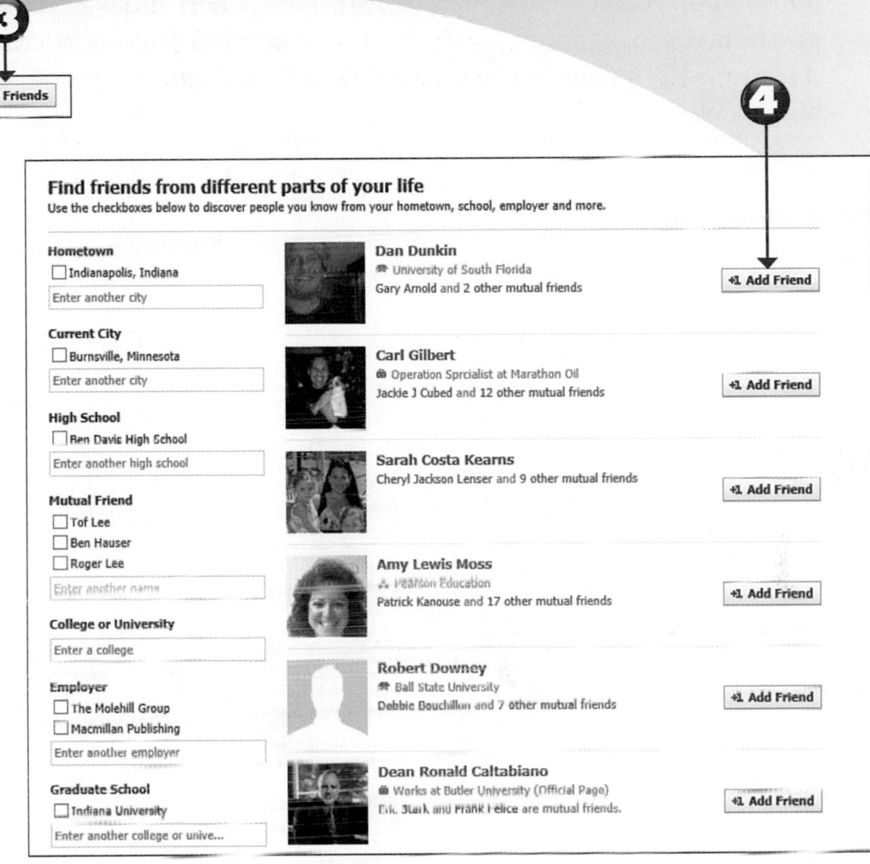

3 When your Friends page appears, click the **Find Friends** button.

4 The next page displays a list of people that Facebook thinks might be friends. To invite any individual to be your friend, click the **Add Friend** button.

End

NOTE

Invitations Facebook doesn't automatically add a person to your friends list. Instead, that person receives an invitation to be your friend; she can accept or reject the invitation. ■

TIP

Accepting a Friend Request To accept or reject any friend requests you've received, click the **Friend Request** button on the Facebook toolbar. ■

COMMENTING ON A FRIEND'S STATUS UPDATE

Sometimes you read a friend's status update and you want to say something about it. To this end, Facebook enables you to comment on your friends' posts; these comments appear under the post in your News Feed. You can also express your approval by "liking" a post with a big thumbs up.

Start

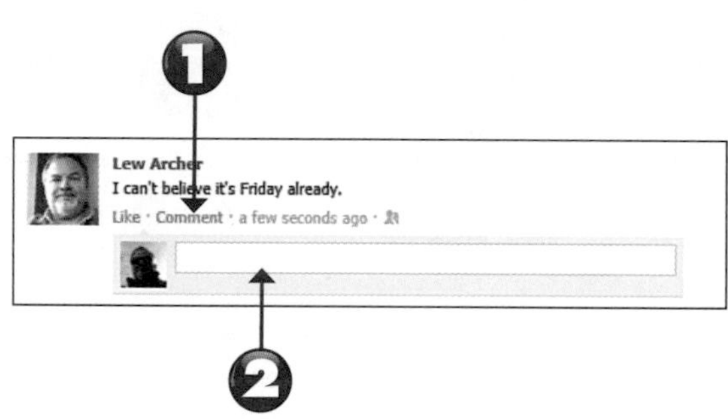
Lew Archer
I can't believe it's Friday already.
Like · Comment · a few seconds ago ·

1. Click the **Comment** link under that post.
2. Enter your comment into the text box that appears, and then press **Enter**.

End

TIP

Liking a Post You can also express your approval for a status update by clicking the **Like** link under the post. This puts a little "thumbs up" icon under the post, along with a message that you "like this." ■

TIP

Read the Book Learn more about Facebook in my companion book, *Easy Facebook* (Que, 2012). ■

VIEWING A FRIEND'S FACEBOOK TIMELINE

You can easily check up on what your Facebook friends are up to by visiting their profile pages. A Facebook profile page contains a "timeline" of that person's posts and major life events. It also displays that person's personal information, uploaded photos and videos, upcoming events, and the like.

Start

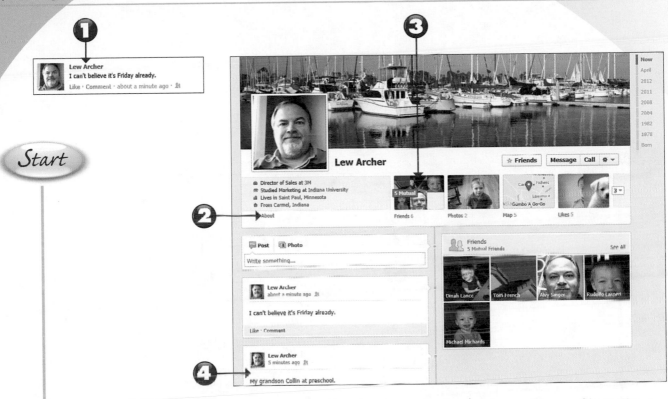

1. Click a person's name anywhere on the Facebook site to display his or her profile or Timeline page.
2. View key personal information under the person's profile picture, or click **About** to view their full personal profile.
3. View a list of this person's friends by clicking **Friends**.
4. View a person's status updates in reverse chronological order (newest first) on the Timeline.

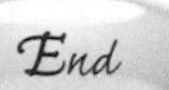

TIP

Posting on a Friend's Page You can post a message on your friend's profile page by entering your text into the Write Something box near the top of the Timeline. ■

TIP

Personalizing Your Profile You can personalize your own profile page in a number of ways. You can change your profile and pictures, edit your personal information, and add and delete items to and from your Timeline. ■

POSTING A STATUS UPDATE

The easiest way to let people know what's what is to post what Facebook calls a *status update*. Every status update you make is broadcast to everyone on your friends list, displayed in the News Feed on their Home pages. A basic status update is text only, but you can also include photos, videos, and links to other web pages in your posts.

Start

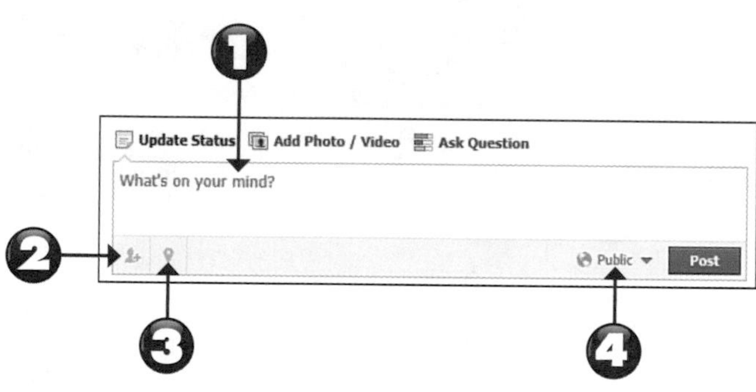

1. On the Facebook home page, type your message into the Publisher box at the top of the page. As you do this, the box expands to contain your text.
2. If you're with someone else and want to mention them in the post, click the **Who Are You With?** button and enter that person's name.
3. If you want to include your current location in your post, click the **Where Are You?** button and enter the city or place you're at.
4. To determine who can read this post, click the **down arrow** next to the Public button and make a selection.

Continued

TIP

Who Sees Your Posts? You can opt to make any post Public (anyone who's subscribed to your posts can read it), visible only to your Friends, visible only to yourself (Only Me), or Custom (you select individuals who can and can't view it). Alternatively, you can select which friends list can view the update. ■

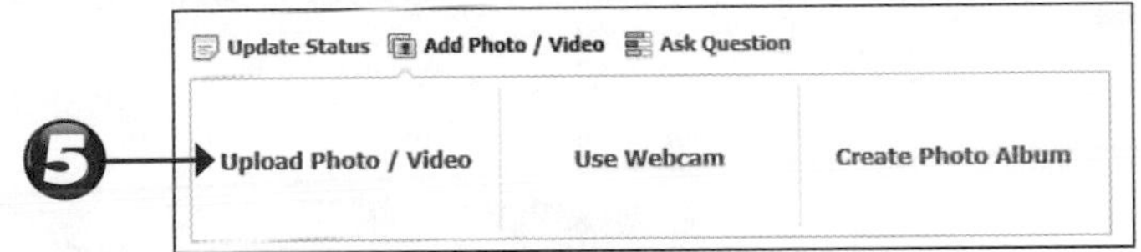

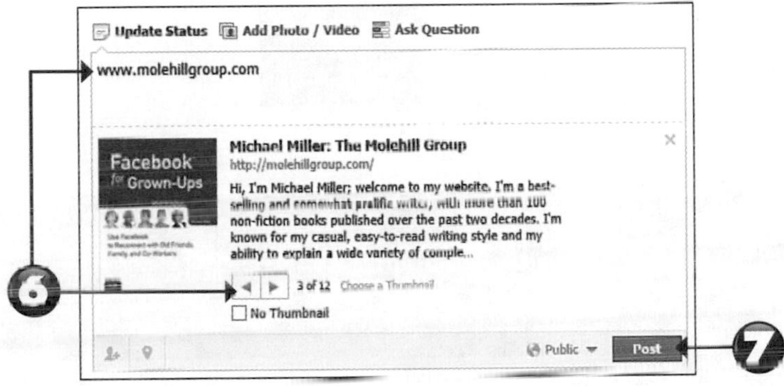

5. To include a picture or video with your post, click **Upload Photo/Video** in the Publisher box. When the panel changes, click the **Browse** button and then select the file you want.

6. To include a link to another web page, simply enter that page's URL in your status update. Facebook should recognize the link and display a Link panel; select a thumbnail image from the web page to accompany the link, or check the **No Thumbnail** box.

7. When you're ready to post your update, click the **Post** button.

End

CAUTION

Social Networking Safety Make sure you and your kids don't post overly personal information or incriminating photographs on Facebook or other social networks; you could attract online stalkers. Similarly, don't broadcast your every move on your profile page—and don't automatically accept friend requests from people you don't know. ■

VIEWING A FRIEND'S PHOTOS

Facebook is a social network, and one of the ways we connect socially is through pictures. Facebook lets any user upload and store photos in virtual photo albums. It's easy, then, to view a friend's photos on the Facebook site.

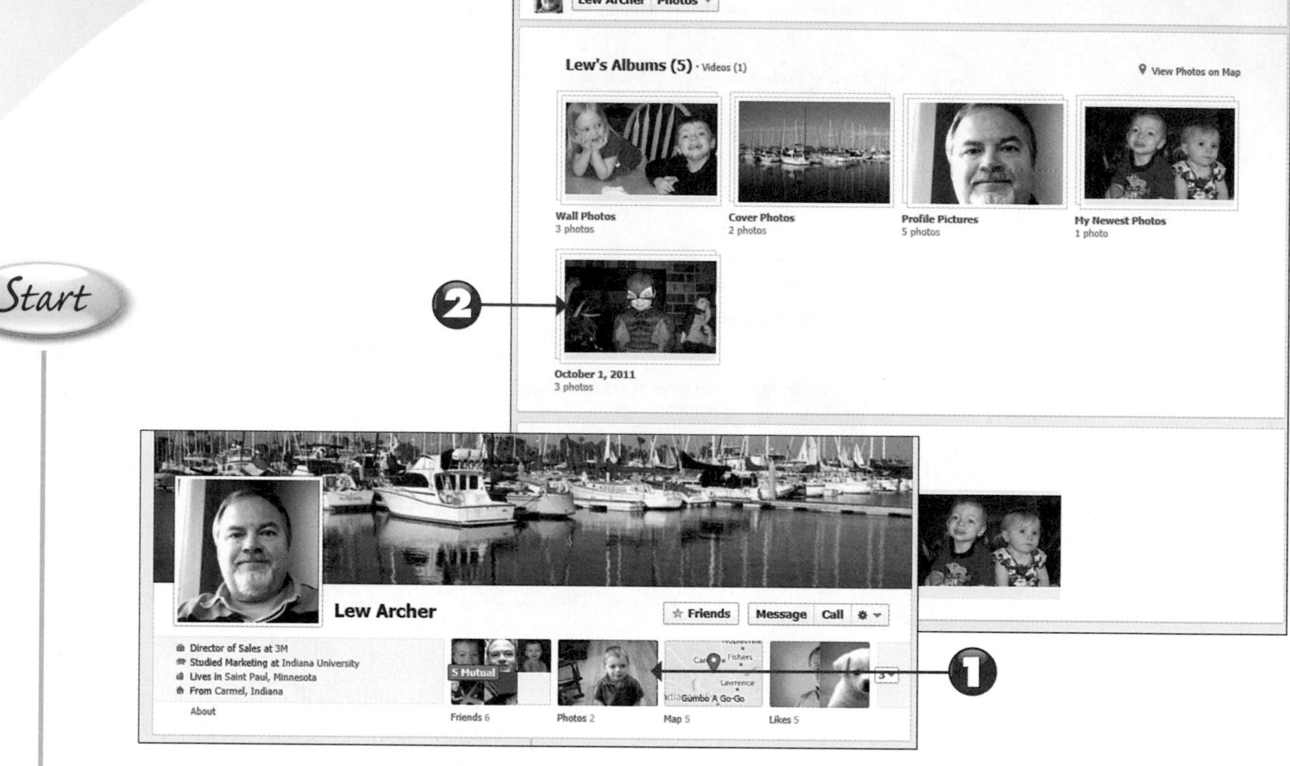

1. Go to your friend's profile/Timeline page and click the **Photos** graphic.
2. When your friend's Photos page appears, click the photo album you want to view.

NOTE

All Photos The top of the Photos page displays your friend's most recent albums; click **See More** to view all albums. The bottom of the Photos page displays photos in which your friend appears. ■

3. Click the thumbnail of the picture you want to view.
4. To go to the next picture, mouse over the current picture to display the navigational arrows then click the **right arrow**.
5. Click the **X** to close the photo viewer.

End

TIP

Commenting and Liking To comment on the current picture, enter your message into the comments box. To like a photo, mouse over the picture and click **Like**. ■

TIP

Downloading a Picture To download the current picture to your own computer, mouse over the photo, click **Options**, and then click **Download** from the pop-up menu. ■

SHARING YOUR PHOTOS ON FACEBOOK

Facebook is a great place to share your personal photos with family and friends. You can upload new photos to an existing photo album or create a new album for newly uploaded photos.

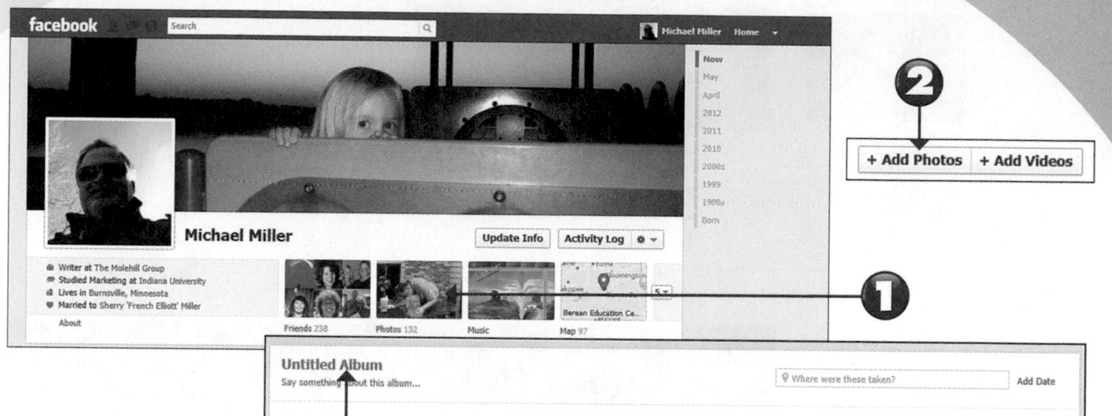

Start

1. From your profile/Timeline page, click the **Photos** graphic to display the Photos page.
2. Click the **Add Photos** button.
3. Enter a name for the new album and where the photos were taken, select who you want to share the album with, and then click the **Select Photos to Upload** button.

Continued

TIP

Uploading to an Existing Photo Album You can also upload photos to an existing photo album. Follow steps 1 and 2, above, and when the Photos page appears, click the photo album you want to upload to. Follow the rest of the steps as instructed. ■

TIP

High-Quality Photos To upload photos at their original resolution, check the **High Quality** option. This enables your friends to download your pictures at an acceptable resolution for printing. ■

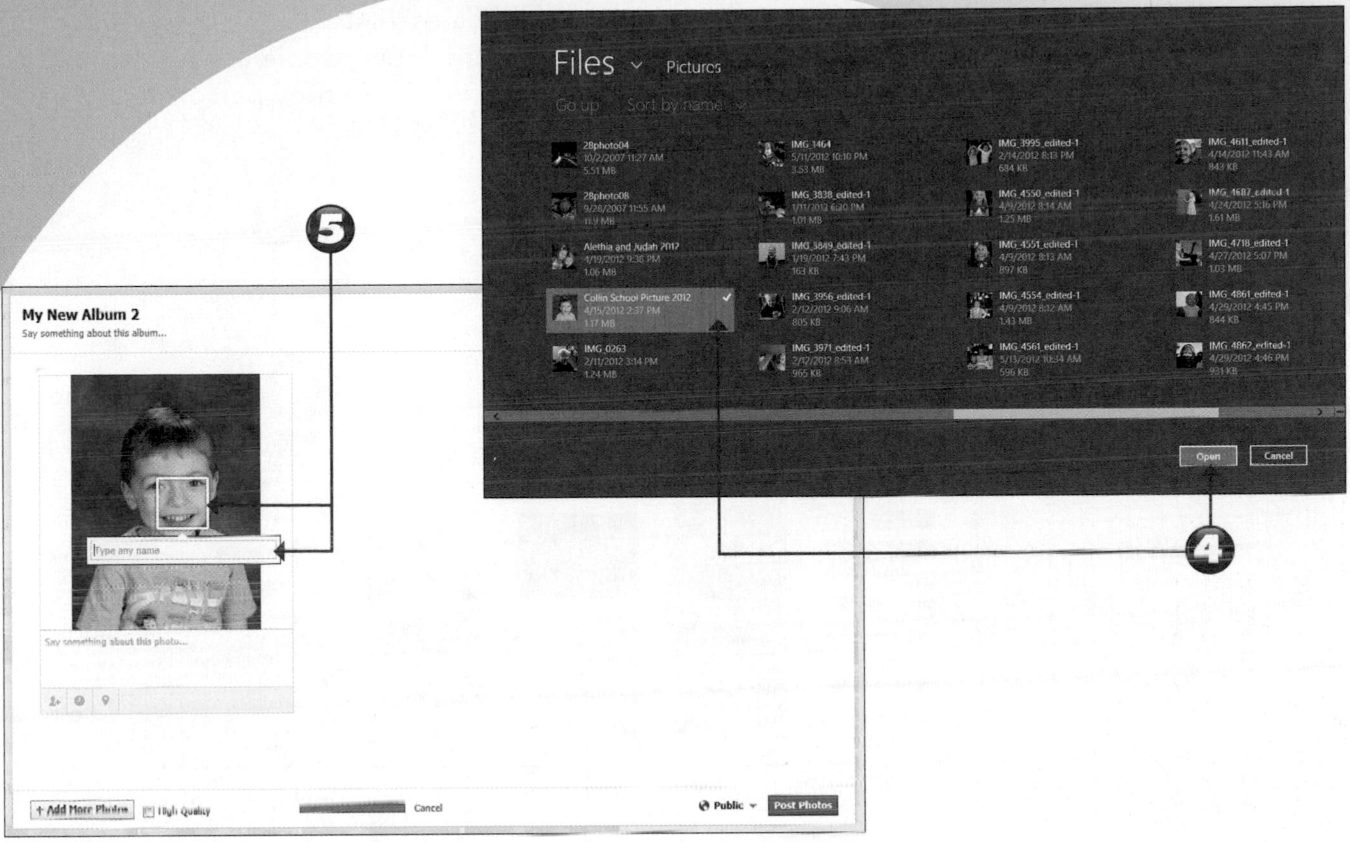

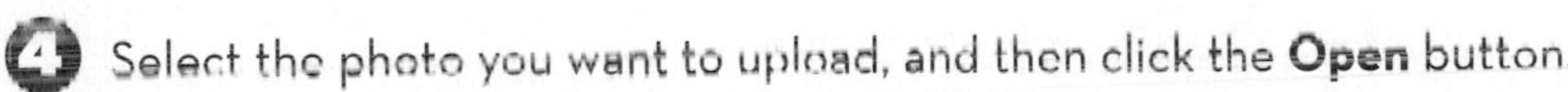

4 Select the photo you want to upload, and then click the **Open** button.

5 If there are people in the photo you've uploaded, Facebook displays the album page with boxes around the faces. To "tag" that person in Facebook, click a face and then enter that person's name.

SHARING INTERESTING IMAGES WITH PINTEREST

Pinterest (www.pinterest.com) is a new social network with particular appeal to women. Unlike Facebook, which lets you post text-based status updates, Pinterest is all about images. The site consists of a collection of virtual online "pinboards" that people use to share pictures they find interesting. Users "pin" photos and other images to their personal message boards, and then share their pins with online friends.

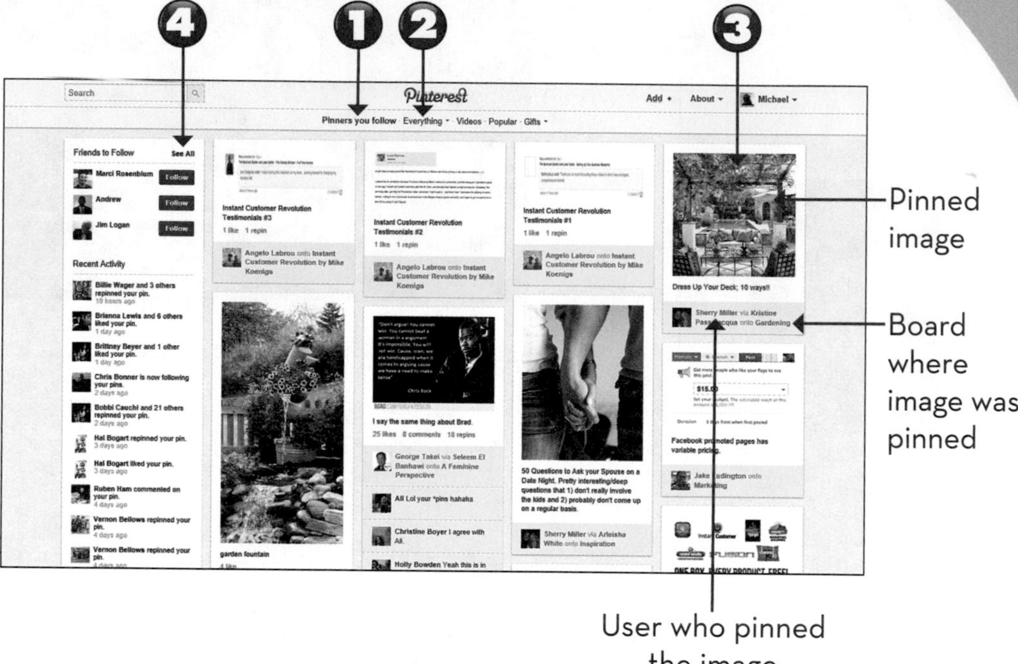

Start

1. Click to display pins from people you follow.
2. Click to display all recent pins on the Pinterest site.
3. Click a pin to view in more detail.
4. Click to see people you may want to follow.

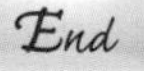

NOTE

What's in a Name? Pinterest is all about pinning items of interest—hence the name, a combination of *pin* and *interest*. ■

NOTE

Request an Invitation As of June 2012, Pinterest was still in a public testing phase—although with close to 15 million users. You can request an invitation from any current Pinterest member or from the Pinterest site at www.pinterest.com. ■

FINDING PEOPLE TO FOLLOW ON PINTEREST

When you find someone who posts a lot things you're interested in, you can follow that person on Pinterest. Following a person means that means that all that person's new pins will display on your Pinterest home page.

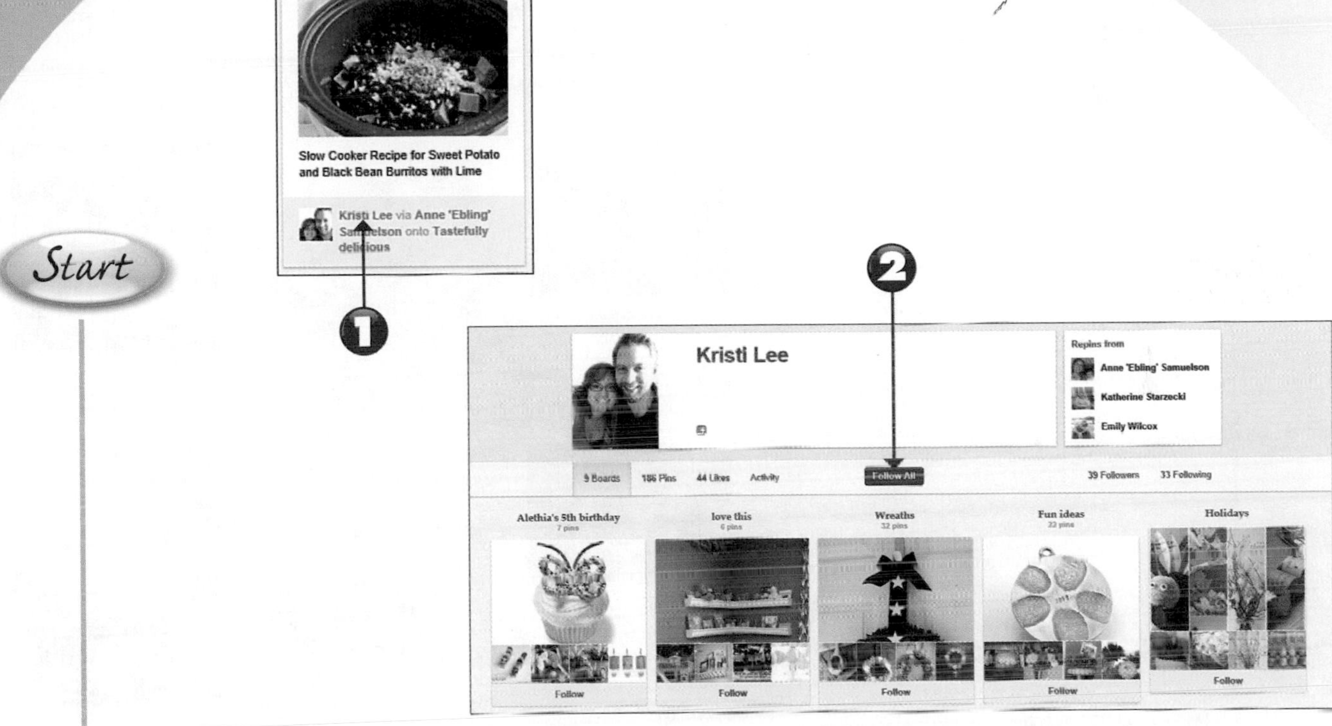

1. When you find a pin you like, click the name of the person who pinned it.

2. You now see that person's personal page. Click the **Follow All** button to follow this person.

End

TIP

Logging In You can log in to Pinterest with the email address and password your created when you signed up or with your Facebook or Twitter credentials. ■

TIP

Following Boards Instead of following all of a person's pins, you can opt to follow only selected pinboards. Just go to that person's personal Pinterest page and click the **Follow** button for the board you want to follow. ■

FINDING AND REPINNING INTERESTING PINS

Some people say that Pinterest is a little like a refrigerator covered with magnets holding up tons of photos and drawings. You can find lots of interesting items pinned from other users—and then "repin" them to your own personal pinboards.

1. Enter the name of something you're interested in into the Search box at the top of any Pinterest page, and then press **Enter**.
2. Pinterest now displays pins that match your query. Mouse over the item you want to repin and click the **Repin** button.

NOTE

Repins About 80% of the pins on Pinterest are actually repins. ■

TIP

Popular Categories The most popular categories on Pinterest are Home, Arts and Crafts, Style and Fashion, and Food. Of these, Food is the most likely category to be repinned. ■

3. When the Repin panel appears, pull down the pinboard list and select which board you want to pin this item to.

4. Accept the previous user's description or add your own to the large text box.

5. Click the red **Pin It** button to repin the item.

End

TIP

Keep or Replace You can keep the original pinner's description or replace it with a new description of your own. If you want to truly personalize your pins, it's best to use your own descriptions, even when you repin. ■

PINNING FROM A WEB PAGE

You can also pin images you find on nearly any web page. It's as easy as copying and pasting the page's web address.

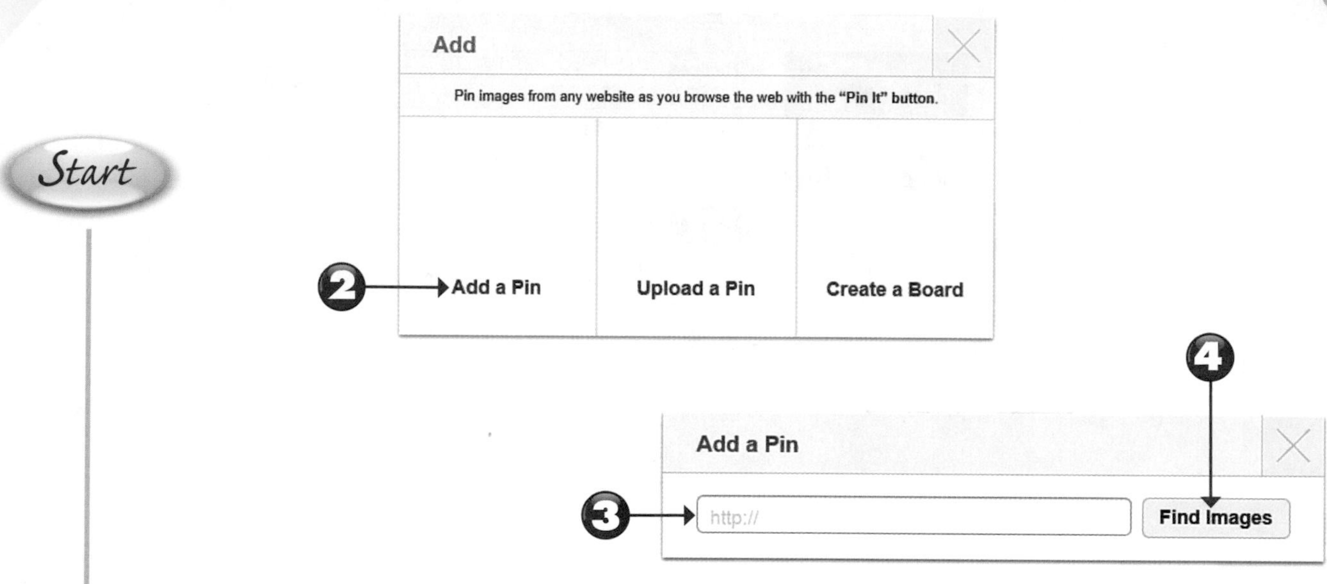

1. Click **Add+** on the Pinterest menu bar to display the Add panel.
2. Click **Add a Pin** to display the Add a Pin panel.
3. Enter the web address (URL) of the page you want to pin into the text box.
4. Click the **Find Images** button.

Continued

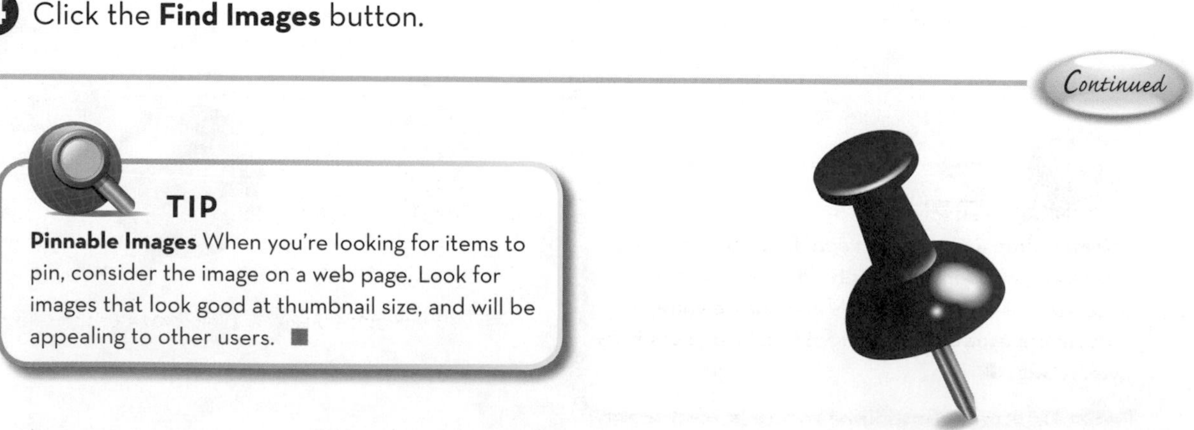

TIP

Pinnable Images When you're looking for items to pin, consider the image on a web page. Look for images that look good at thumbnail size, and will be appealing to other users. ■

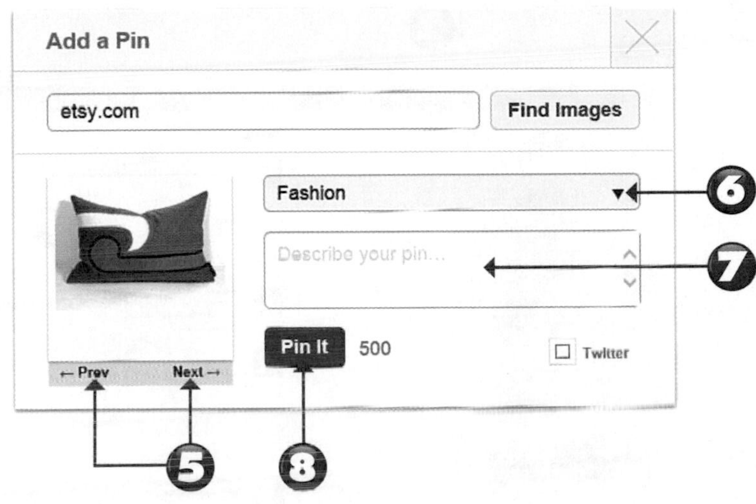

5. The Add a Pin panel now changes to display a slideshow of images found on the selected web page. Click the **Next** or **Prev** buttons to cycle through the images until you find the one you want to pin.
6. Pull down the pinboard list and select the board to which you want to pin this image.
7. Enter a short (500 characters or less) text description of or comment on this image into the Describe Your Pin box.
8. Click the red **Pin It** button when done.

End

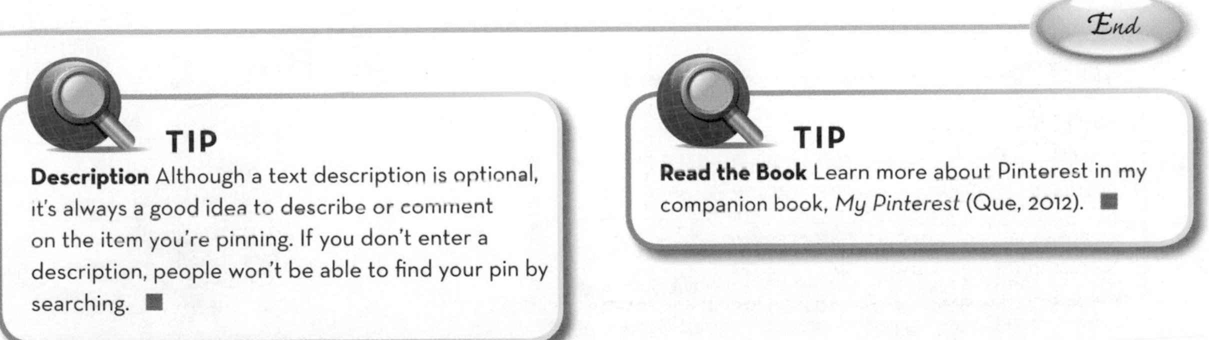

TIP

Description Although a text description is optional, it's always a good idea to describe or comment on the item you're pinning. If you don't enter a description, people won't be able to find your pin by searching. ■

TIP

Read the Book Learn more about Pinterest in my companion book, *My Pinterest* (Que, 2012). ■

TWEETING WITH TWITTER

Twitter is a *microblogging* service that lets you create short (up to 140 characters in length) text posts that keep your friends and family informed of your latest activities. Anyone subscribing to your posts receives updates via the Twitter site.

1. Go to Twitter's home page (www.twitter.com).
2. Enter up to 140 characters into the Compose New Tweet box, and then press **Enter.**

NOTE

Microblogging A *blog* (short for *web blog*) is a means of sharing personal observations over the Internet, kind of like a web-based diary. While a normal blog post can be of any length, a *microblog* is limited to very short messages—like the text message you send via mobile phone. ■

FOLLOWING OTHER TWITTER USERS

Twitter lets you "follow" what other users are doing on Twitter. Once you've registered and signed in, the Twitter home page displays "tweets" from users you've decided to follow.

1. From the #Discover page on the Twitter site, click **Find Friends**.
2. Enter a person's email address or username into the Search box.
3. Click the **Search Twitter** button.
4. Click the **Follow** button for the user you want to follow.

End

NOTE

Other Ways to Search You can also search for Twitter users on other email networks (such as Gmail, Yahoo!, and Hotmail), invite nonusers to join Twitter, and view a list of suggested users you might want to follow. ■

VIEWING ALL YOUR SOCIAL ACTIVITY FROM THE WINDOWS PEOPLE APP

If you follow a lot of friends on multiple social networks, it can be quite time-consuming. Fortunately, the Windows 8 People app consolidates messages from several major social networks and your email accounts. You can view the latest updates from your friends all in one place, as well as comment on and retweet those updates—without having to visit the social networking sites themselves. The People app also serves to organize all the contacts you have in your email and similar programs.

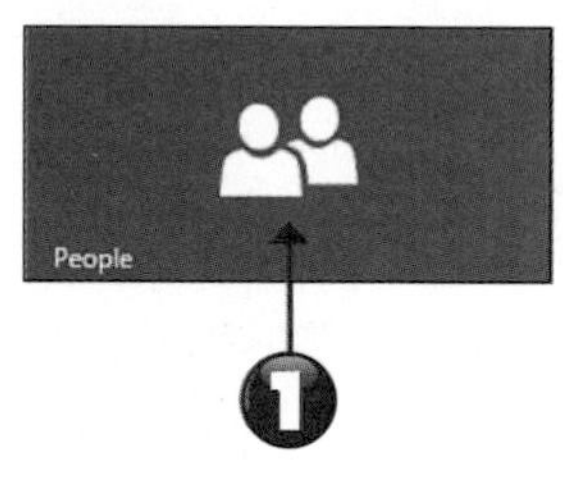

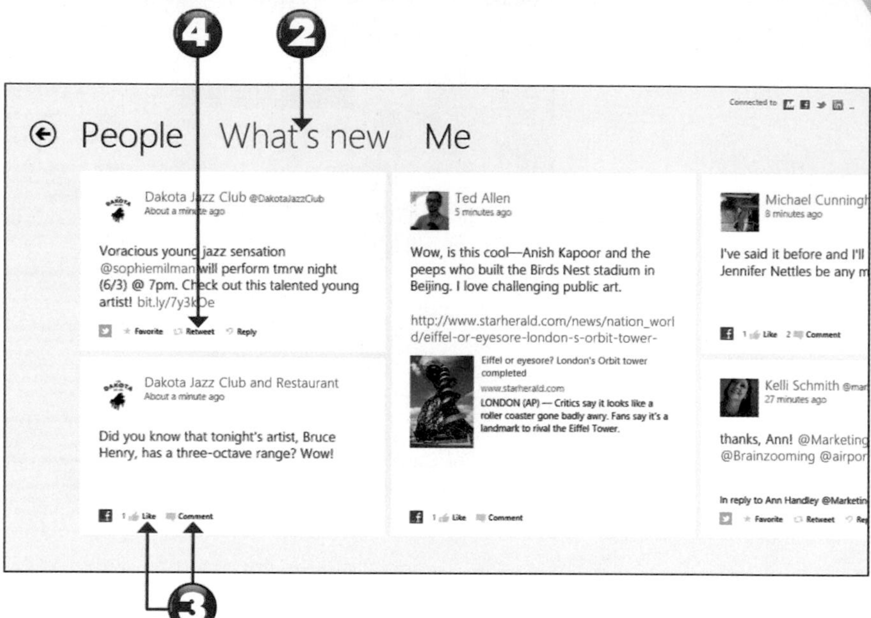

1. To launch the People app, click or tap the **People** tile on the Start screen. (This is a "live" tile, displaying the latest activity from your connected friends.)
2. To view what your friends are posting on Facebook and other social networks, click **What's New.** Each status update or tweet is displayed in its own panel.
3. To like or comment on a Facebook post, click the **Like** or **Comment** links.
4. To retweet a Twitter post, click **Retweet**.

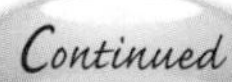

NOTE

Connecting with the People App The People app automatically connects to the Microsoft Account you used to create your Windows account. You can manually connect the People app to your Facebook, Google+, LinkedIn, and Twitter social network accounts, as well as your Gmail, Hotmail, and Microsoft Exchange email accounts. ■

TIP

Commenting and Liking To "like," comment on, or retweet a given post, click or tap that post to open it on a new page and proceed from there. ■

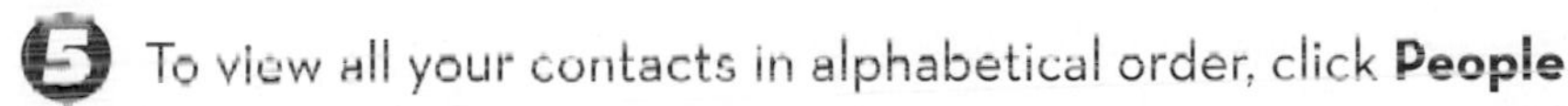

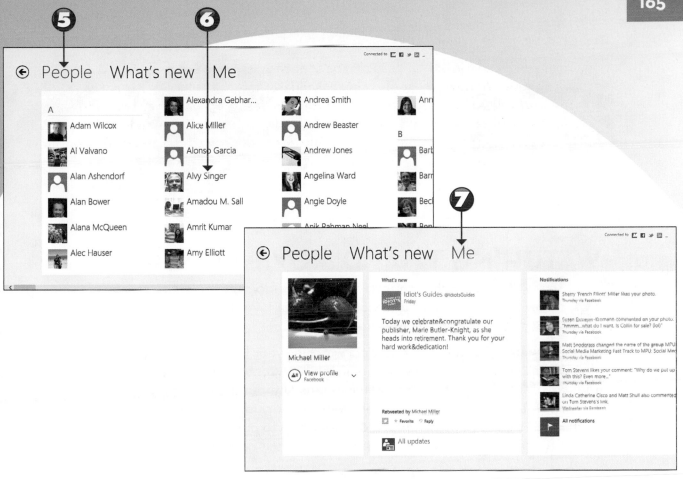

5. To view all your contacts in alphabetical order, click **People**.

6. Click or tap a person's name to view full details about this person.

7. To view your own online profile, including your latest social posts, click **Me**.

End

TIP

Adding a New Contact To add a new contact to the People app, display the options bar and click **New**. When the New Contact page appears, enter the contact's information, and then click **Save**. ■

TIP

Connecting a New Account To manually connect new accounts to the People app, display the charms bar, click **Settings**, and then click **Accounts**. When the Accounts pane appears, click or tap **Add an Account**. When the Add an Account pane appears, click or tap the account you want to add and follow the onscreen instructions specific to that type of account. ■

WATCHING TV AND MOVIES ONLINE

Want to rewatch last night's episode of *American Idol*? Or the entire season of *NCIS*? How about a classic music video from your favorite band? Or that latest "viral video" you've been hearing about?

Here's the latest hot thing on the Web: watching your favorite television programs, films, and videos online, via your web browser. Assuming you have a fast enough Internet connection, you can find tens of thousands of free and paid videos to watch at dozens of different websites, including YouTube, Hulu, and Netflix. You can even use Windows 8's Video app to purchase and download videos to your PC—and watch them anytime, at your convenience.

PLAYING A VIDEO WITH THE VIDEO APP

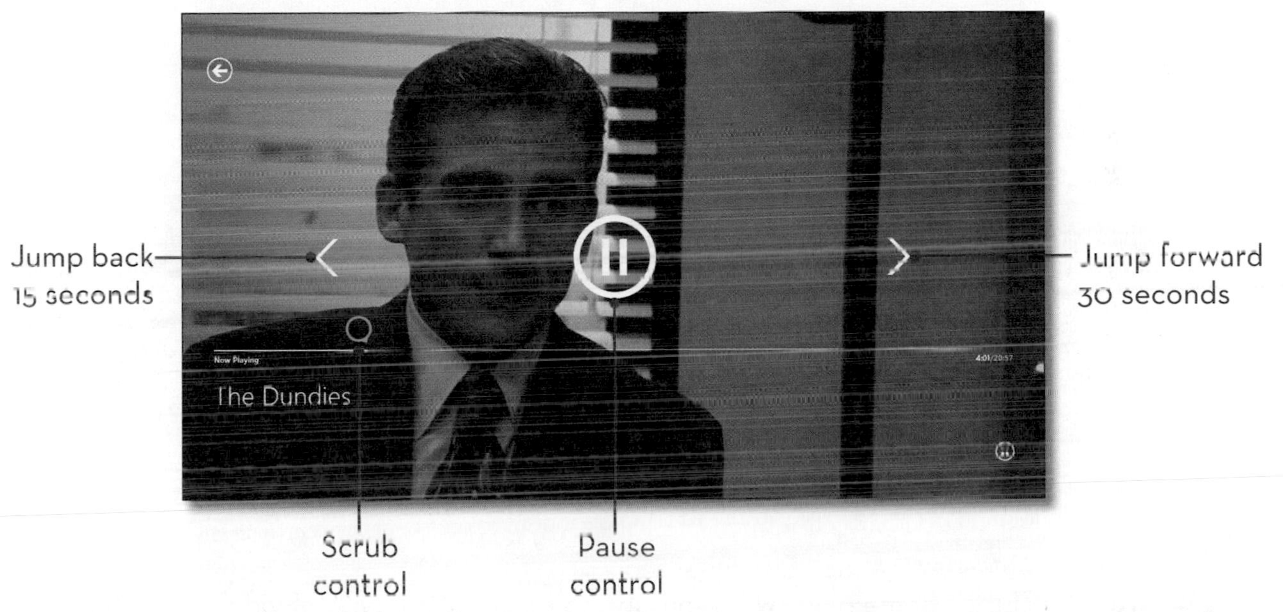

WATCHING VIDEOS ON YOUTUBE

The most popular video site on the web is YouTube. This site is a video sharing community; users can upload their own videos and watch videos uploaded by other members. (YouTube also offers a number of commercial movies, TV shows, and music videos.)

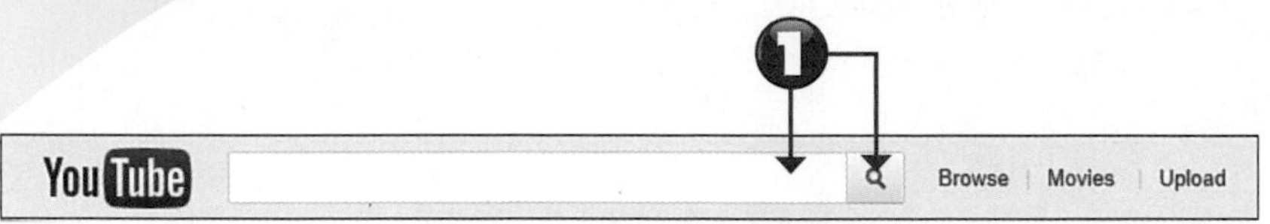

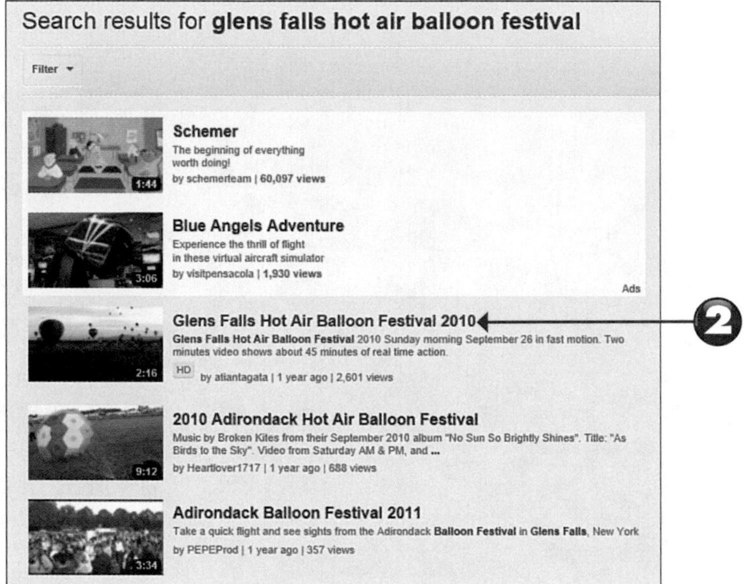

1. From YouTube's home page (www.youtube.com), enter the type of video you're looking for into the Search box, and then press **Enter** or click the **Search** (magnifying glass) button.
2. When the list of matching videos appears, click the video you want to watch.

Continued

TIP

Movies To view commercial movies on YouTube, click **Movies** at the top of any page. Some movies are free; others can be "rented" on a 48-hour pass for as low as $1.99. ■

TIP

Playlists To add a video to a playlist, click the **Add To** button under the video player, and then click a playlist. You can view your playlists favorites by clicking the down arrow next to your name (at the top of the page); click a playlist to begin playback. ■

3. When the video page appears, the video begins playing automatically.
4. Click the **Pause** button to pause playback; click the button again to resume playback.
5. Click the **full-screen** button to view the video on your entire computer screen.
6. Click the **thumbs-up** button to "like" the video.

End

TIP

Sharing Videos Find a video you think a friend would like? Click the **Share** button under the video player. You can then opt to email a link to the video, "like" the video on Facebook, or tweet a link to the video on Twitter. ■

TIP

Uploading Your Own Videos To upload your own home movies to YouTube, click **Upload** at the top of any page. On the next screen, click **Select Files from Your Computer**, and then navigate to and select the video you want to upload. After the video is uploaded, you can add a title and description, as well as choose a thumbnail image for the video. ■

WATCHING TV SHOWS ON HULU

Hulu offers episodes from major-network TV shows, as well as new and classic feature films, for online viewing. The standard free membership offers access to a limited number of videos; upgrade to Hulu Plus ($7.99/month) for a larger selection of newer shows.

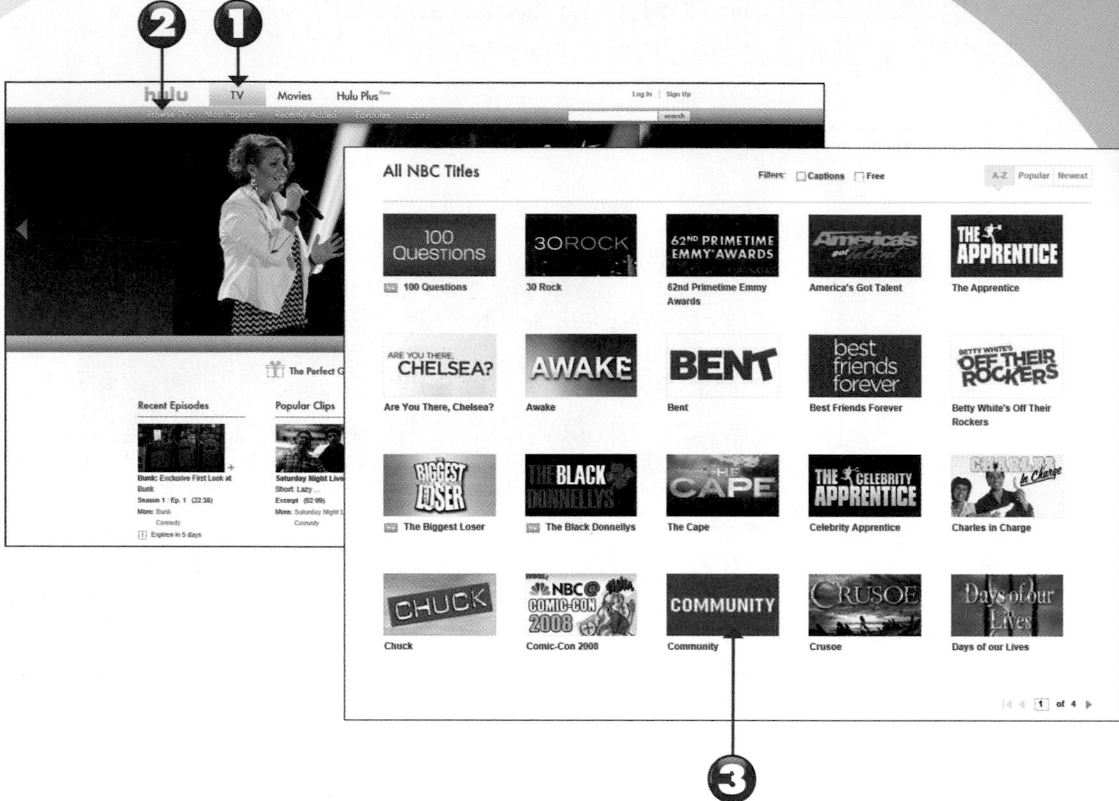

Start

1. Go to the Hulu home page (www.hulu.com) and click the **TV** tab to view television programming.
2. Click **Browse TV** to browse through programming by genre, or use the Search box to search for specific shows.
3. When you find a show you want, click its title or thumbnail.

Continued

TIP

Browsing You can browse Hulu's TV programming by series name, network, or genre. ■

TIP

Movies Hulu also offers a variety of movies for online viewing. The standard free membership has a very limited selection of movie programming, typically documentaries and movie trailers. The $7.99 Hulu Plus membership offers a much larger selection of movies. ■

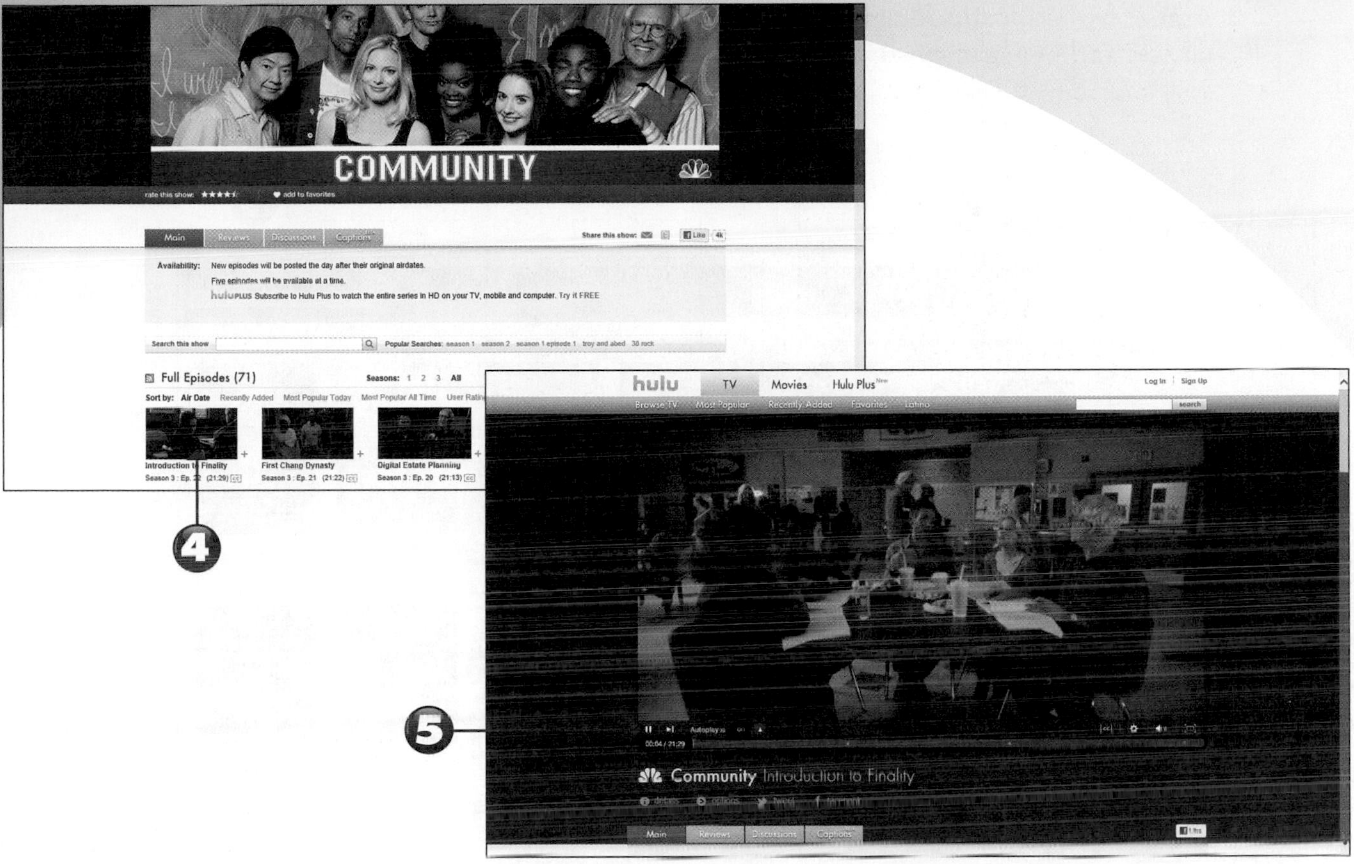

4 You now see the page for this series. Scroll down the page to see specific episodes; click an episode to begin viewing.

5 Playback of the selected episode begins automatically. Mouse over the video to display the playback controls.

End

TIP

Reviews and Discussions Most television programming offered on Hulu is accompanied by user reviews and discussions. Click the **Reviews** and **Discussions** tabs on the series page to view what's available.

WATCHING MOVIES ON NETFLIX

Arguably the most popular site for streaming movies is Netflix. This site offers a mix of both classic and newer movies, as well as classic television programming.

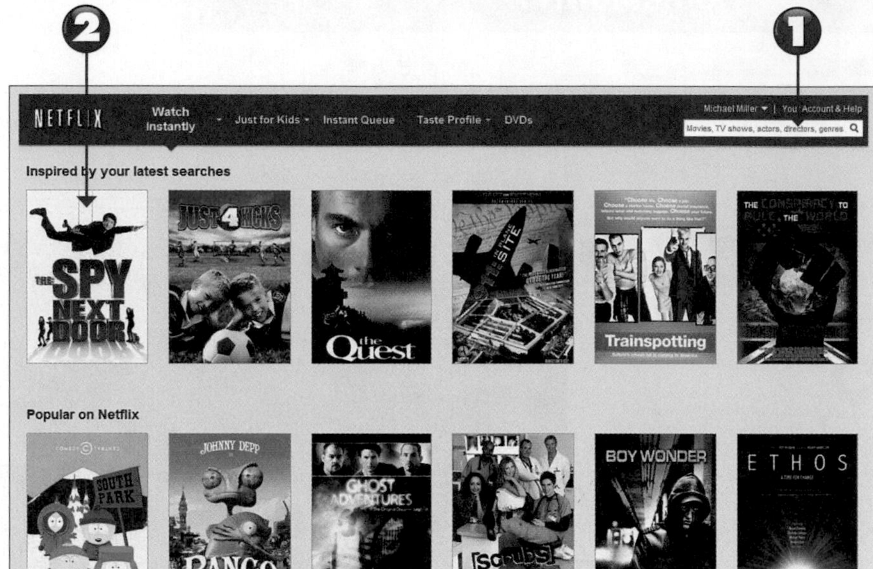

Start

1. Log on to the Netflix home page (www.netflix.com) and scroll through Netflix's suggestions or use the Search box to find the something you want to watch.
2. Click the movie you want to watch.

Continued

TIP

Subscription Fees Netflix isn't free. You pay $7.99/month for unlimited streaming video online. ■

CAUTION

Open on Desktop Netflix may require you to open the desktop version of Internet Explorer for viewing. ■

3 Netflix begins streaming the movie to your computer. Mouse over the movie to display the playback controls.

End

TIP

Recommendations Netflix analyzes your past viewing to suggest new movies you might like to watch. It also organizes programming by genre. ■

NOTE

DVD Rental Netflix also offers a separate DVD-by-mail rental service, with separate subscription fee. ■

DOWNLOADING AND WATCHING MOVIES VIA THE WINDOWS VIDEO APP

If you've downloaded movies or other videos to your PC, you can watch them with Windows 8's Video app. This app lets you play videos you've downloaded to your PC, as well as lets you purchase new videos to watch.

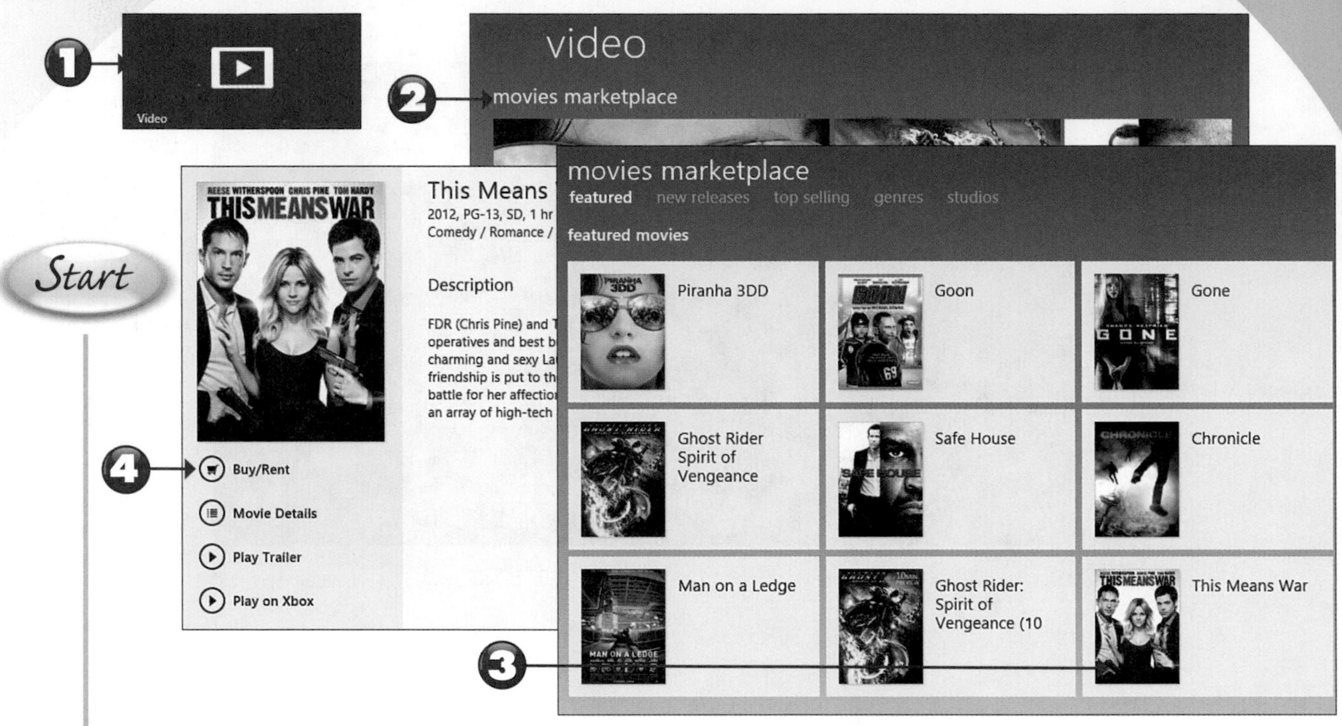

Start

1. Launch the app by clicking or tapping the **Video** tile on the Start screen.
2. To purchase and download new movies or TV programming, scroll to and click either **Movies Marketplace** or **TV Marketplace**.
3. When you find an item you want to purchase, click or tap the tile for that item.
4. Click or tap the **Buy** or **Buy/Rent** button to purchase and download the selected item.

Continued

TIP

Purchasing Videos The Video app lets you purchase movies and TV programming from Microsoft's Xbox Marketplace (formerly known as the Zune Marketplace). You don't pay for items directly, however; instead, you have to purchase the proper number of Microsoft Points required for the item. A typical TV episode costs 240 points (approximately $3), and a typical movie costs 360 points (approximately $4). ■

NOTE

Renting Movies Movies are usually "rented" for a limited time (14 days), rather than downloaded for you to own permanently. ■

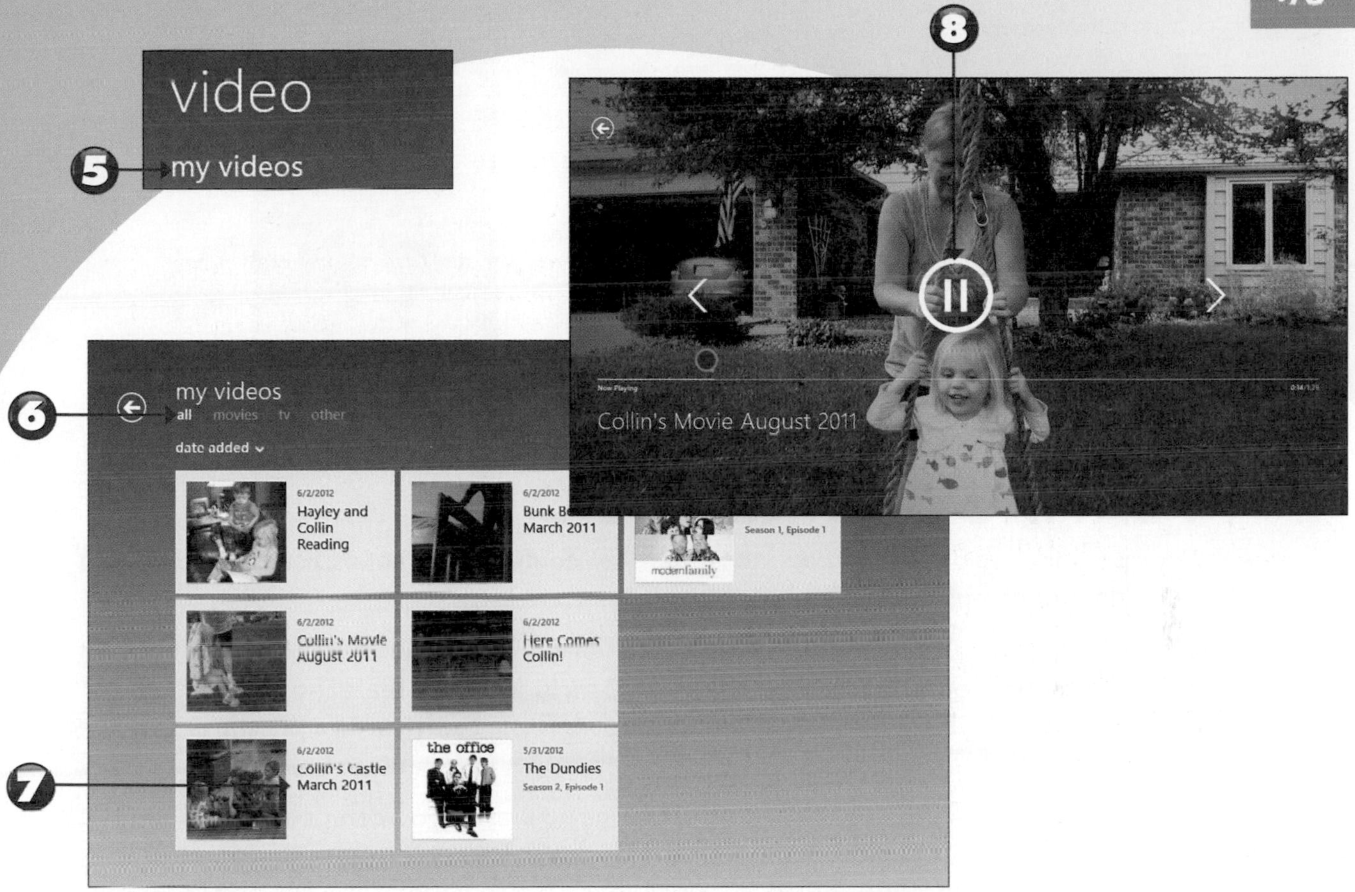

5. To view all the videos in your collection scroll left and click **My Videos**.

6. You now see your video collection, organized by All, Movies, TV, and Other; click or tap a selection at the top of the screen to view that particular type of video.

7. Click or tap the video you want to view.

8. Click or tap the screen to display and use the playback controls.

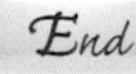

TIP

Playback Controls The Video app lets you pause or resume playback; you can also tap the left or right arrows to jump back 15 seconds or forward 30 seconds in the video. (This is great for skipping recorded commercials.) There's also a scrub control you can drag left or right to skip to a specific point in the video. ■

TIP

Other Places to Purchase Many other sites online let you purchase or "rent" movies and TV shows for viewing on your PC. For example, if you have an iPhone or iPod, you can purchase video programming from the iTunes Store. ■

PLAYING DIGITAL MUSIC

Your personal computer can do more than just compute. It can also serve as a fully functional music player!

That's right, you can use your PC to listen to your favorite music, either on CD or downloaded from the Internet. Windows 8 includes a full-featured Music app for music playback; you can also use Apple's iTunes software to purchase and download music to listen to.

And, if you have an iPhone or iPod portable music player, you can use your PC to manage all of your digital music with the iTunes software. It's easy to download music from the iTunes Store, connect your iPod to your computer, and then transfer your music to your iPod. You can even use the iTunes software to burn your own music CDs!

EXPLORING THE MUSIC APP

PLAYING MUSIC IN WINDOWS

All the music you've purchased and downloaded online, as well as music you've ripped from your own CDs, is stored in the Music library on your computer's hard drive. You can view and play music from your library using Windows 8's Music app. The Music app is the central hub for all your music-related activities on your computer.

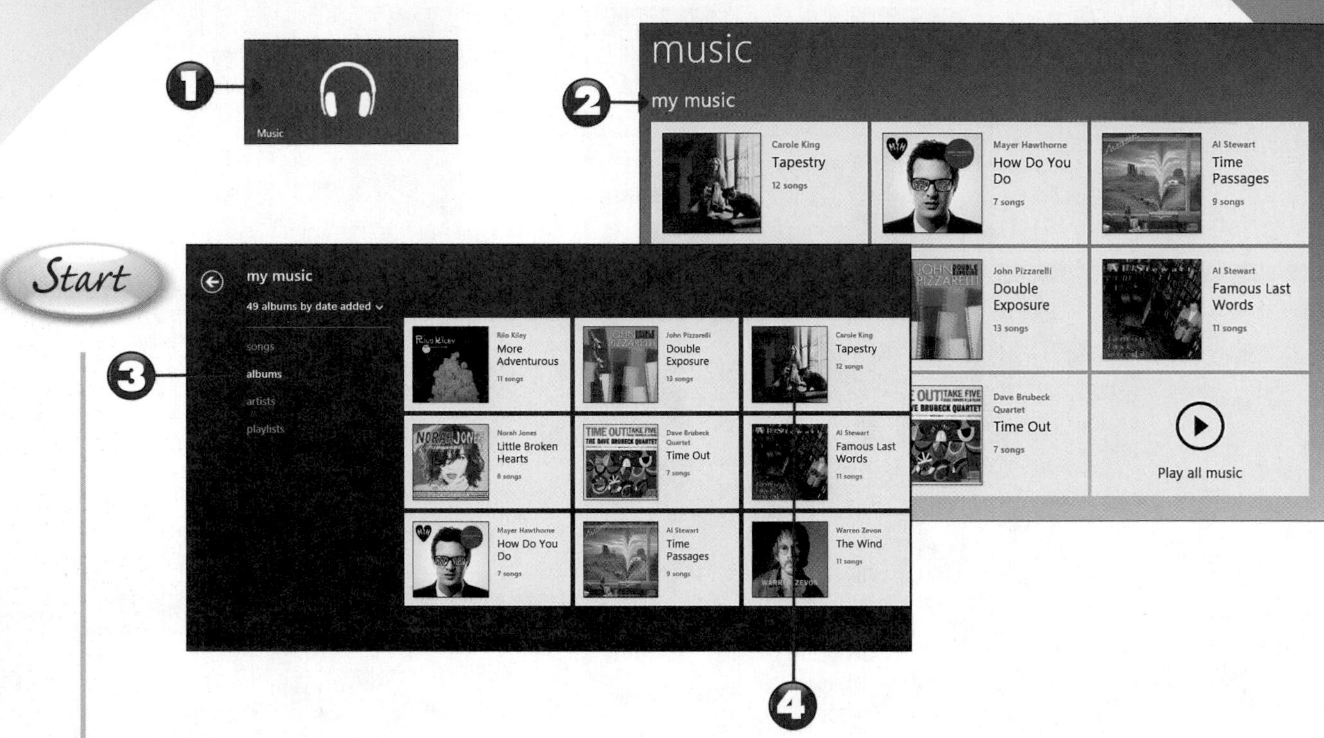

1. From the Windows Start screen, click or tap the **Music** tile to launch the Music app.
2. Scroll left and click or tap **My Music**.
3. You now see all the music stored on your computer. Click **Songs** to display the individual songs in your collection. Click **Albums** to display complete albums. Click **Artists** to display your collection organized by recording artist. Or click **Playlists** to view any playlists you've created.
4. Click the album or track you want to play.

Continued

TIP

Playback from the Home Screen You can also play music directly from the Music app's home screen, by clicking an album's tile. To play your entire collection, click the **Play All Music** tile. ■

TIP

Windows Media Player If you need more fully featured music playback and management, check out the Windows Media Player app that runs on the traditional desktop. To launch this app, right-click the **Start** screen and click **All Apps**; when the Apps screen appears, scroll to and click the **Windows Media Player** icon. ■

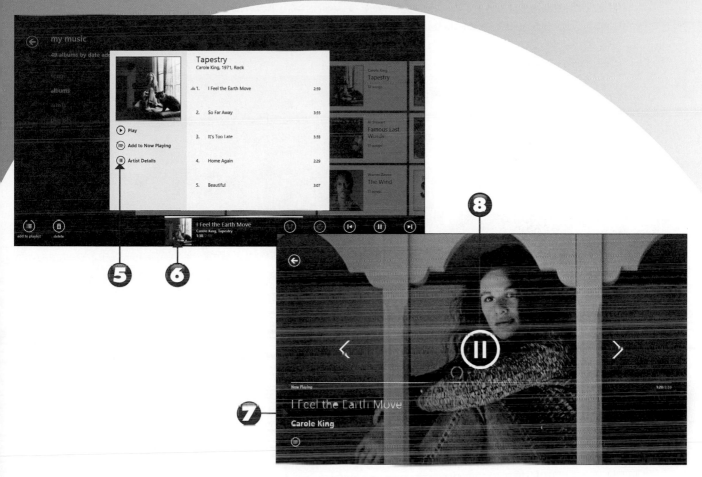

5 The Music app displays a pane for that item. Click the **Play** button to begin playback.

6 To display the album in full screen, right-click to display the options bar and click the album cover.

7 The Music app now begins playback and displays either artwork from this artist or a collage of all your albums. Click or tap the screen to display album information and playback controls.

8 Click the **Pause** button to pause playback; click the **Play** button to resume playback.

End

TIP

Different Ways to Display By default, the Music app displays albums by date added. You can also sort your music in alphabetic order, or by release year or genre. In addition, you can opt to display artists or individual tracks instead of albums.

TIP

Listening While Working You can switch to any other app in Windows, or to the Start screen, while your music is playing. To pause or change the playback, however, you'll have to switch back to the Music app.

FINDING MUSIC TO PURCHASE IN WINDOWS

The Windows 8 Music app also lets you to purchase new music online. You can purchase individual tracks or complete albums from Microsoft's Xbox Music store (formerly known as the Zune Music store).

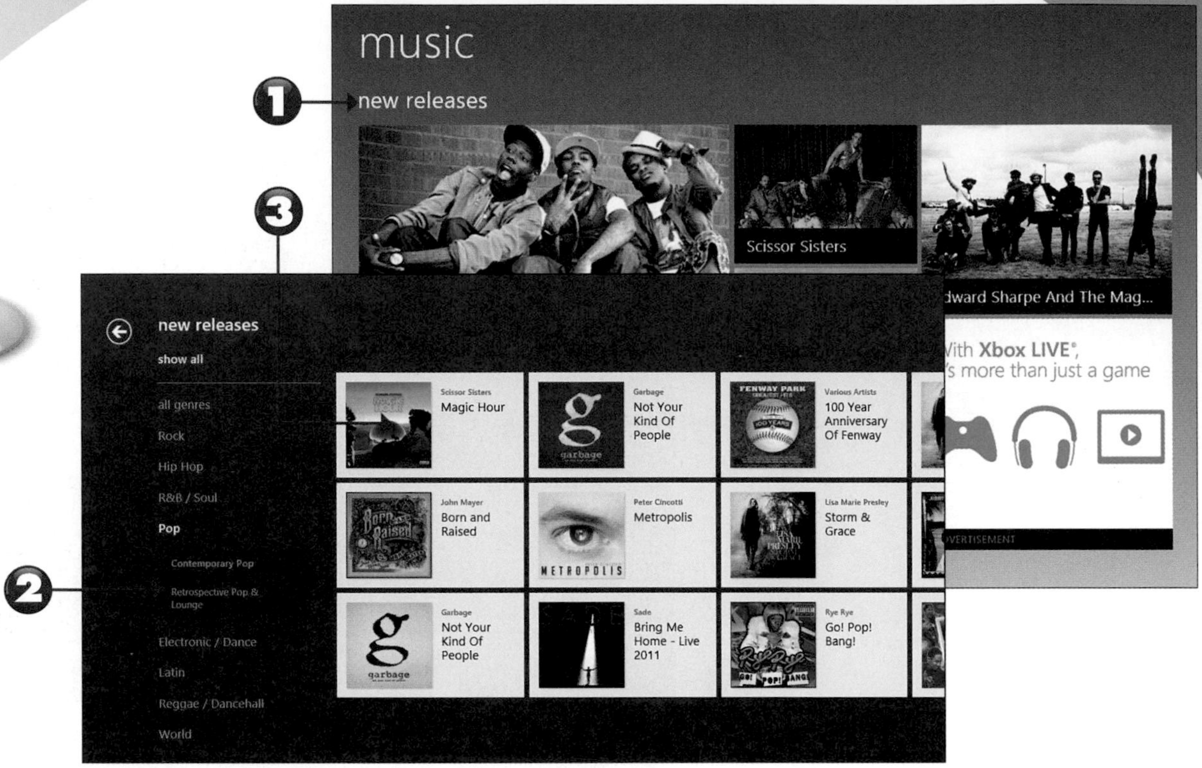

Start

1. From within the Music app, scroll to and click either **New Releases** or **Popular**.
2. Browse the featured albums or click a genre (Rock, Hip Hop, and so on) to view albums within that genre.
3. Click or tap the item want to buy; this displays a large panel for that item.

Continued

TIP

Other Online Music Stores You can buy downloadable music at many online music stores, including the iTunes Store (www.apple.com/itunes/) and Amazon MP3 Store (www.amazonmp3.com). Many online music services, such as Spotify (www.spotify.com) and Pandora (www.pandora.com), stream music to your computer over the Internet for a flat monthly fee. ■

TIP

Tracks or Albums You can purchase both individual tracks and complete albums. ■

4 Click or tap **Buy Album** to display the Confirm Purchase screen.

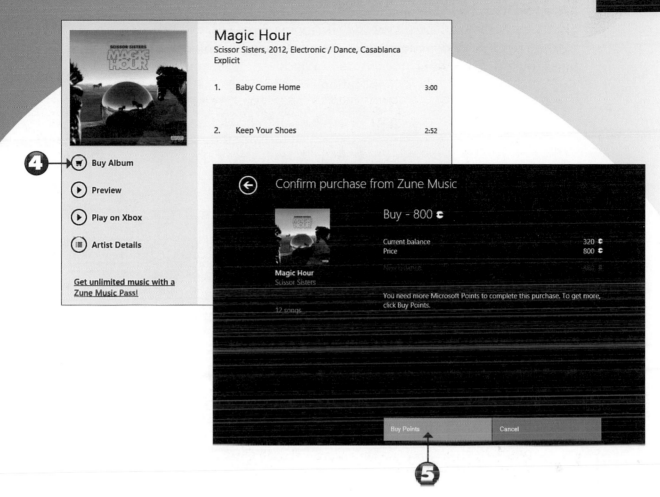

5 Click or tap the **Buy Points** button to purchase enough Microsoft Points to complete the purchase.

End

TIP

Microsoft Points Items in Microsoft's Xbox Music Store must be purchased with Microsoft Points, not actual dollars. It costs $4.99 to purchase 400 Microsoft Points, or $9.99 to purchase 800 Points. A typical album costs 800 Microsoft Points, which equates to a $9.99 purchase. ■

NOTE

Downloading Purchases Once you make the purchase, the album is downloaded to your computer and added to your Music library. This takes a few minutes; once the download is complete, you can play your new album. ■

DOWNLOADING MUSIC FROM THE ITUNES STORE

The largest online music store today is Apple's iTunes Store, with more than 20 million tracks available for downloading, at prices ranging from 69 cents to $1.29 each. You can play music purchased at the iTunes Store in Windows' Music app, on your iPod or iPhone, or with Apple's iTunes music player application—which you also need to access the iTunes Store.

Start

1. In the iTunes software, click **iTunes Store** in the navigation pane.

2. The iTunes software now connects to the Internet and displays the iTunes Store's main page. To view music for purchase, click **Music** in the navigation bar at the top of the screen.

3. To search for a specific song or artist, enter your query into the Search box and press **Enter**.

Continued

TIP

iTunes Software You must download and install the iTunes software to shop the iTunes Store, as well as to manage the music on your iPod or iPhone. You can download the iTunes app for free at www.apple.com/itunes/. ■

TIP

Browsing by Genre You can also browse the iTunes store by type of music—Alternative, Country, Classical, and so on. Just click the down arrow next to the **Music** button and click the genre you're interested in. ■

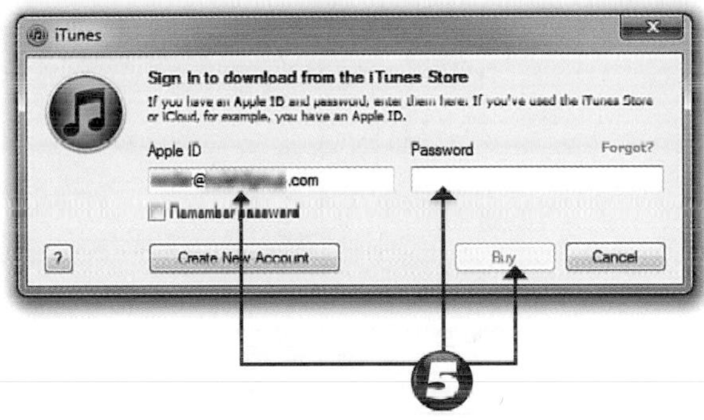

4 The iTunes Store now displays all the albums and tracks that match your search. To purchase an item, click the **Buy** button.

5 When prompted to sign in and download the item, enter your Apple ID and Password, and then click the **Buy** button.

End

TIP

Apple Account Before you can purchase items from the iTunes Store, you have to create an Apple account and enter your credit card information. You may be prompted to do this the first time you click to purchase, or you can create your account manually, at any time, by clicking the **Sign In** button at the top right of the iTunes window and, when prompted, clicking the **Create New Account** button. ■

TIP

More in the Store The iTunes Store offers more than just music for download. iTunes also sells movies, TV shows, music videos, podcasts, audiobooks, and ebooks. You also get access to iTunes U, which offers all manner of educational materials, as well as Apple's App Store for the iPhone and iPad. ■

PLAYING A CD WITH ITUNES

You can also use the iTunes program to play audio CDs—if your computer has a CD drive, that is.

Start

1. Insert a CD into your PC's CD drive and launch the iTunes software.
2. The CD automatically appears in the iTunes window. All the tracks of the album are listed in the main window.

TIP

Playing Downloaded Music You can also use the iTunes software to play music you've downloaded or ripped to your PC. Just select **Music** in the Library section of the navigation pane, and then click the track or album you want to play. ■

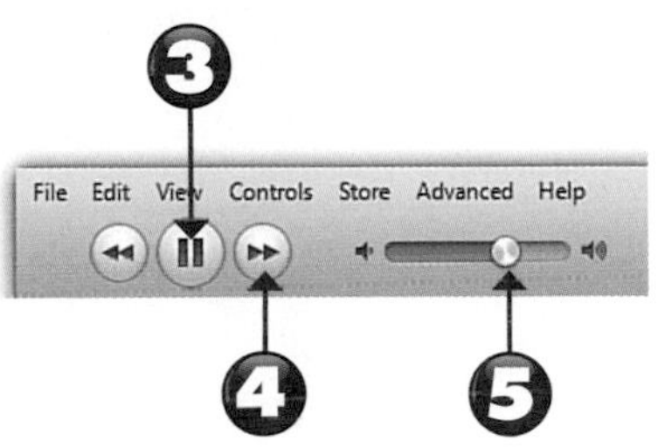

3. Click the **Play** button to begin playback; the button now changes to a Pause button. Click the **Pause** button to pause playback.

4. Click the **Forward** button to skip to the next track.

5. Use the volume slider to adjust the volume louder or softer.

End

TIP

Shuffle and Repeat To play the songs on a CD in a random order, click on the **Shuffle** button at the bottom left of the iTunes window. iTunes also offers a repeat function, which repeats the selected songs over and over. You activate this function by clicking on the **Repeat** button, which is next to the Shuffle button. ■

RIPPING A CD TO YOUR HARD DISK WITH ITUNES

In addition to downloading music from the Internet, you can store digital music on your PC by *ripping* tracks from CDs you own. Before you begin ripping CDs, however, you first have to configure the iTunes software to use the desired file format and bitrate for the songs it rips.

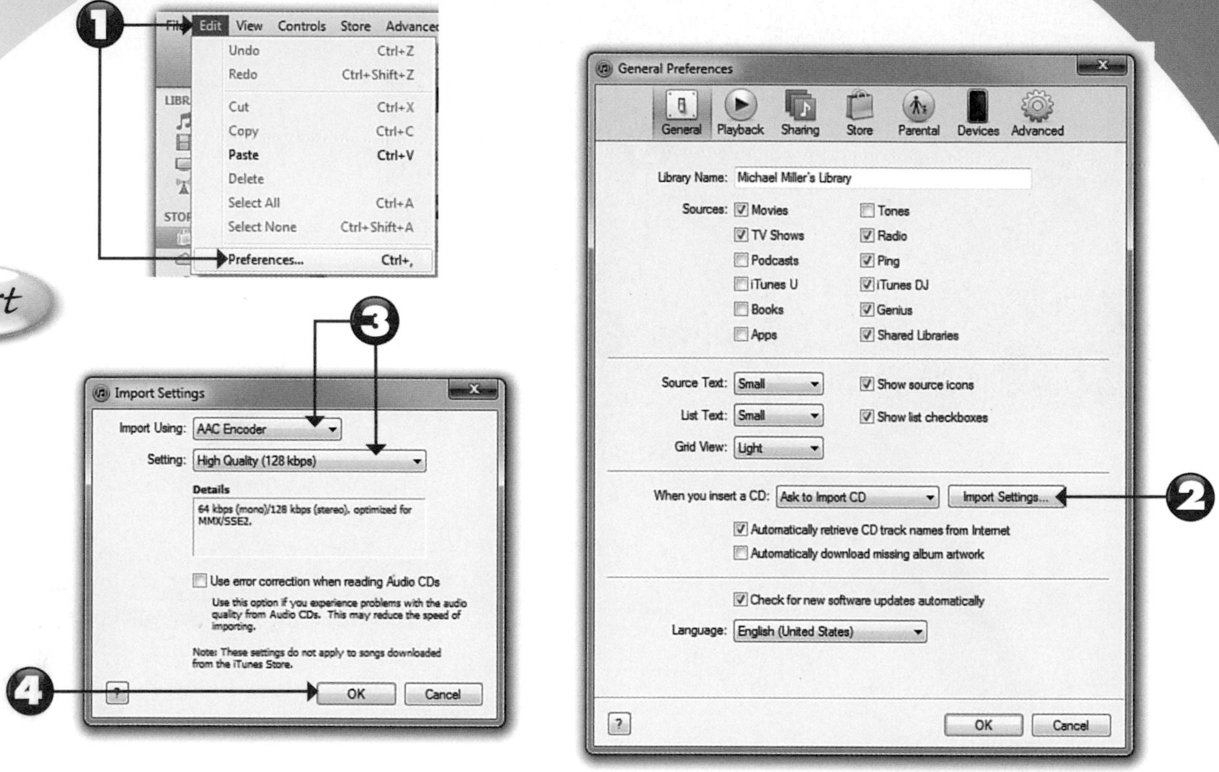

1. From within iTunes, Select **Edit, Preferences** to open the General Preferences dialog box.
2. Select the General tab, and then go to the When You Insert a CD section and click the **Import Settings** button.
3. When the Import Settings dialog box appears, pull down the **Import Using** list and select the desired file type, and then pull down the **Setting** list and select the desired rip quality.
4. Click **OK** when done.

TIP

File Format For near-universal compatibility with other music player software and hardware, rip to the MP3 format. For slightly better audio quality with smaller file sizes, rip to the AAC format. ■

TIP

Bit Rate The higher the bit rate you select for audio quality, the better the sound. For WMA format files, 128Kbps is the default; 192Kbps is a good setting for MP3 files. ■

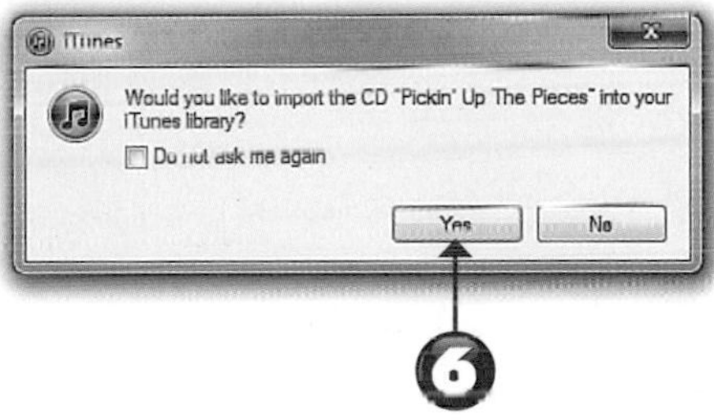

5 After you've configured the iTunes rip settings, insert the CD you want to rip into your PC's CD drive.

6 When iTunes asks if you'd like to import the CD, click **Yes**.

End

TIP

Connect Before You Rip Make sure you're connected to the Internet before you start ripping, so that iTunes can download album and track details. If you don't connect, you won't encode track names or CD cover art—and will have to do so manually, later. ■

NOTE

Added to the Library After iTunes extracts the selected tracks from the CD and converts them to the file format you selected, the ripped files are automatically added to the iTunes Music library. ■

CONNECTING AN IPOD TO YOUR PC

To manage the music stored on your iPod or iPhone, you have to connect your device to your computer. The actual music management is done with Apple's iTunes software. This is called synchronizing or "syncing" tracks from your computer to your portable device.

Start

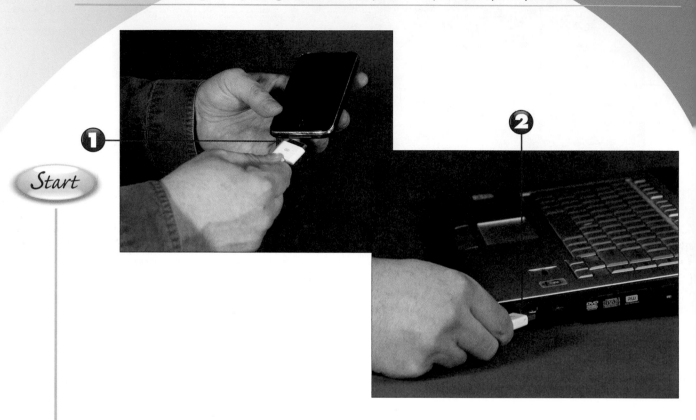

1. Connect one end of the USB cable to your iPod.
2. Connect the other end of the USB cable to a USB port on your PC.

Continued

TIP

Manually Syncing You can also manually select which tunes are copied to your iPod or iPhone. Just access the Music tab on the connection screen and opt to sync only selected tracks and playlists—those items checked in your iTunes library. ■

TIP

Autofill and the iPod Shuffle If you have an iPod shuffle, iTunes offers an Autofill option. This lets the software automatically choose songs to sync to your iPod—which is useful if you have more songs on your hard disk than you have storage capacity on your shuffle. ■

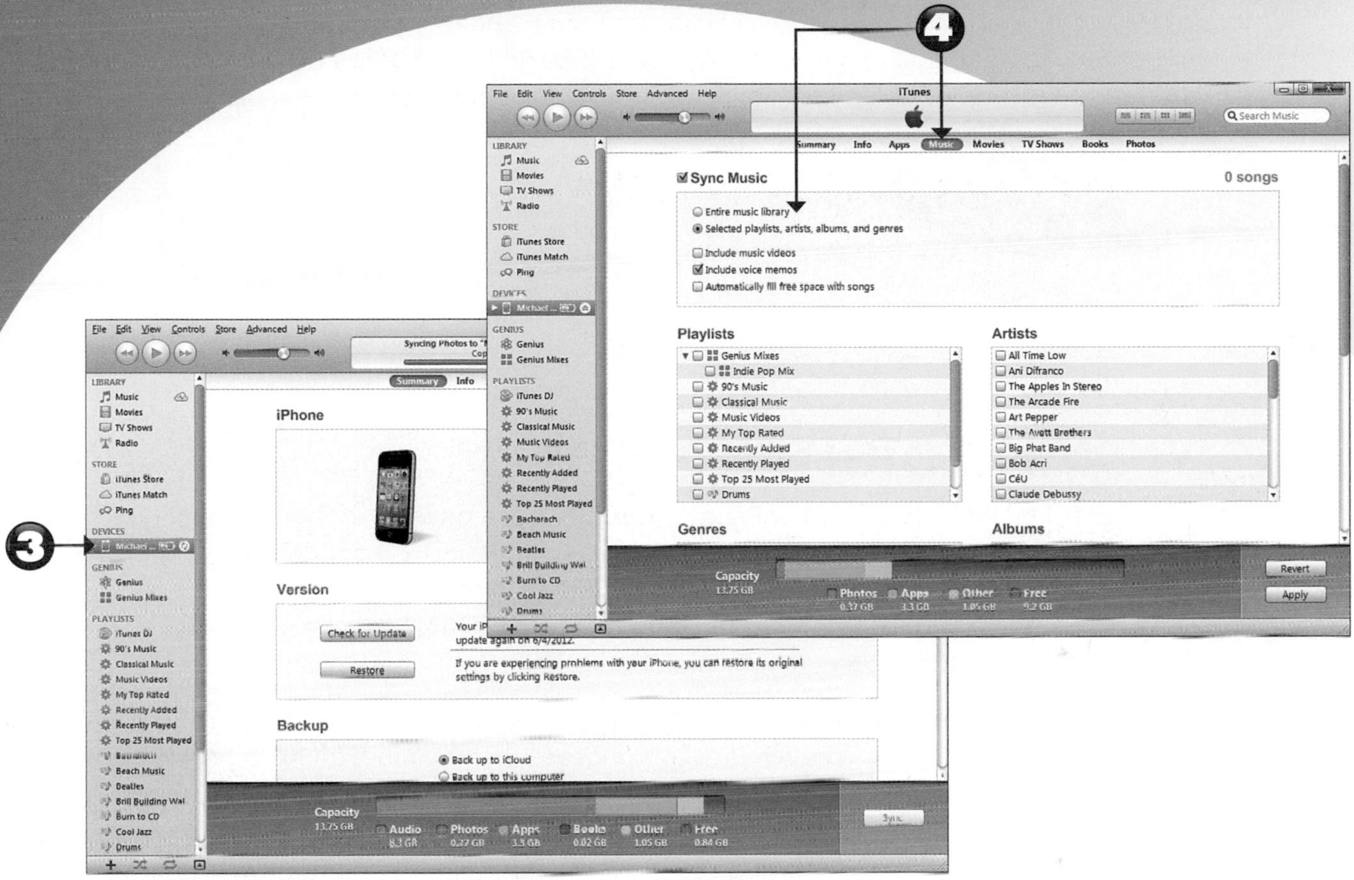

3 The iTunes software now launches on your PC and displays the screen for your device. iTunes automatically syncs all selected tracks and playlists to your portable device.

4 To configure what music files are synced to your portable device, access the Music tab, and choose to sync everything in your Music library or just selected playlists, artists, albums, or genres. Check those items you want to sync.

End

TIP

Apply Your Changes After you make a change on the Music tab, click the **Apply** button to register the change and make the new sync. ■

CAUTION

Finish Before Disconnecting Make sure that your iPod or iPhone is done synchronizing before you disconnect it form your PC. You should never disconnect your device in the middle of a sync, as this can damage the music stored on your portable device. ■

VIEWING DIGITAL PHOTOS

The traditional film camera is a thing of the past. These days, everybody uses a digital camera—which you can easily connect to your PC. Once connected, you can transfer all the photos you take to your computer's hard disk, view them on your computer monitor, share them with friends and family via Facebook and social media, and even edit your pictures to make them look even better.

Windows 8 includes a new Photos app that helps you find and view all the photos stored on your PC. It even displays photos stored online, on Facebook, Flickr, or your Microsoft SkyDrive account.

If you want to print your photos, there are a number of services you can use. You can take your photos (on a memory card or USB drive) to your local Target, Wal-Mart, Walgreens, or other similar store to print in person. Or you can use an online service to upload your photos and send you prints via postal mail. Digital photo printing in this fashion is relatively inexpensive and quite easy to do.

NAVIGATING THE PHOTOS APP

View photos stored on your PC

View photos uploaded to your SkyDrive account

View photos uploaded to Facebook

View photos uploaded to Flickr

View photos stored on an external device

TRANSFERRING PICTURES FROM A MEMORY CARD

If your PC includes a memory card reader, it may be easier to copy your digital photos via your camera's memory card. When you insert a memory card, your PC recognizes the card as if it were another disk on your system. You can then copy files from the memory card to your computer's hard disk.

Start

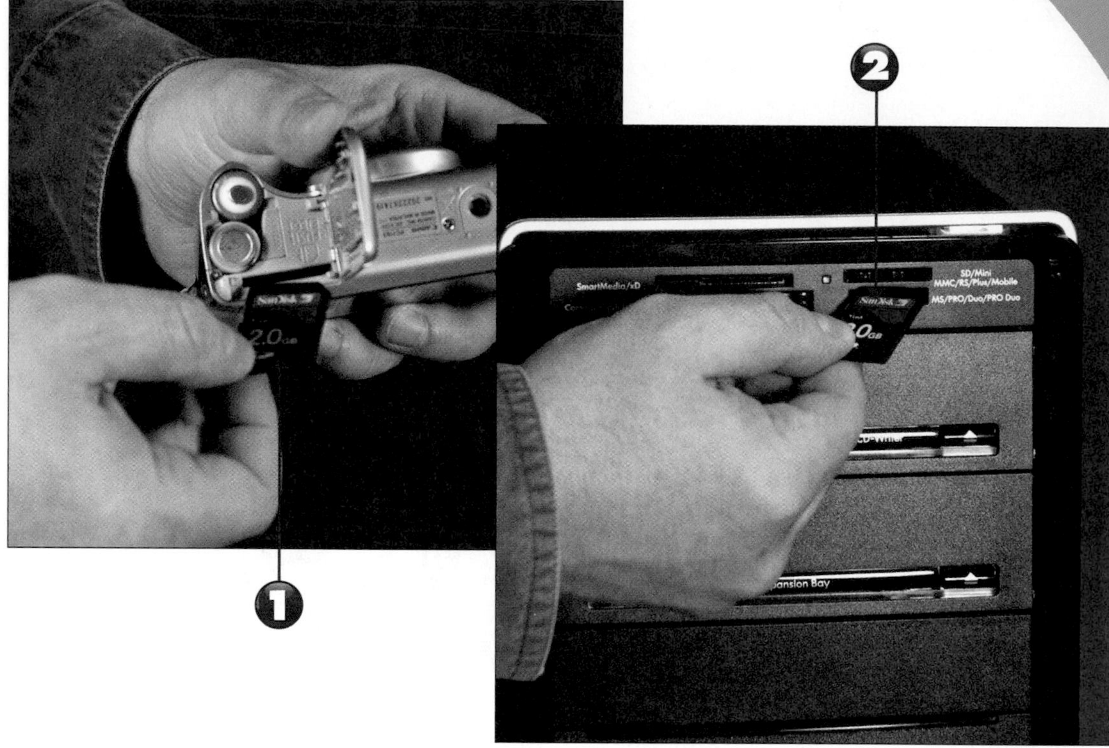

1. Turn off your digital camera and remove the flash memory card.
2. Insert the memory card from your digital camera into the memory card slot on your PC.

Continued

TIP

Connecting via USB You can also transfer photos by connecting your digital camera to your computer via USB. Windows should recognize when your camera is connected and automatically download the pictures in your camera, while displaying a dialog box that notifies you of what it's doing. ■

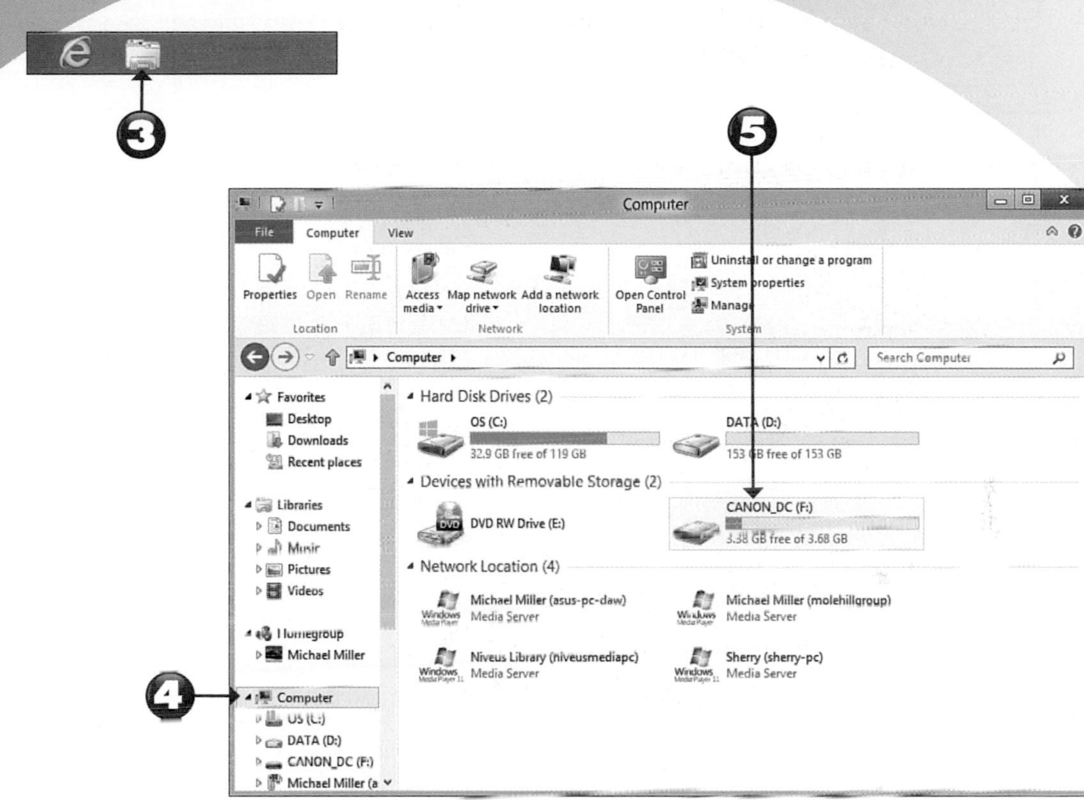

3. Open the Windows desktop and click **File Explorer** on the taskbar.

4. When Windows Explorer opens, click **Computer** in the navigation pane.

5. Click the drive for your memory card reader drive.

Continued

NOTE

Copying Automatically Windows may recognize that your memory card contains digital photos and start to download those photos automatically—no manual interaction necessary. ■

CAUTION

Other Opening Apps Depending on what apps you have installed on your system, you may get multiple prompts to download photos when you connect your camera. If this happens, pick the program you prefer to work with and close the other dialog boxes. ■

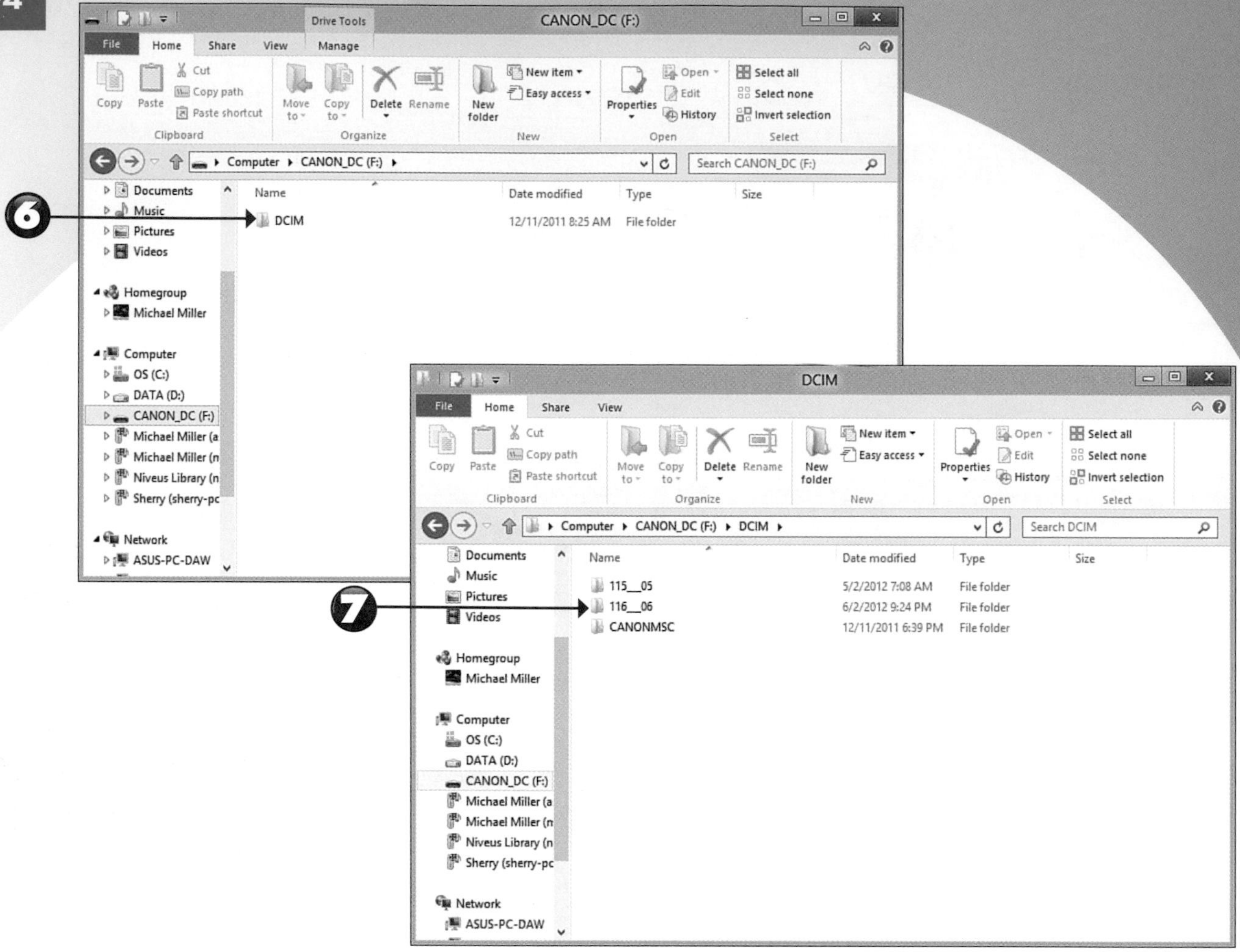

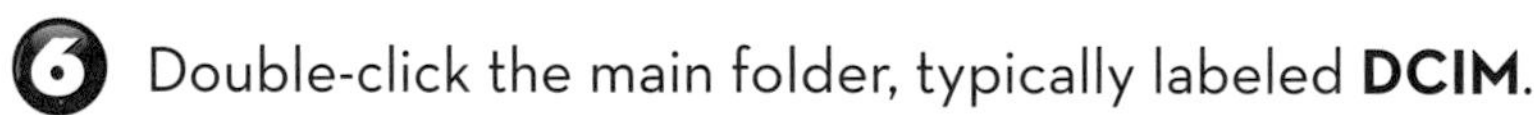

6 Double-click the main folder, typically labeled **DCIM**.

7 Double-click the appropriate subfolder within the DCIM folder to see your photos.

Continued

TIP

Different Folder Names Some cameras might use a name other than DCIM for the main folder. ■

TIP

Printing from a Memory Card Many color photo printers include memory card slots that let you print directly from your camera's memory card, bypassing your computer entirely. ■

8. Hold down the **Ctrl** key and click each photo you want to transfer.

9. Select the **Home** ribbon and click **Copy To**.

10. Click **Pictures** in the Library section of the navigation pane.

11. Select the **Home** ribbon and click **Paste**.

TIP

Buy a Bigger Card To store more pictures (and higher-resolution pictures) on your camera, invest in a higher-capacity flash memory card. The bigger the card, the more photos you can store before transferring to your computer. ■

VIEWING YOUR PHOTOS IN WINDOWS

To view your photos, you can use Windows 8's Photos app. The Photos app consolidates photos stored in a number of places, including on your computer, in the Pictures library; online on Facebook; online on Flickr; and online in your Microsoft SkyDrive account, if you've uploaded any photos there. (It will also display any photos stored on memory devices connected to your computer.)

Start

1. From the Windows Start screen, click or tap the **Photos** tile.

2. To view photos stored in a specific location, click or tap the tile for that location. For example, to view photos stored on your computer, click or tap the **Pictures Library** tile.

Continued

NOTE

Flickr Flickr (www.flickr.com) is a popular photo-sharing site for digital photography enthusiasts. You can upload and share your photos on Flickr for free. ■

TIP

Number of Photos The number of photos stored in each location is noted as a small number beneath the main tile. ■

3 Click through the folders and subfolders until you find a photo you want to view, and then click that photo to view it full screen.

4 To view a slide show of your pictures, right-click the screen to display the options bar, and then click or tap **Slide Show.**

5 To delete the current picture, right-click the screen to display the options bar, and then click or tap **Delete.**

End

TIP

Photo Editing If you want to edit your photos—for cropping, red-eye removal, and the like—you'll need to install a separate photo editing app, such as (www.picasa.com) or Adobe Photoshop Elements (www.adobe.com). ■

TIP

Lock Screen Picture To use the current picture as the image on the Windows Lock screen, display the photo full screen, and then right-click the screen to display the options bar and click or tap **Set As, Lock Screen.** ■

ORDERING PRINTS ONLINE

It's easy to order print copies of your digital photos. You can copy your photo files to a memory card or USB drive and deliver them by hand to your local photo finisher or use an online photo-finishing service. This latter option is convenient for many users; all you have to do is upload the photos you want to print and wait for the prints to be delivered in the mail.

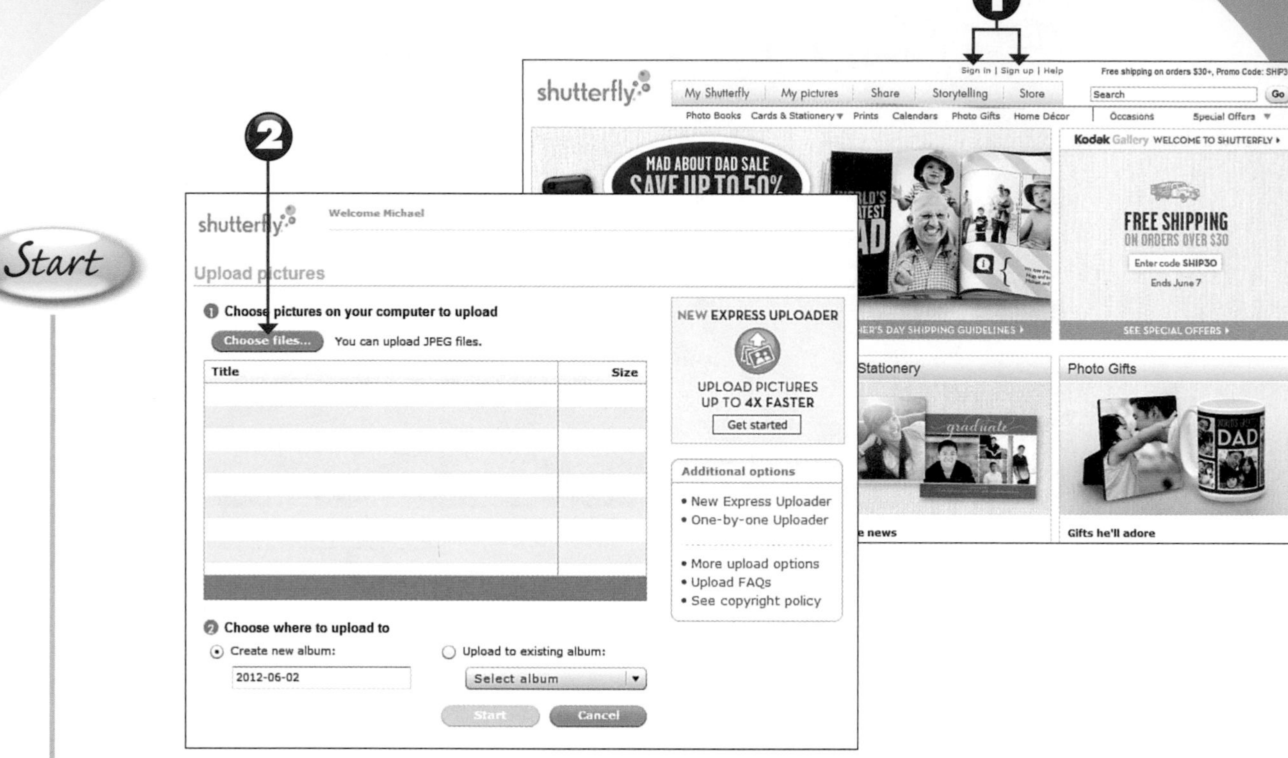

1. Use Internet Explorer to go to the website of the photo printing service, such as Shutterfly (www.shutterfly.com), and create or sign into your account.

2. Upload the pictures you want to print.

Continued

TIP

Local Prints Most local camera shops, chain drugstores, and mass-merchant retailers (such as Target and Wal-Mart) offer in-person photo printing services. Many of these locations also let you upload your photos from your PC at home and then pick up the prints in person. ■

TIP

Photo Printing Services Some of the most popular online photo printing services include dotPhoto (www.dotphoto.com), Nations Photo Lab (www.nationsphotolab.com), Shutterfly (www.shutterfly.com), and Snapfish (www.snapfish.com). ■

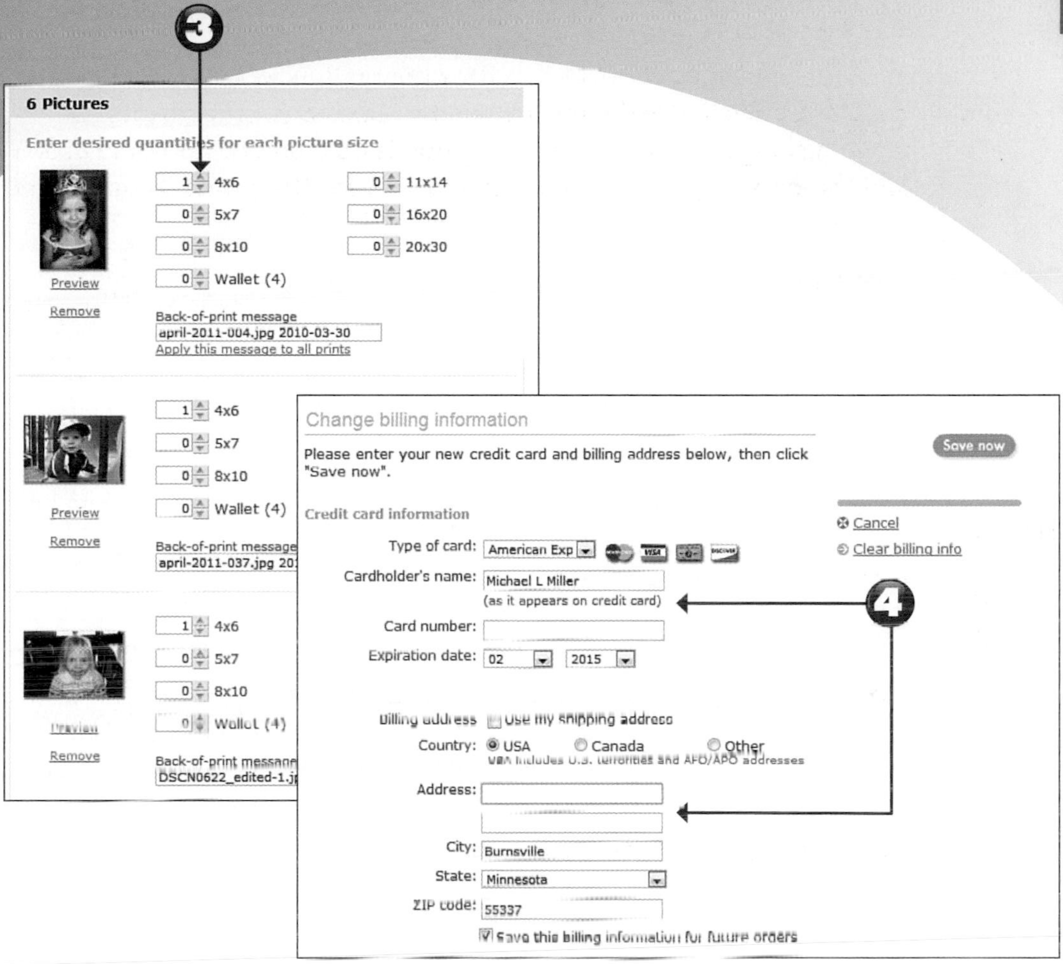

3. Select the size and number you want printed of each photo.

4. Enter payment and shipping information, as necessary.

End

TIP

Pricing At most photo printing sites, the 4-inch x 6-inch size is the most affordable, at around 15 cents a print (before shipping). Other print sizes run a dollar or more a copy. ■

TIP

Emailing Photos If you intend to email photos to a friend or family member, you'll want to use your photo-editing program to resize the photo files so that they're no larger than 100KB or so. Sending photos larger than 1MB in size will likely cause problems in sending and receiving via email. ■

WORKING WITH FILES AND FOLDERS

All the data for documents and programs on your computer is stored in electronic files. These files are then arranged into a series of folders and subfolders—just as you'd arrange paper files in a series of file folders in a filing cabinet.

In Windows 8, you use File Explorer on the traditional desktop to view and manage your folders and files. You open File Explorer by opening the desktop and then clicking the **File Explorer** icon on the taskbar.

FILE EXPLORER

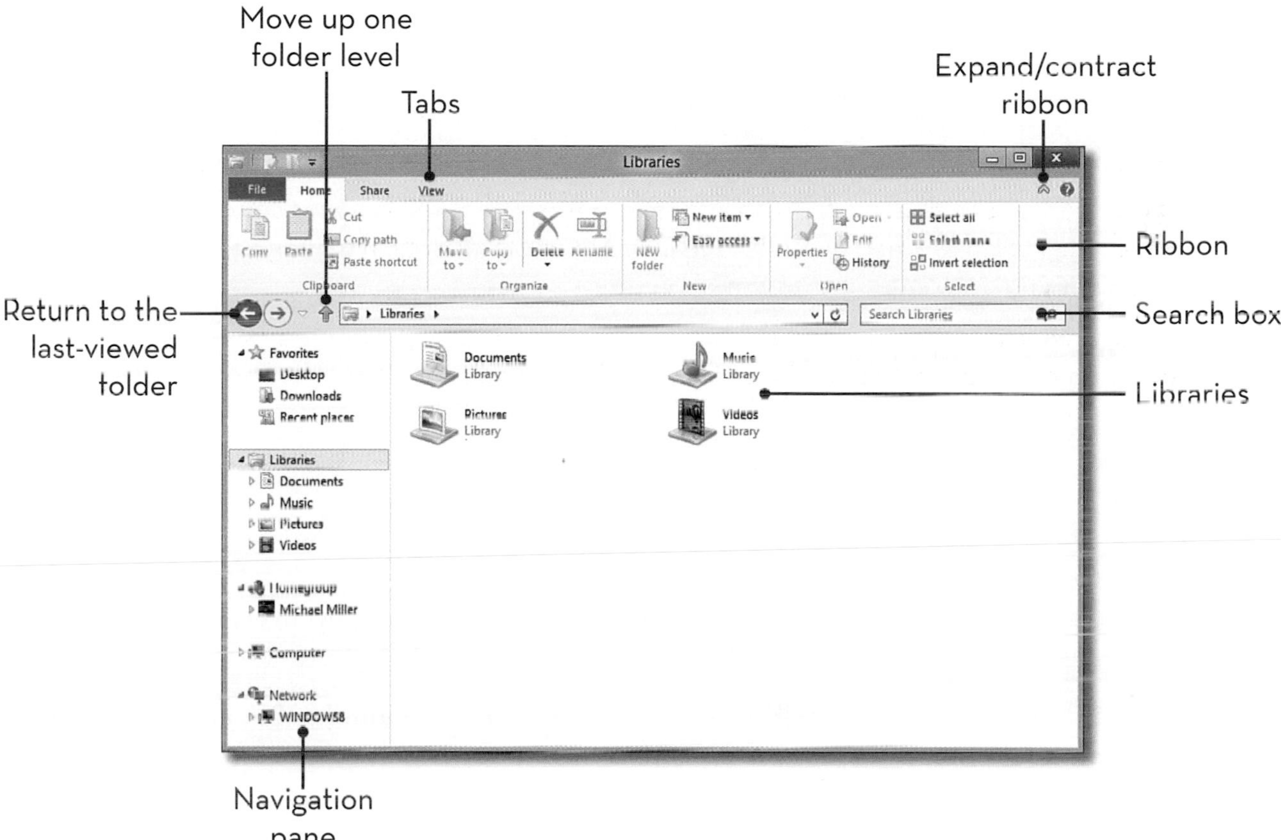

NAVIGATING FOLDERS

You can navigate through the folders and subfolders in File Explorer in several ways.

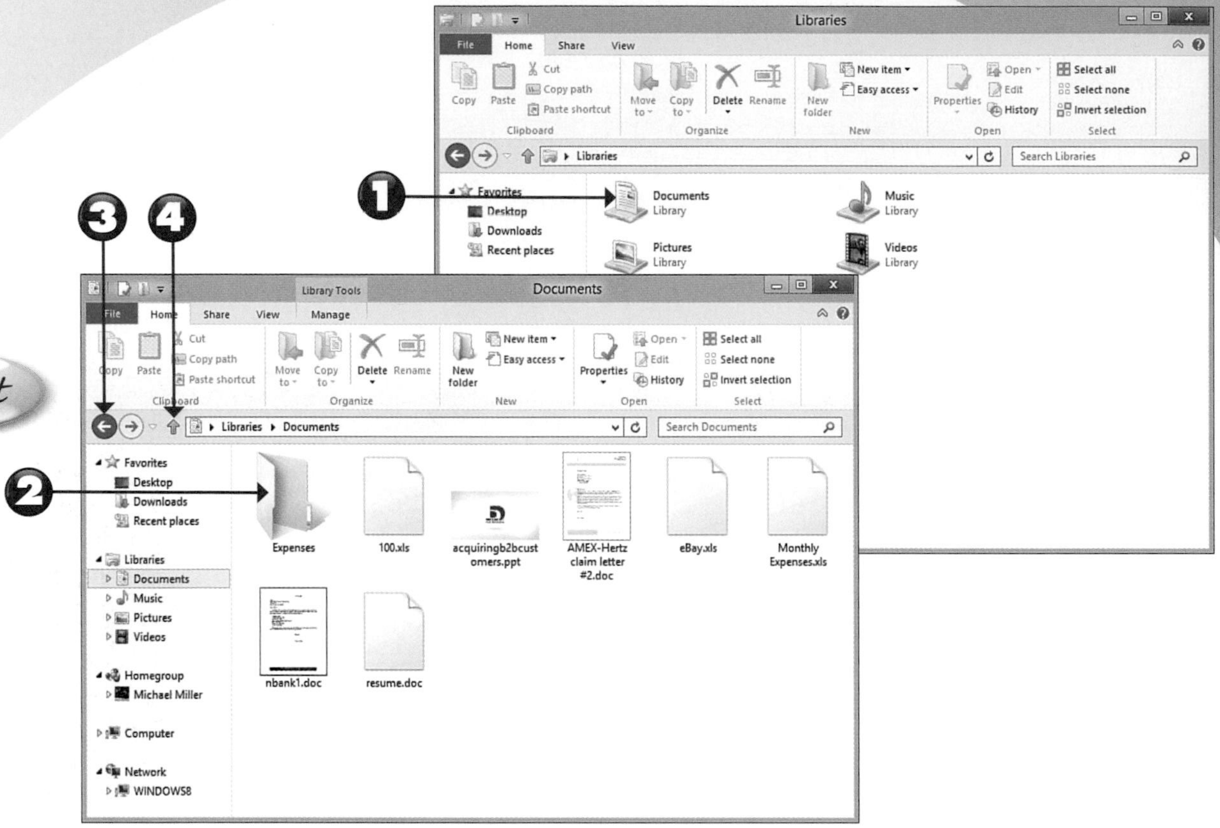

Start

1. In File Explorer's default view, your documents are organized into Documents, Music, Pictures, and Videos libraries. Double-click any library to view the contents.
2. A given library may contain multiple folders and subfolders. Double-click any item to view its contents
3. To move back to the disk or folder previously selected, click the **Back** button on the toolbar.
4. To move up the hierarchy of folders and subfolders to the next highest item, click the **up-arrow** button on the toolbar.

End

NOTE

Libraries In Windows, a *library* is kind of a virtual folder; it doesn't physically exist on your hard disk, but instead points to the subfolders and files you place within it. Windows includes four main libraries: Documents, Music, Pictures, and Videos. The Documents library, for example, contains all the documents on your PC, no matter where they're actually stored. ■

TIP

Breadcrumbs The list of folders and subfolders in File Explorer's address box presents a "breadcrumb" approach to navigation. You can view even earlier folders by clicking the separator arrow next to the folder icon in the Address box; this displays a pull-down menu of the recently visited and most popular items. ■

NAVIGATING WITH THE NAVIGATION PANE

Another way to navigate your files and folders is to use the navigation pane. This pane, on the left side of the File Explorer window, displays both favorite links and hierarchical folder trees for your computer, libraries, and networks.

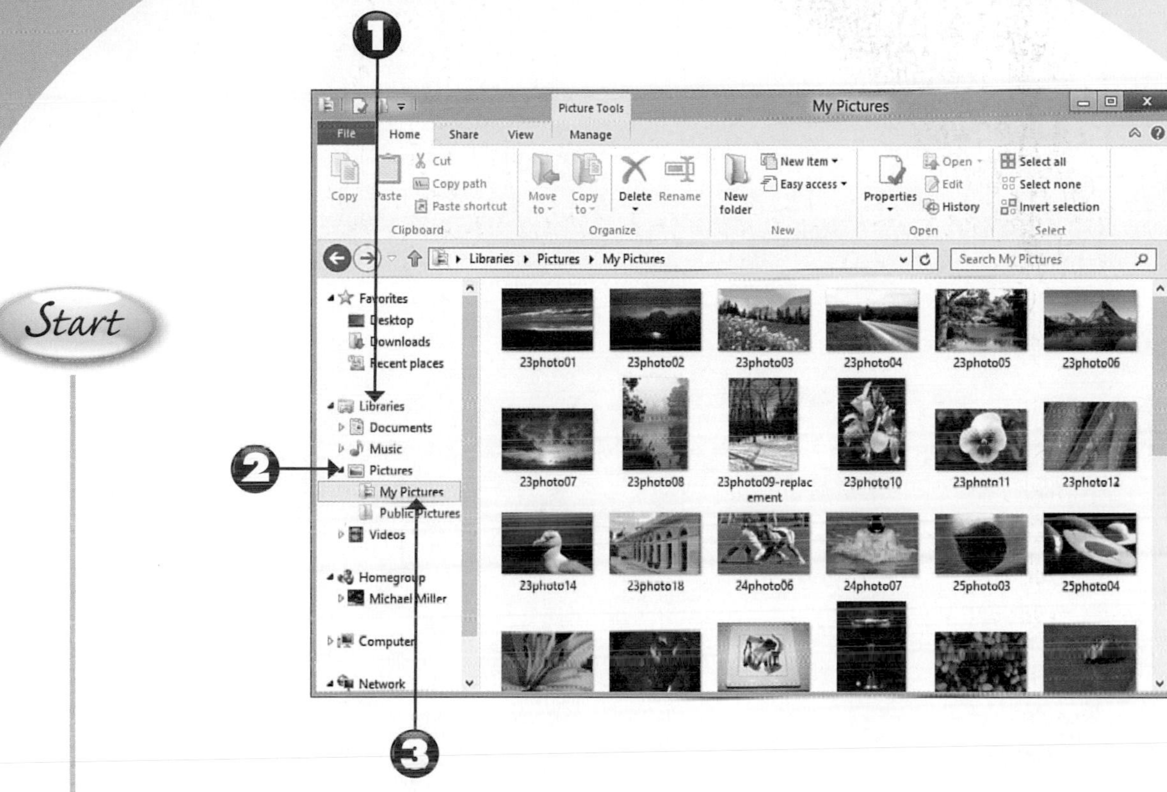

1. Click an icon in the navigation pane to open the contents of the selected item.

2. Click the arrow icon next to any folder to display all the subfolders it contains.

3. Click a folder to display its contents in the main File Explorer window.

End

NOTE

Favorites By default, Windows Favorites include Desktop, Downloads, and Recent Places. Other Favorites may be added, depending on your own individual usage. ■

TIP

Computer To navigate all the drives and folders on your computer, click the **Computer** folder in the navigation pane. ■

CHANGING THE WAY FILES ARE DISPLAYED

You can choose to view the contents of a folder in a variety of ways. The icon views are nice in that they show a small thumbnail preview of any selected file.

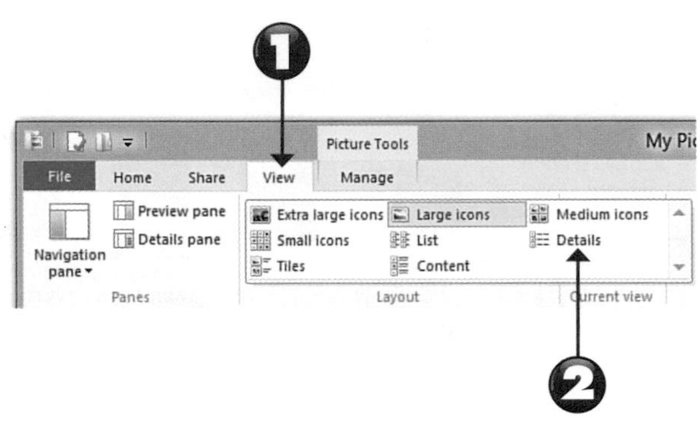

1. Click the **View** tab on the ribbon bar.
2. Go to the Layout section and click one of the following view options: **Content**, **Tiles**, **Details**, **List**, **Small Icons**, **Medium Icons**, **Large Icons**, or **Extra Large Icons**.

End

TIP

Which View Is Best? Any of the larger icon views are best for working with graphics files. Details view is best if you're looking for files by date or size. ■

NOTE

Windows Explorer In previous versions of Windows, File Explorer was known as Windows Explorer—or, more colloquially, as either the My Computer or My Documents folder. ■

SORTING FILES AND FOLDERS

When viewing files in File Explorer, you can sort your files and folders in a number of ways. To view your files in alphabetic order, choose to sort by **Name**. To see all similar files grouped together, choose to sort by **Type**. To sort your files by the date and time they were last edited, select **Date Modified**.

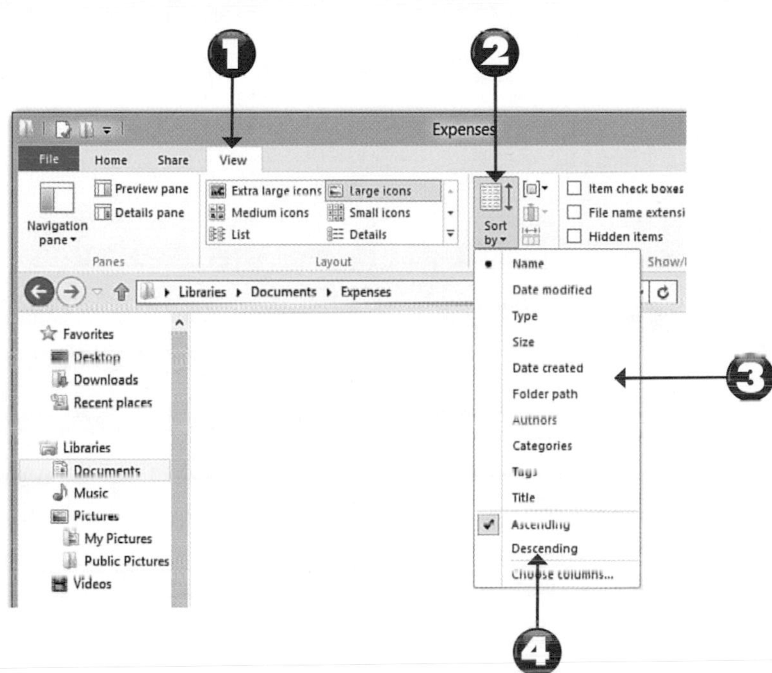

1. Click the **View** tab on the ribbon bar.
2. Click the **Sort By** button.
3. Choose to sort by **Name**, **Date Modified**, **Type**, **Size**, **Date Created**, **Folder Path**, **Authors**, **Categories**, **Tags**, or **Title**.
4. By default, Windows sorts items in ascending order. To change the sort order, click **Descending**.

End

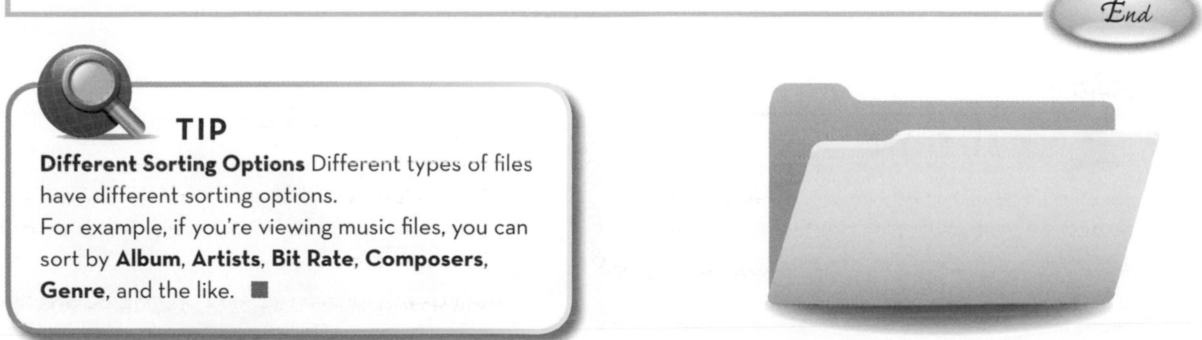

TIP

Different Sorting Options Different types of files have different sorting options.
For example, if you're viewing music files, you can sort by **Album**, **Artists**, **Bit Rate**, **Composers**, **Genre**, and the like. ■

CREATING A NEW FOLDER

The more files you create, the harder it is to organize and find things on your hard disk. When the number of files you have becomes unmanageable, you need to create more folders—and subfolders—to better categorize your files.

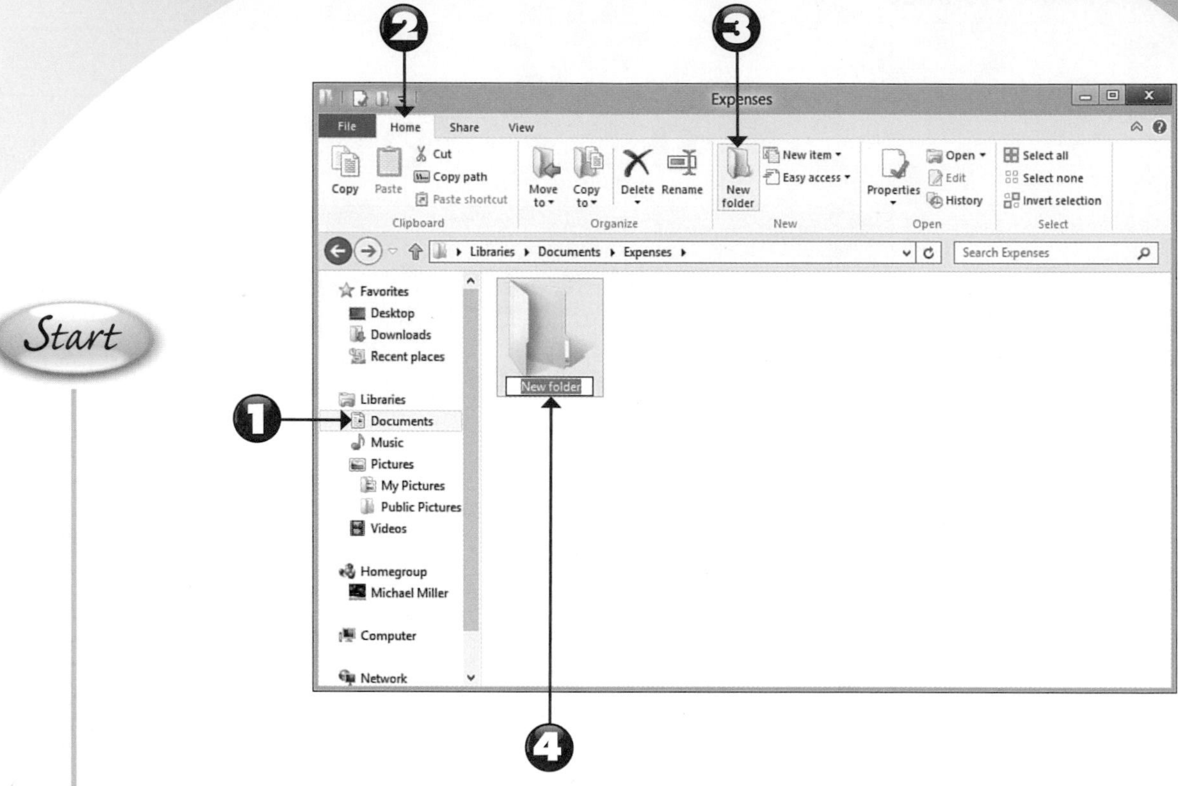

Start

1. Navigate to the drive or folder where you want to place the new folder.

2. Click the **Home** tab on the ribbon bar.

3. Click the **New Folder** button.

4. A new, empty folder now appears with the filename New Folder highlighted. Type a name for your folder and press **Enter**.

End

CAUTION

Illegal Characters Folder names and filenames can include up to 255 characters—including many special characters. You *can't*, however, use the following "illegal" characters: \ / : * ? " < > |. ■

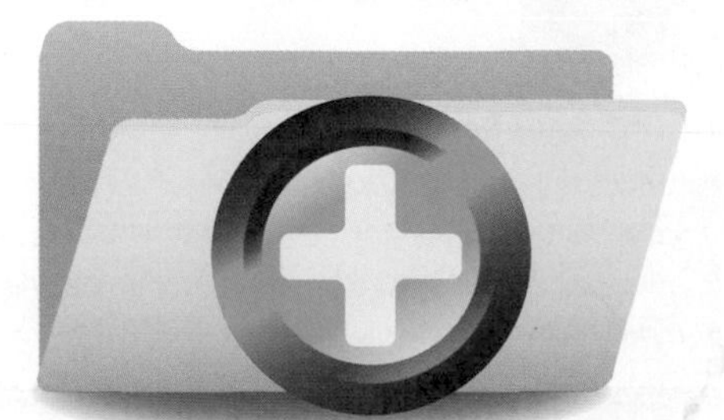

RENAMING A FILE OR FOLDER

When you create a new file or folder, it helps to give it a name that describes its contents. Sometimes, however, you might need to change a file's name. Fortunately, Windows makes renaming an item relatively easy.

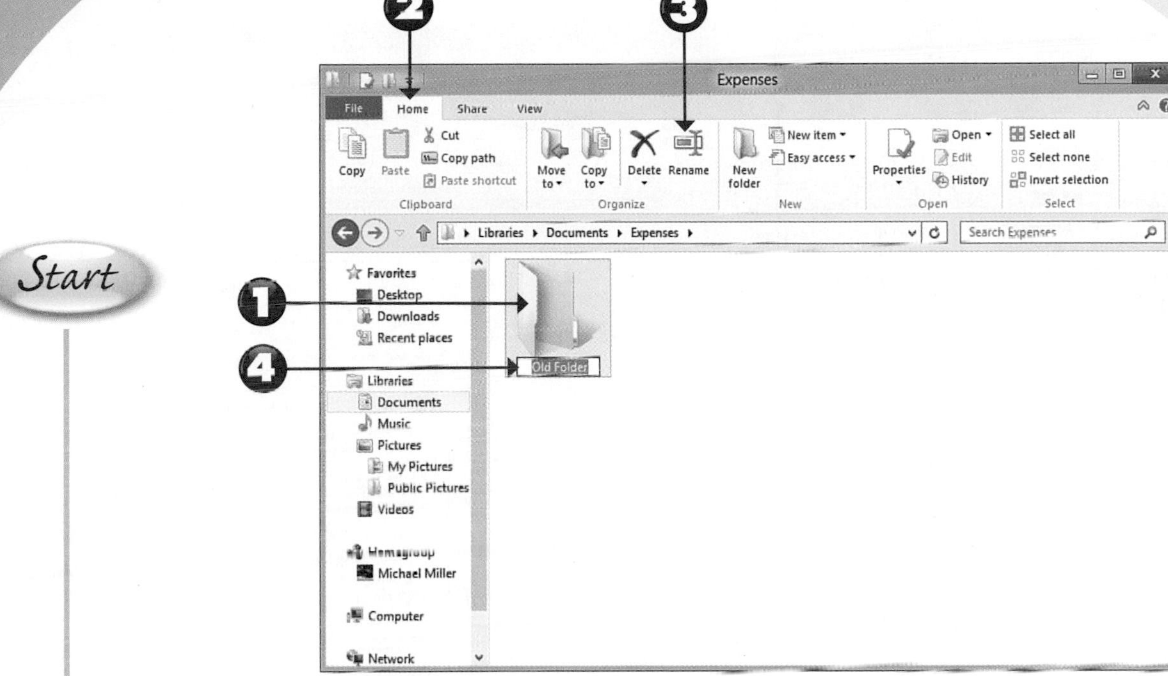

1. Click the file or folder you want to rename.
2. Click the **Home** tab on the ribbon bar.
3. Click the **Rename** button; this highlights the filename.
4. Type a new name for your folder (which overwrites the current name), and press **Enter**.

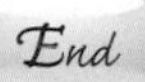

CAUTION

Don't Change the Extension The one part of the filename you should never change is the extension—the part that comes after the final "dot" if you choose to show file extensions. Try to change the extension, and Windows will warn you that you're doing something wrong. ■

TIP

Keyboard Shortcut You can also rename a file by selecting the file and pressing **F2** on your computer keyboard. This highlights the filename and readies it for editing. ■

COPYING A FILE OR FOLDER

There are many ways to copy a file in Windows 8. The easiest method is to use the Copy To button on the Home ribbon.

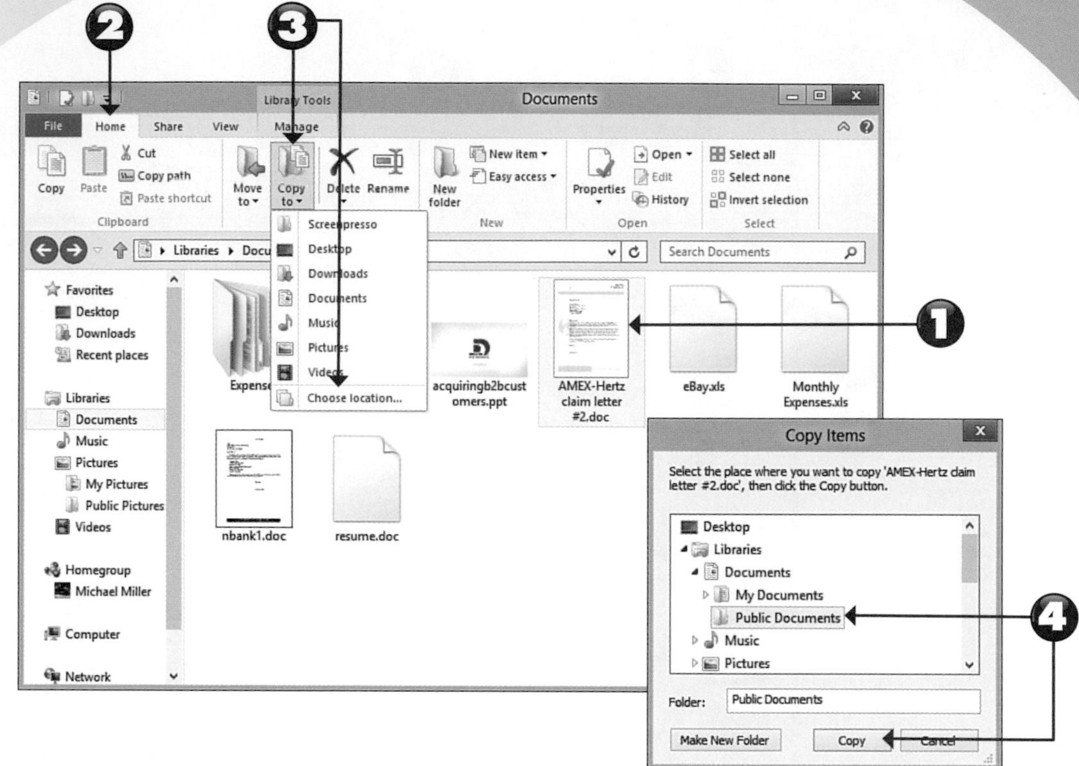

Start

1. Click the item you want to copy.
2. Click the **Home** tab on the ribbon bar.
3. Click the **Copy To** button and select **Choose Location** from the pull-down menu.
4. When the Copy Items dialog box appears, navigate to the new location for the item then click the **Copy** button.

End

TIP

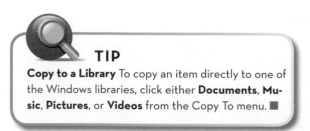

Copy to a Library To copy an item directly to one of the Windows libraries, click either **Documents**, **Music**, **Pictures**, or **Videos** from the Copy To menu. ■

MOVING A FILE OR FOLDER

Moving a file or folder is different from copying it. Moving cuts the item from its previous location and pastes it into a new location. Copying leaves the original item where it was *and* creates a copy of the item elsewhere.

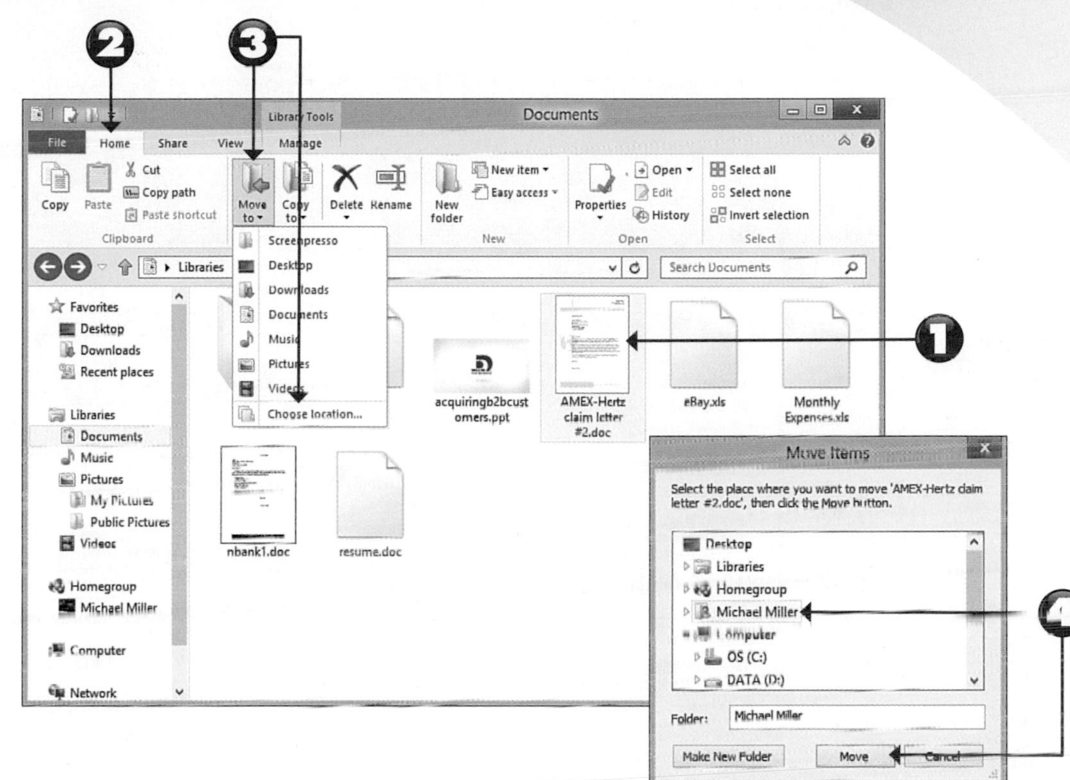

Start

1. Click the item you want to move.
2. Click the **Home** tab on the ribbon bar.
3. Click the **Move To** button and select **Choose Location** from the pull-down menu.
4. When the Move Items dialog box appears, navigate to the new location for the item, and then click the **Move** button.

End

TIP

Move to a Library To move an item directly to one of the Windows libraries, click either **Documents**, **Music**, **Pictures**, or **Videos** from the Move To menu. ■

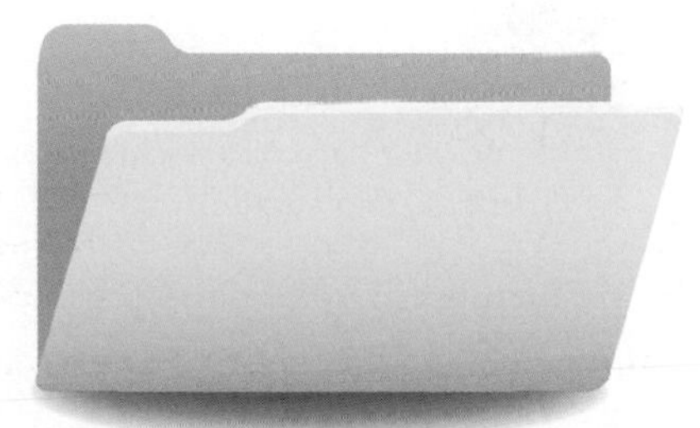

SEARCHING FOR A FILE

As organized as you might be, you might not always be able to find the specific files you want. Fortunately, Windows 8 offers an easy way to locate difficult-to-find files, via the new Instant Search function. Instant Search lets you find files by extension, filename, or keywords within the file.

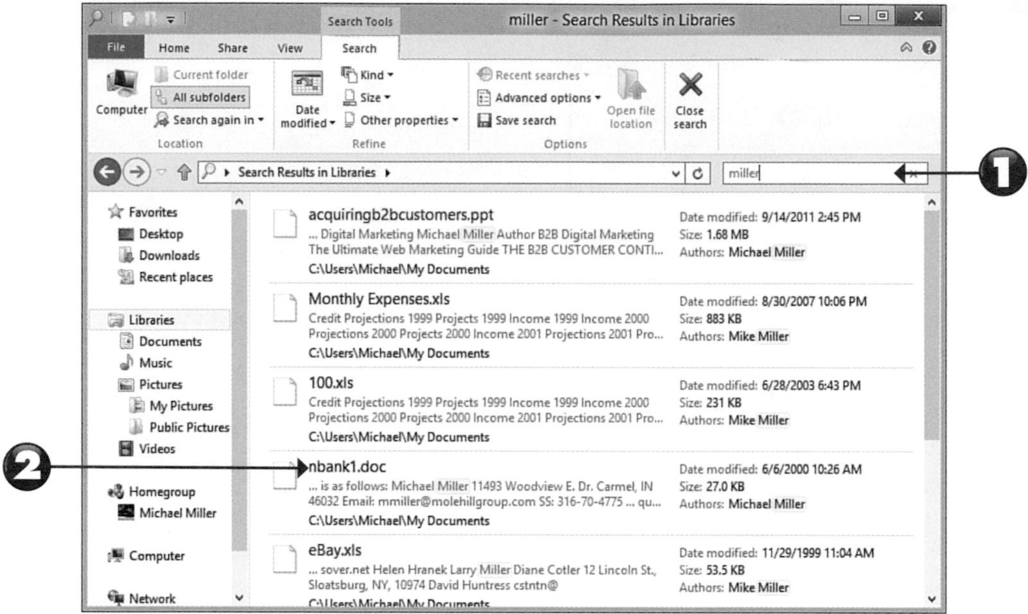

1. From within File Explorer, enter one or more keywords into the Search box and press **Enter.**
2. Windows now displays a list of files that match your search criteria. Double-click any icon to open that file.

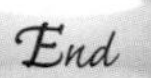

TIP

Search Index Instant Search indexes all the files stored on your hard disk (including email messages) by type, title, and contents. ■

DELETING A FILE OR FOLDER

Keeping too many files eats up too much hard disk space—which is a bad thing. Because you don't want to waste disk space, you should periodically delete those files (and folders) you no longer need. When you delete a file, you send it to the Windows Recycle Bin, which is kind of a trash can for deleted files.

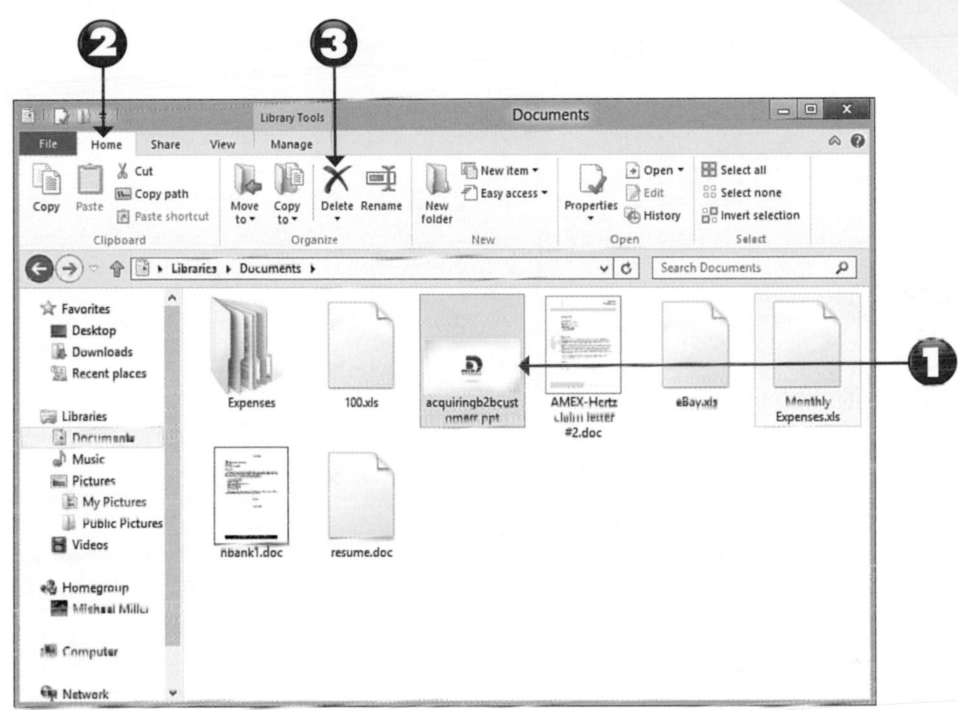

1. Click the file you want to delete.
2. Click the **Home** tab on the ribbon bar.
3. Click the **Delete** button.

End

TIP

Other Ways to Delete You can also delete a file by dragging it from the folder window onto the Recycle Bin icon on the desktop, or by highlighting it and pressing the **Delete** key on your computer keyboard. ■

RESTORING DELETED FILES

Have you ever accidentally deleted the wrong file? If so, you're in luck. Windows stores the files you delete in the Recycle Bin, which is actually a special folder on your hard disk. For a short period of time, you can "undelete" files from the Recycle Bin back to their original locations.

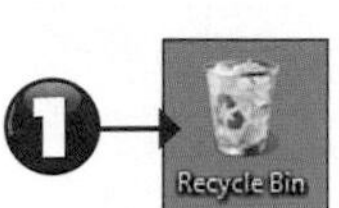

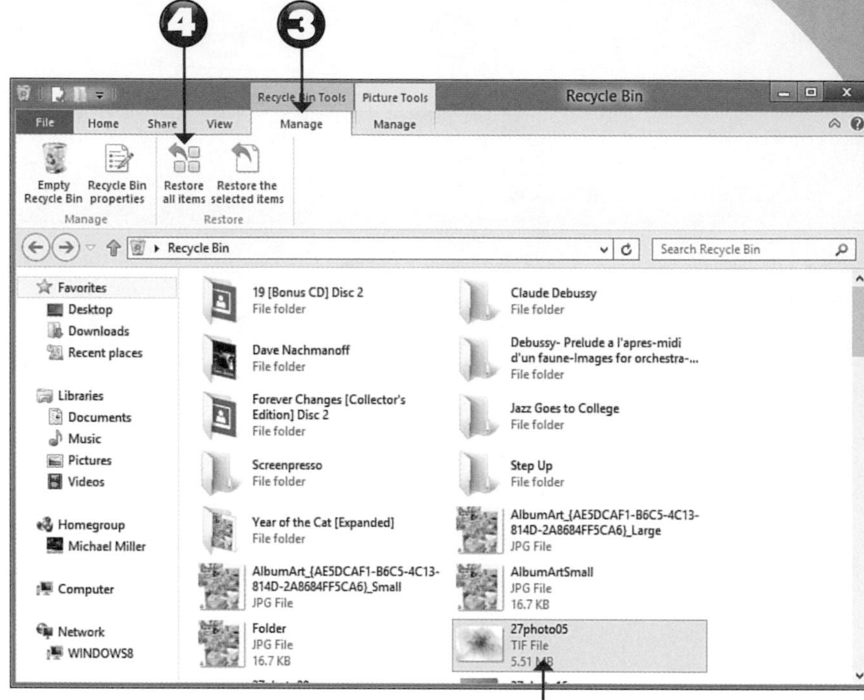

1. From the Windows desktop, double-click the **Recycle Bin** icon to open the Recycle Bin folder.
2. Click the file you want to restore.
3. Click the **Manage** tab on the ribbon bar.
4. Click the **Restore the Selected Items** button.

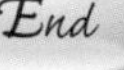

EMPTYING THE RECYCLE BIN

By default, the deleted files in the Recycle Bin can occupy 4GB plus 5% of your hard disk space. When you've deleted enough files to exceed this limit, the oldest files in the Recycle Bin are automatically and permanently deleted from your hard disk. You can also manually empty the Recycle Bin and thus free up some hard disk space.

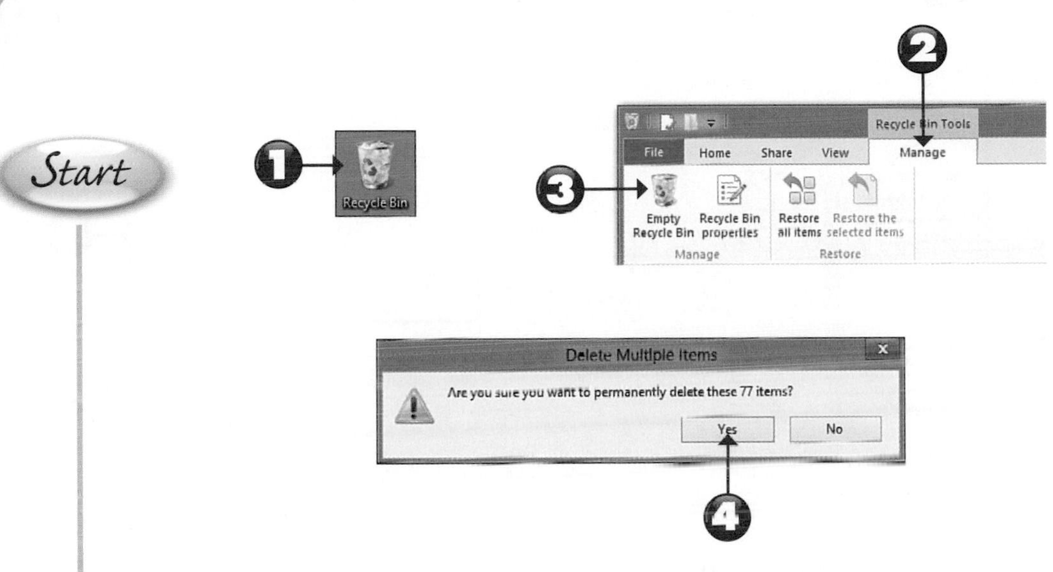

1. From the Windows desktop, double-click the **Recycle Bin** icon to open the Recycle Bin folder.
2. Click **Manage** tab on the ribbon bar.
3. Click the **Empty the Recycle Bin** button.
4. When the Delete Multiple Items dialog box appears, click **Yes** to completely erase the files.

End

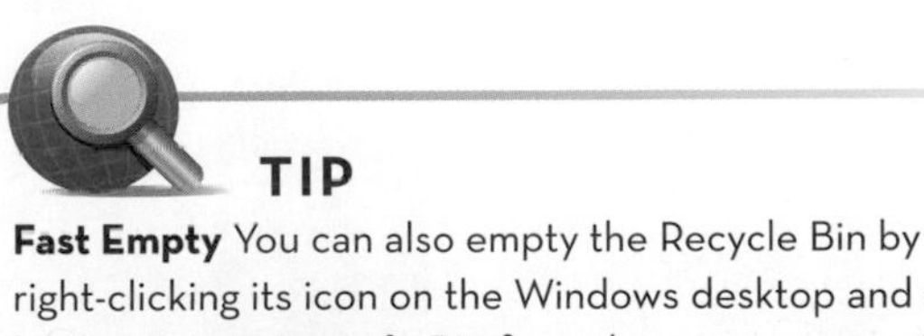

TIP

Fast Empty You can also empty the Recycle Bin by right-clicking its icon on the Windows desktop and selecting **Empty Recycle Bin** from the pop-up menu. ■

COMPRESSING A FILE

Really big files can be difficult to copy or share. Fortunately, Windows lets you create *compressed* folders, which take big files and compress them in size (called a "zipped" file). After the file has been transferred, you can then uncompress the file back to its original state.

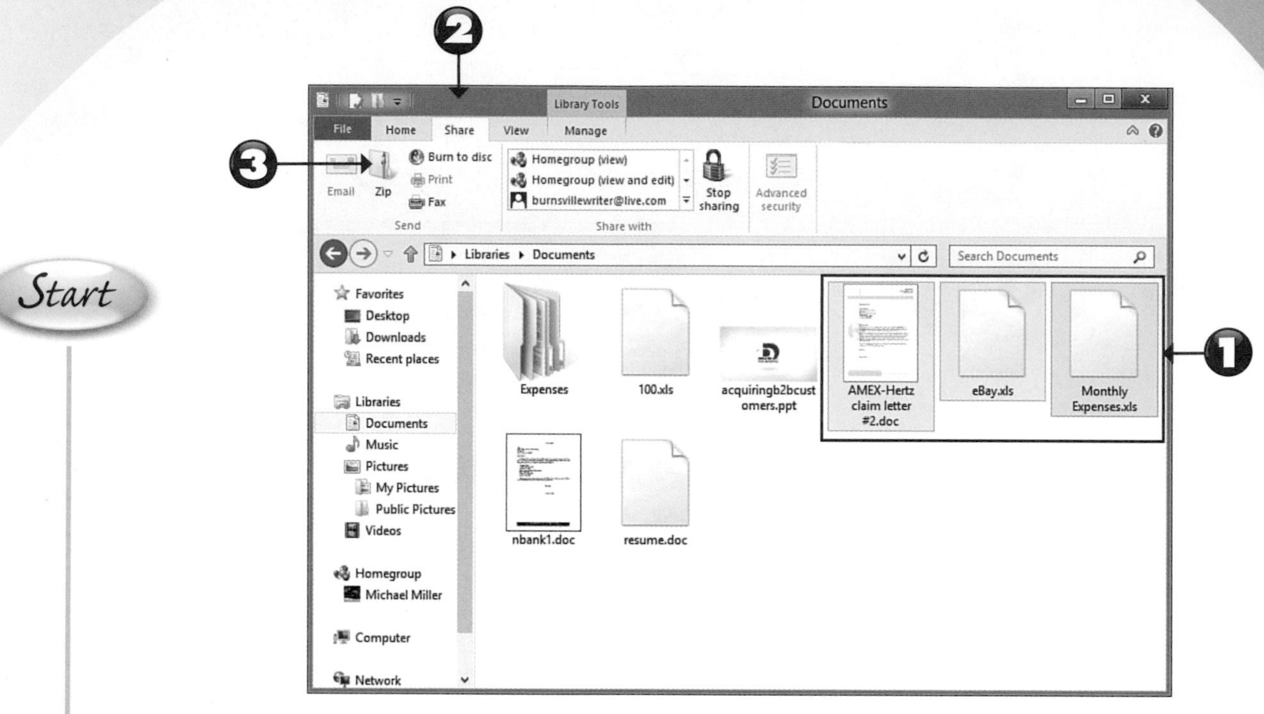

1. Click the files you want to compress. (To select more than one file, hold down the **Ctrl** key when clicking.)

2. Click the **Share** tab on the ribbon bar.

3. Click the **Zip** button. Windows now creates a new folder that contains compressed versions of the files you selected.

End

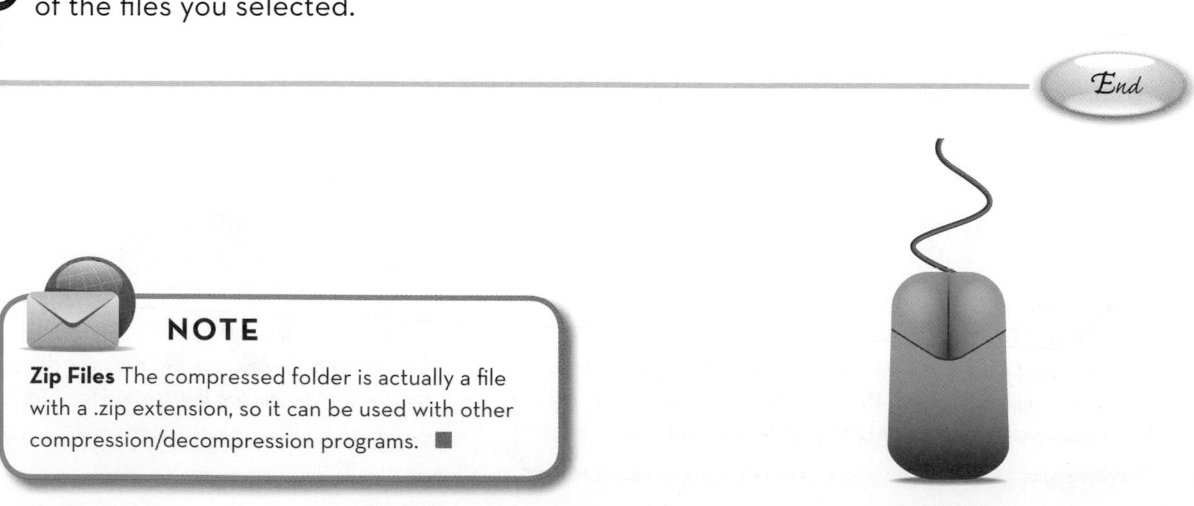

NOTE

Zip Files The compressed folder is actually a file with a .zip extension, so it can be used with other compression/decompression programs. ■

EXTRACTING FILES FROM A COMPRESSED FOLDER

The process of decompressing a file is actually an *extraction* process. That's because you extract the original files from the compressed folder to the desired location on your computer's hard drive.

Start

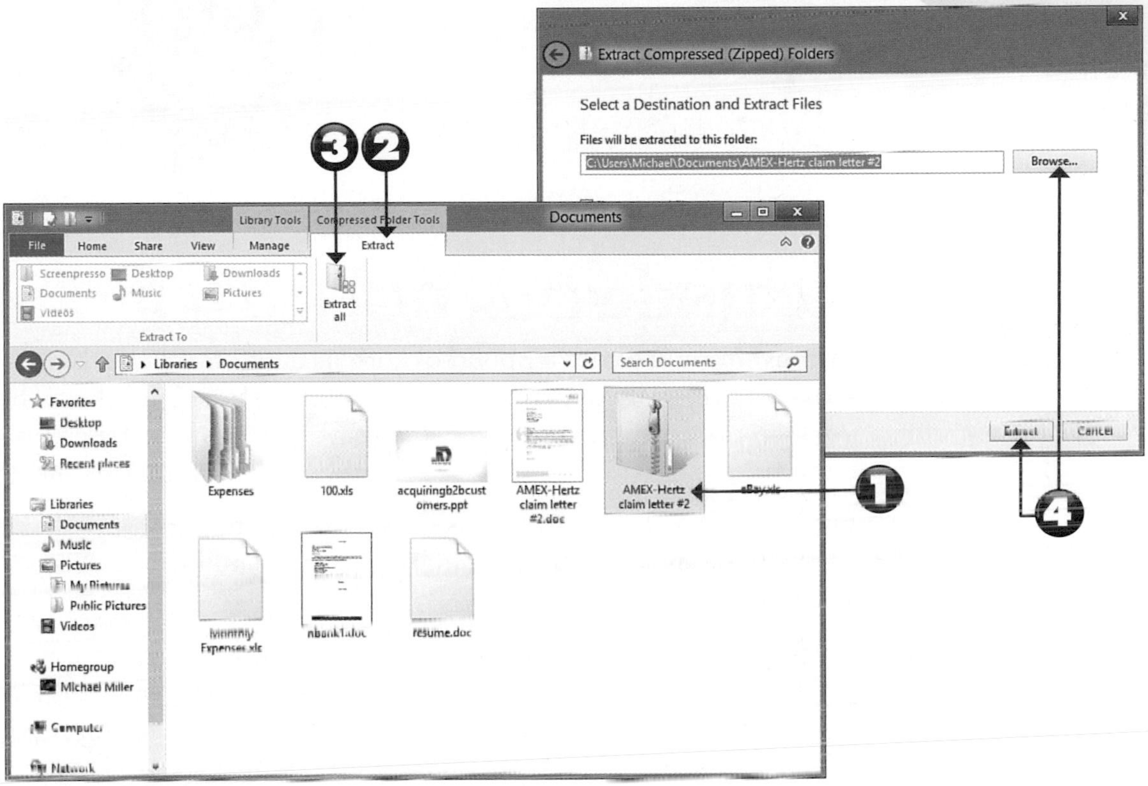

1. Select the compressed folder.
2. Click the **Extract** tab on the ribbon bar.
3. Click the **Extract All** button.
4. When the Extract dialog box appears, click the **Browse** button to select a location for the extracted files, and then click the **Extract** button.

End

TIP

Extracted Folder By default, compressed files are extracted to a new folder with the same name. You can change this, however, to extract to any folder you like. ■

TIP

Zipper Icon Compressed folders are distinguished by the little zipper on the folder icon. ■

PROTECTING YOUR COMPUTER

"An ounce of prevention is worth a pound of cure" is a bit of a cliché, but it's also true—especially when it comes to your computer system. Spending a few minutes a week on preventive maintenance can save you from costly computer problems in the future.

This is doubly true when your computer is connected to the Internet. That's because there's a whole new world of potential dangers online—viruses, spyware, computer attacks, and more.

To ease the task of protecting and maintaining your system, Windows 8 includes several utilities to help you keep your computer running smoothly. You should use these tools as part of your regular maintenance routine—or if you experience specific problems with your computer system.

WINDOWS CONTROL PANEL

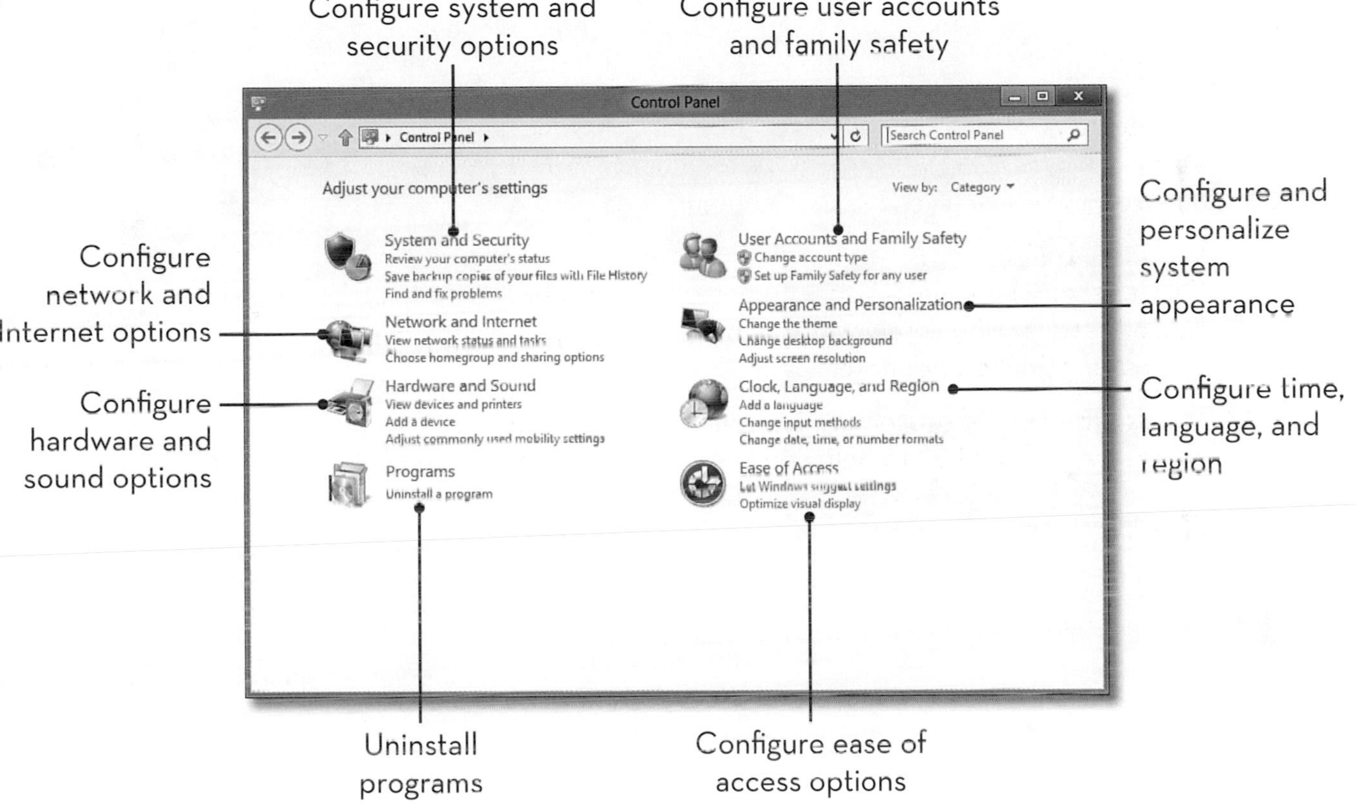

OPENING THE CONTROL PANEL

Many Windows system utilities are accessed from the Control Panel. This utility runs on the traditional Windows desktop and provides access to a number of system configuration options.

Start

1. From the Windows desktop (*not* the Start screen!), display the charms bar and click **Settings.**
2. When the Settings panel appears, click **Control Panel**.

End

TIP

System Settings The Control Panel duplicates most of the configuration options found on the PC Settings screen, and adds several more. Because casual users will find the PC Settings screen easier to use, you should use it for basic system configuration. To access the PC Settings screen, display the charms bar, click **Settings**, and then click **Change PC Settings**. ■

USING THE WINDOWS ACTION CENTER

In Windows 8, the best way to manage your PC's maintenance and security is via the Action Center. This built-in utility centralizes many maintenance operations, error reporting, and troubleshooting operations, and will alert you to any action you need to take to protect and maintain your system.

1. Open the Windows Control Panel and click **System & Security**.
2. On the next screen, click **Action Center**.
3. The main Action Center screen notifies you of actions you need to take or problems you need to resolve.

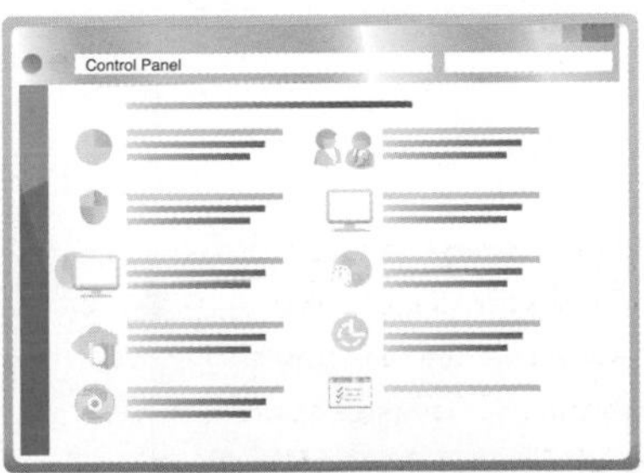

DEFENDING AGAINST MALWARE WITH WINDOWS DEFENDER

Computer viruses and spyware (collectively known as malicious software, or *malware*) install themselves on your computer, typically without your knowledge, and then either damage critical system files or surreptitiously send personal information to some devious third party. You can protect your system from viruses and spyware by using an anti-malware program, such as Windows Defender, which is built in to Windows 8.

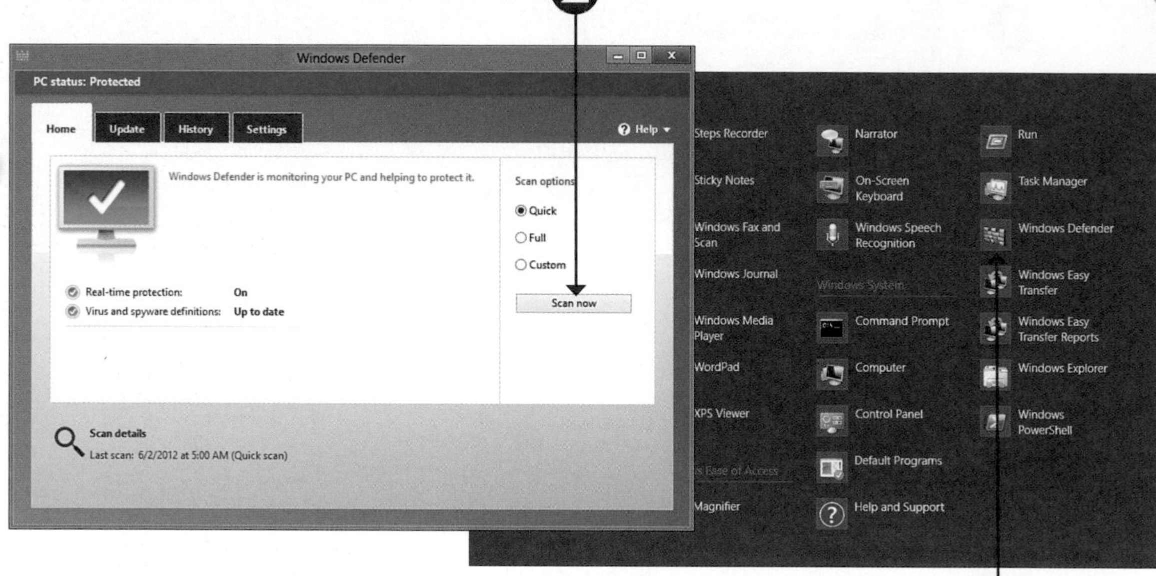

1. Windows Defender runs in the background, monitoring your computer against malware threats. To open Windows Defender, right-click the Windows Start screen to display the options bar, click **All Apps**, and when the Apps screen appears, scroll to and click **Windows Defender**.

2. While Defender automatically scans your system on its own schedule, you can perform a manual scan at any time by clicking the **Scan Now** button.

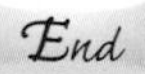

TIP

Other Anti-Malware Utilities Your computer manufacturer may substitute or supplement Windows Defender with other antivirus utilities, such as AVG Anti-Virus (www.avg.com), Kaspersky Anti-Virus (www.kaspersky.com), McAfee VirusScan AntiVirus Plus (www.mcafee.com), and Norton AntiVirus (www.symantec.com). Other antispyware utilities include Ad-Aware (www.lavasoftusa.com) and Spybot Search & Destroy (www.safer-networking.org). ■

CAUTION

How to Catch a Virus Computer viruses and spyware are most commonly transmitted via infected computer files. You can receive virus-infected files via email or instant messaging or by downloading files from unsecure websites. ■

KEEPING YOUR COMPUTER IN TIP-TOP SHAPE

Not all preventive maintenance takes place from within Windows. There are also some physical things you should do to keep your computer operating in tip-top shape.

Start

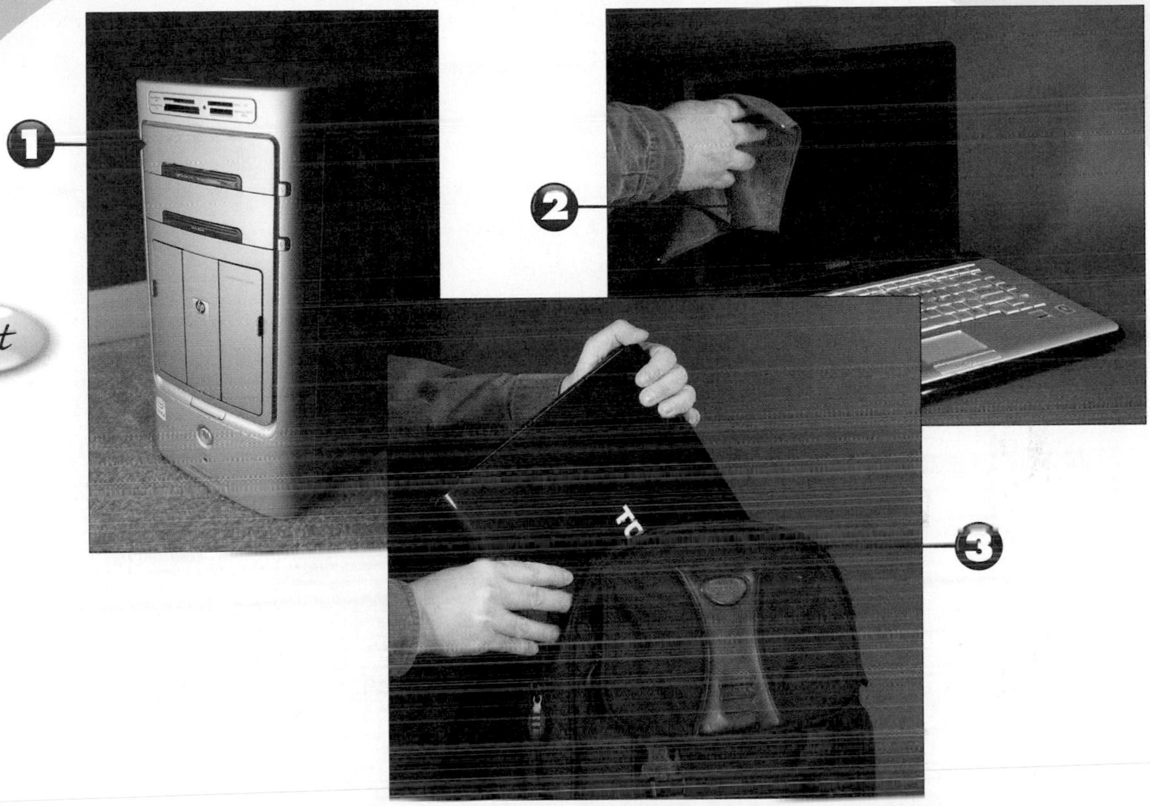

1. Position your computer in a clean, dust-free environment. Keep it away from direct sunlight and make sure there's plenty of air flow around them to keep it from overheating.

2. Clean your computer's LCD display with plain water or specially formulated display cleaner on a lint-free cloth. Spray the cleaner on the cloth, not directly on the screen.

3. Carry your notebook PC in a well-padded case. Travel with the CD/DVD drive *up*, so as not to jar it when you set down the case.

End

TIP

Keyboard Cleaning Clean your computer keyboard with cotton swabs or a can of compressed air (to *blow* the dirt away). ■

CAUTION

Avoid Alcohol and Ammonia When cleaning your computer screen, do not use any cleaner that contains alcohol or ammonia; these chemicals may damage an LCD screen. You can, however, use commercial cleaning sprays and wipes specially formulated for LCD screens. ■

DELETING UNNECESSARY FILES

Even with today's humongous hard disks, you can still end up with too many useless files taking up too much hard disk space. Fortunately, Windows includes a utility that identifies and deletes unused files. The Disk Cleanup tool is what you should use when you need to free up extra hard disk space for more frequently used files.

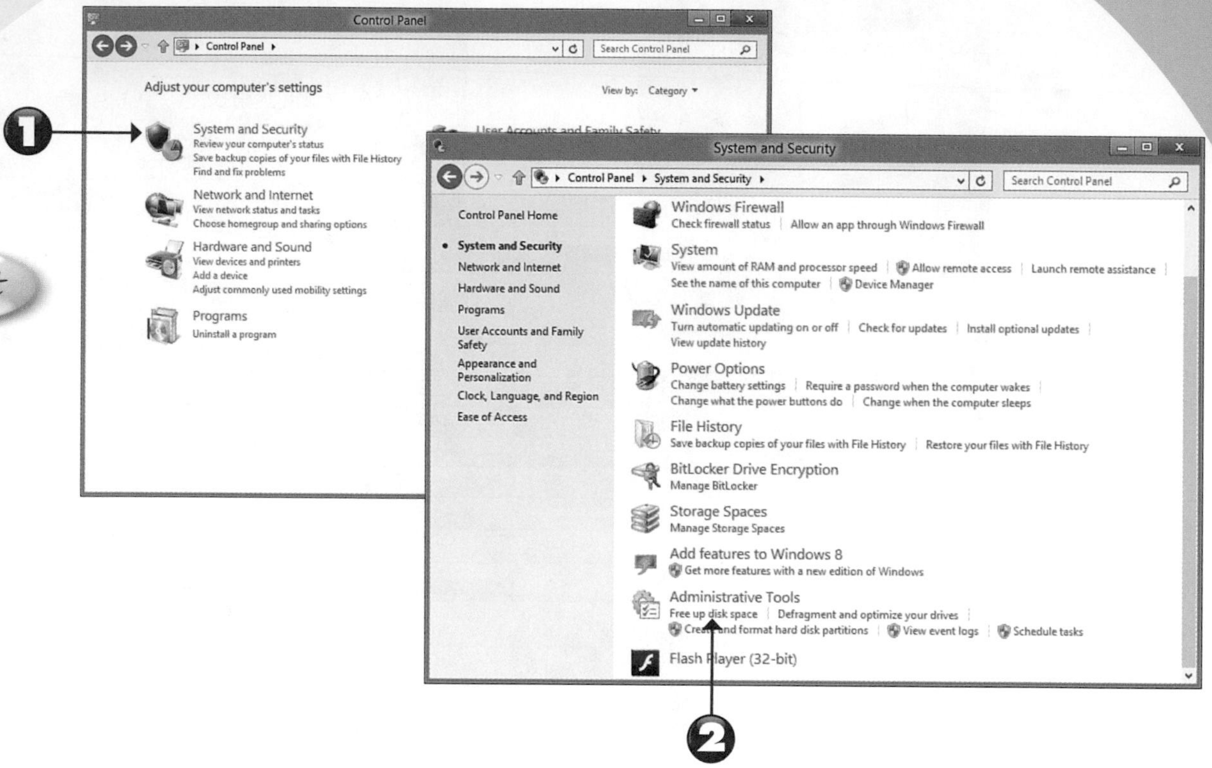

Control Panel
Control Panel
Search Control Panel
Adjust your computer's settings
View by: Category
System and Security
Review your computer's status
Save backup copies of your files with File History
Find and fix problems
Network and Internet
View network status and tasks
Choose homegroup and sharing options
Hardware and Sound
View devices and printers
Add a device
Adjust commonly used mobility settings
Programs
Uninstall a program

System and Security
Control Panel ▸ System and Security
Search Control Panel
Control Panel Home
System and Security
Network and Internet
Hardware and Sound
Programs
User Accounts and Family Safety
Appearance and Personalization
Clock, Language, and Region
Ease of Access
Windows Firewall
Check firewall status | Allow an app through Windows Firewall
System
View amount of RAM and processor speed | Allow remote access | Launch remote assistance
See the name of this computer | Device Manager
Windows Update
Turn automatic updating on or off | Check for updates | Install optional updates
View update history
Power Options
Change battery settings | Require a password when the computer wakes
Change what the power buttons do | Change when the computer sleeps
File History
Save backup copies of your files with File History | Restore your files with File History
BitLocker Drive Encryption
Manage BitLocker
Storage Spaces
Manage Storage Spaces
Add features to Windows 8
Get more features with a new edition of Windows
Administrative Tools
Free up disk space | Defragment and optimize your drives
Create and format hard disk partitions | View event logs | Schedule tasks
Flash Player (32-bit)

Start

1. From the Control Panel, click **System and Security**.

2. On the next screen, scroll to the Administrative Tools section and click **Free Up Disk Space**.

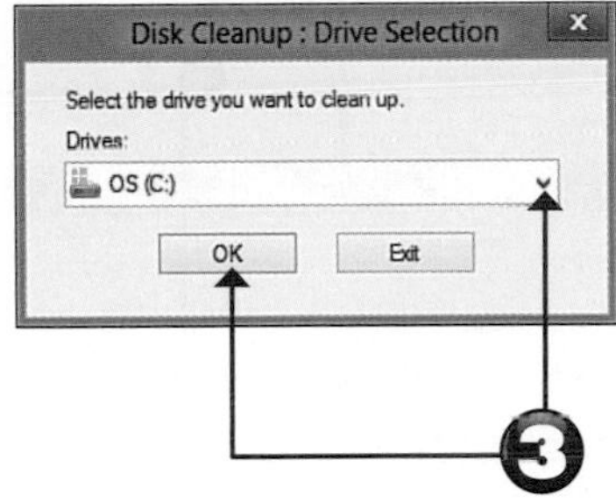

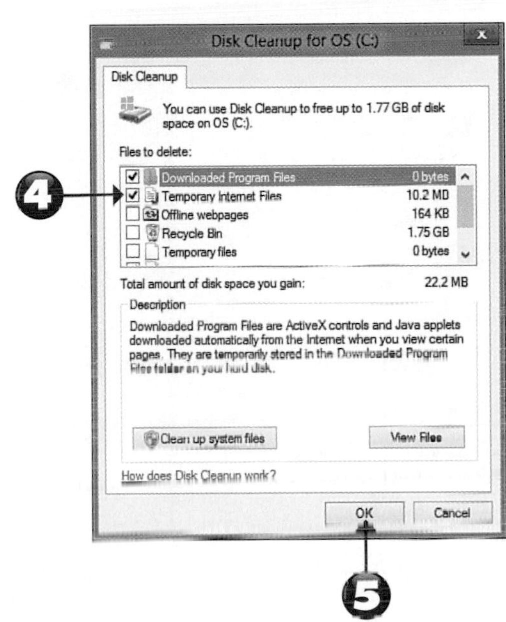

3. When prompted, select the drive you want to clean up, and then click **OK**.
4. Disk Cleanup automatically analyzes the contents of your hard disk drive. When it's finished analyzing, it presents its results in the Disk Cleanup dialog box. Select which types files you want to delete.
5. Click OK to begin deleting.

End

TIP

Which Files to Delete? You can safely choose to delete all these files *except* the setup log files and hibernation files, which are needed by the Windows operating system. ■

DELETING UNUSED PROGRAMS

Another way to free up valuable hard disk space is to delete those programs you never use. This is accomplished using the Uninstall or Change a Program utility.

Start

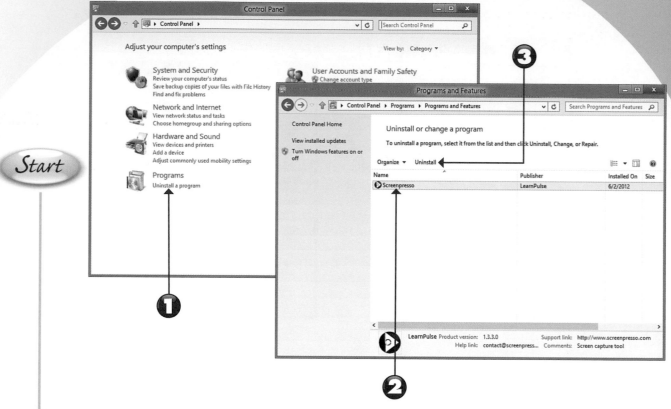

1. From the Control Panel, click **Uninstall a Program** (in the Programs section).
2. When the Programs and Features screen appears, click the program you want to delete.
3. Click **Uninstall**.

End

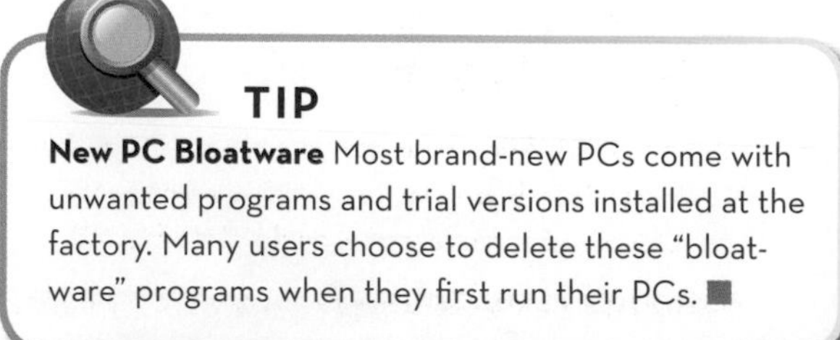

TIP

New PC Bloatware Most brand-new PCs come with unwanted programs and trial versions installed at the factory. Many users choose to delete these “bloat-ware” programs when they first run their PCs. ■

DEFRAGMENTING YOUR HARD DISK

If you're system is taking longer and longer to open and close files or run applications, it's probably because little fragments of files are spread all over your hard disk. You fix the problem when you put all the pieces of the puzzle back in the right boxes—which you do by defragmenting your disk. In Windows 8, the Disk Defragmenter utility runs automatically in the background, but you can also choose to run the utility manually, for more immediate results.

Start

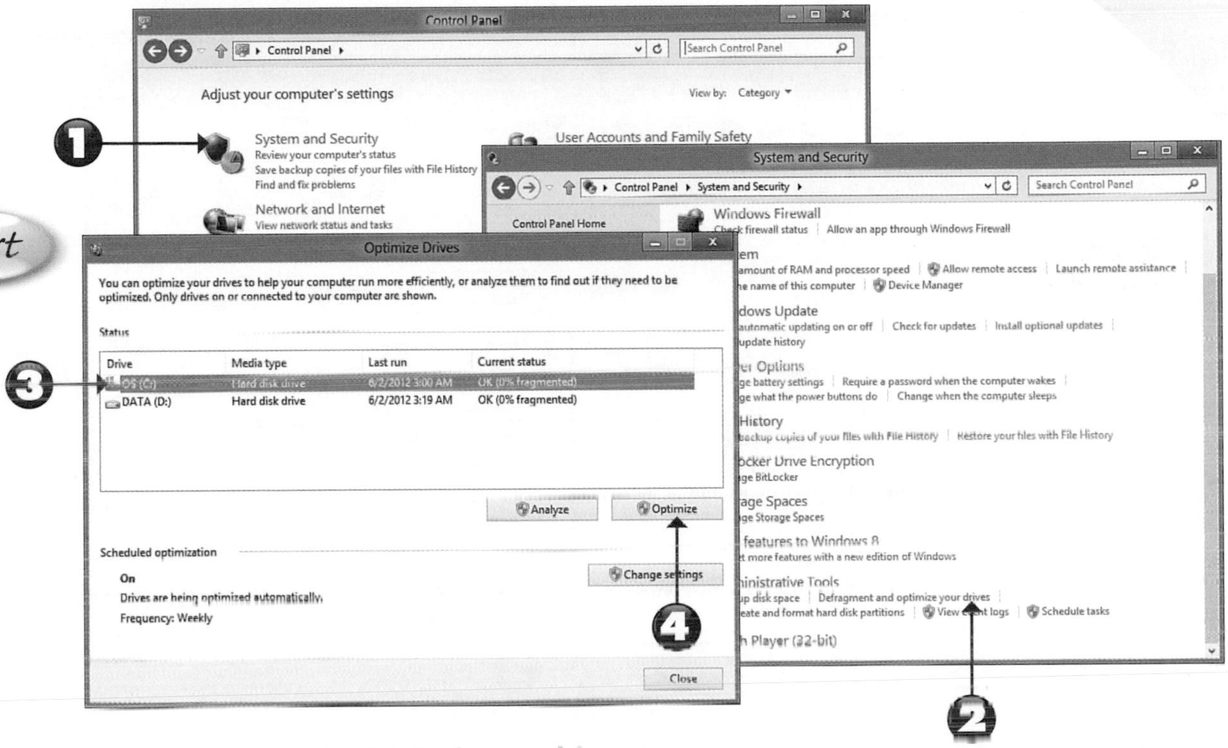

1. From the Control Panel, click **System and Security**.
2. On the next screen, scroll to the Administrative Tools section and click **Defragment and Optimize Your Drives.**
3. When the Optimize Drives window appears, select the drive you want to defragment (typically drive C:).
4. Click the **Optimize** button.

End

TIP

It Takes Time Defragmenting your drive can take an hour or more, especially if you have a large hard drive or your drive is really fragmented. ■

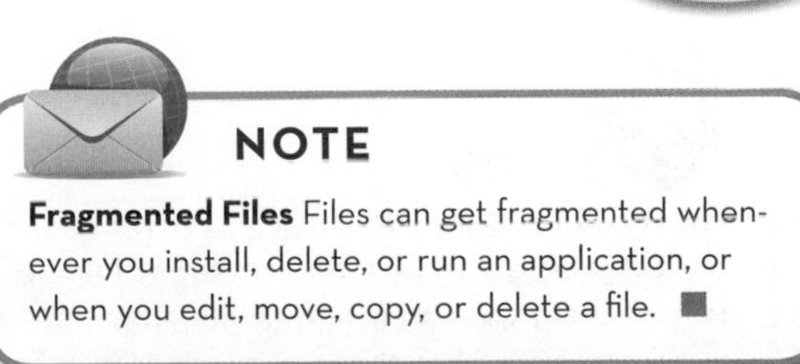

NOTE

Fragmented Files Files can get fragmented whenever you install, delete, or run an application, or when you edit, move, copy, or delete a file. ■

CHECKING YOUR HARD DISK FOR ERRORS

Any time you move or delete a file or accidentally turn off the power while the system is running, you run the risk of introducing errors to your hard disk. Fortunately, you can find and fix most of these errors directly from within Windows, using the ScanDisk utility.

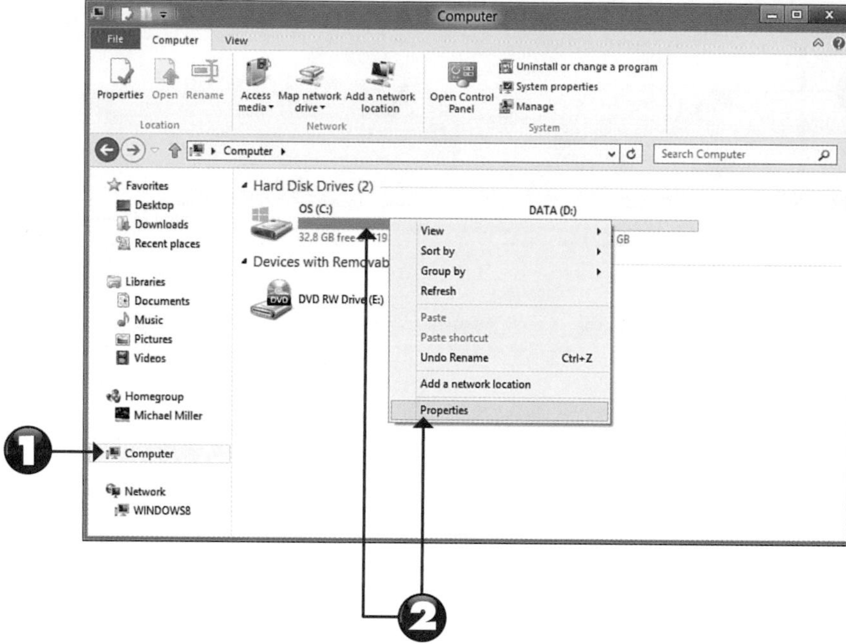

1. Launch File Explorer and click **Computer** in the navigation pane.
2. Right-click the icon for the drive you want to scan, and then select **Properties** from the pop-up menu.

Continued

TIP

How Often to Run? It's a good idea to run all these system utilities at least once a month, just to ensure that your system stays in tip-top condition. ■

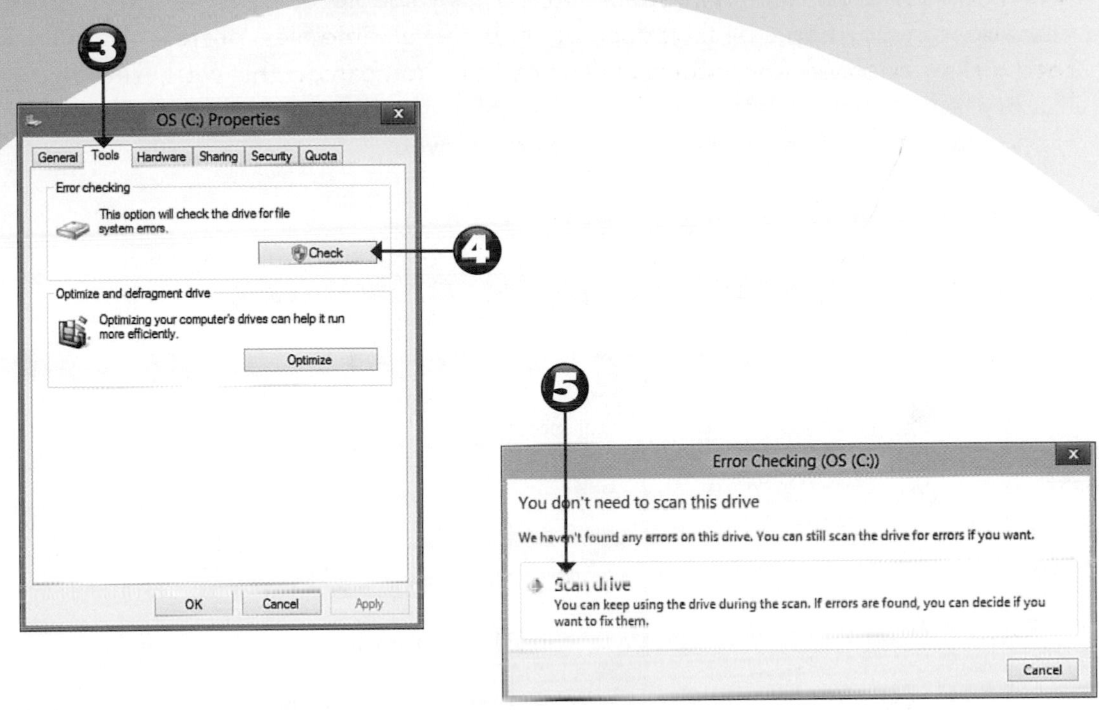

3. When the Properties dialog box appears, select the **Tools** tab.
4. Click the **Check** button in the Error-Checking section.
5. When the Error Checking dialog box appears, click **Scan Drive**.

End

TIP

Scanning and Fixing ScanDisk not only scans your hard disk for errors but also automatically fixes any errors it finds. (If it finds errors, however, you may need to reboot your system.) ■

TIP

Rebooting You may be prompted to reboot your PC if you're checking your computer's C: drive. ■

BACKING UP YOUR FILES WITH FILE HISTORY

The data stored on your computer's hard disk is valuable, and perhaps irreplaceable. That's why you want to keep a backup copy of all these valuable files, preferably on an external hard disk or another computer on your network. You can do this with Windows 8's new File History feature, which lets you keep copies of all the different versions of your files and then restore them in case they get lost or destroyed.

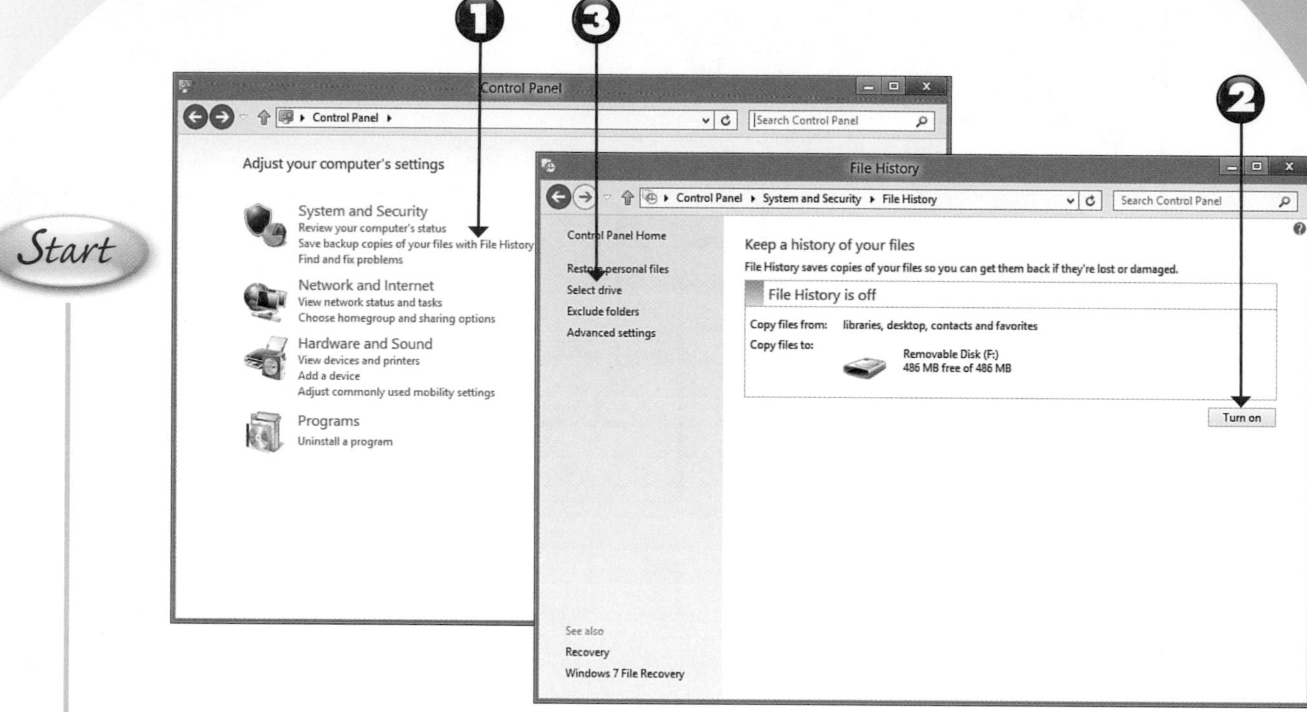

1. From the Windows Control Panel, go to the System and Security section and click **Save Backup Copies of Your Files with File History**.

2. When the File History screen appears, click the **Turn On** button.

3. File History automatically uses the first external drive on your system for its backup. If you want to use a different backup drive, click **Select Drive** in the navigation pane and, when the next screen appears, select a different drive or network location.

TIP

External Hard Drives The easiest way to perform a backup is to use an external hard disk drive. These drives provide lots of storage space for a relatively low cost, and they connect to your PC via USB. There's no excuse not to do it! ■

TIP

Backup Schedule By default, File History saves copies of files every hour, and keeps all saved versions forever. You can change these settings by clicking **Advanced Settings** in the navigation bar of the File History window. ■

RESTORING BACKUP FILES

File History makes it easy to restore any or all files you've backed up. It's a matter of selecting which files to restore, and to where.

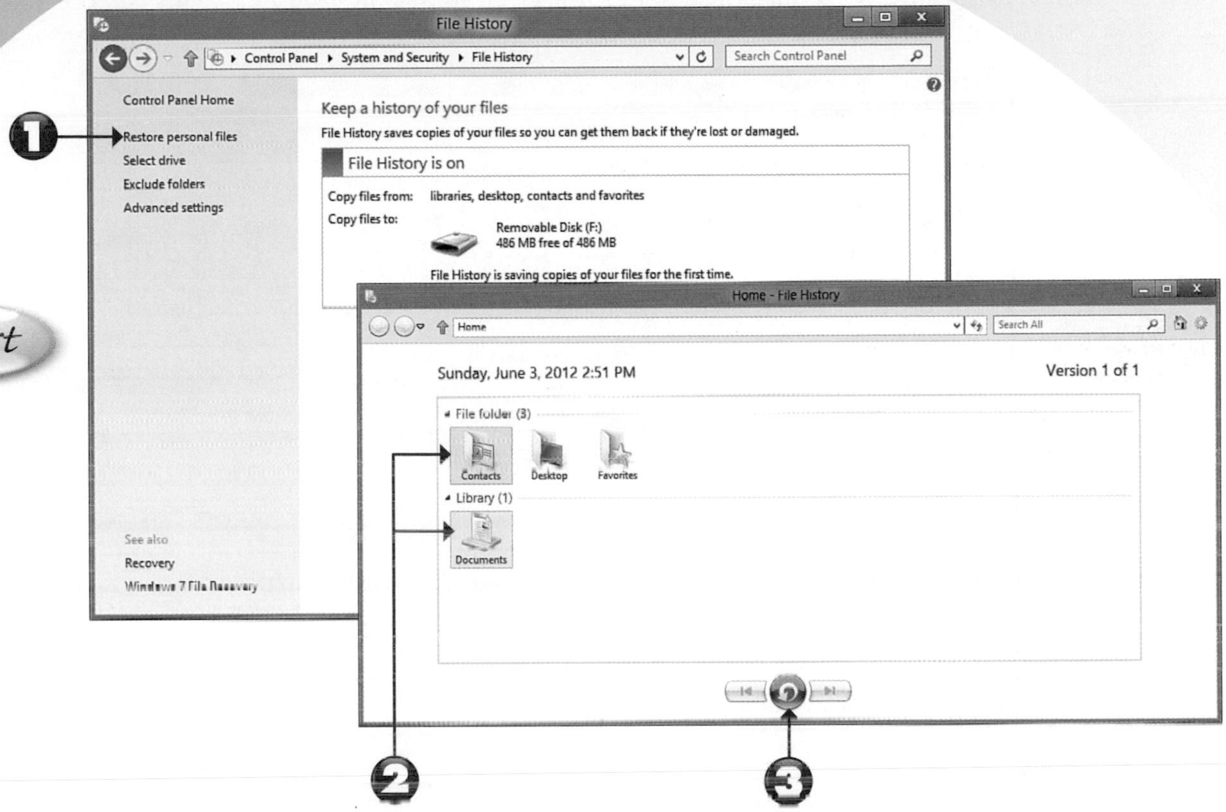

Start

1. From the File History screen, click **Restore Personal Files** from the navigation pane.
2. When the Home screen appears, navigate to and select those files you wish to restore.
3. Click the blue **Restore** button to restore these files to their original locations.

End

TIP

Restoring Changed Files You can also use File History to restore a given file to an earlier state. This is useful if you're editing a document, for example, and want to use an earlier version of the document before more recent editing. ■

TIP

Restoring to a Different Location To restore backup files to a different location than the original, click the **Settings** button on the Home screen, select **Restore To** from the menu, and then select a new location. ■

RESTORING YOUR COMPUTER AFTER A CRASH

If your computer system ever crashes or freezes, your best course of action is to run the System Restore utility. This utility can automatically restore your system to the state it was in before the crash occurred—and save you the trouble of reinstalling any damaged software programs. It's a great safety net for when things go wrong!

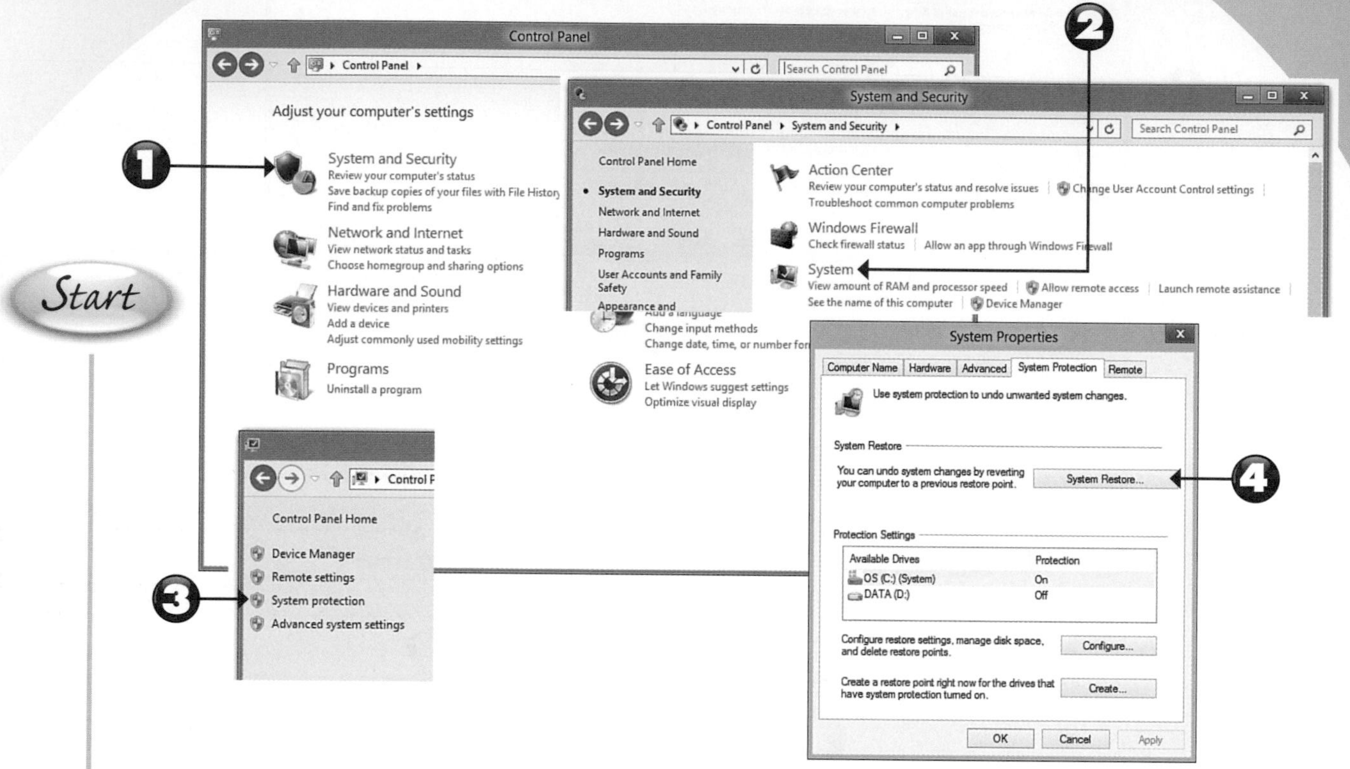

1. From the Windows Control Panel, click **System and Security**.
2. On the next screen, click **System**.
3. On the next screen, click **System Protection** in the navigation pane.
4. When the System Properties dialog box appears, make sure the **System Protection** tab is selected, and then click the **System Restore** button.

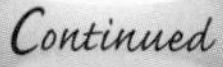

TIP

Restoring Your System Be sure to close all programs before you use System Restore because Windows will need to be restarted when it's done. The full process might take a half-hour or more. ■

CAUTION

System Files Only—No Documents System Restore will help you recover any damaged programs and system files, but it won't help you recover any documents or data files. This is why you need to use the File History utility to back up all your data on a regular basis—and restore that backed-up data in the case of an emergency. ■

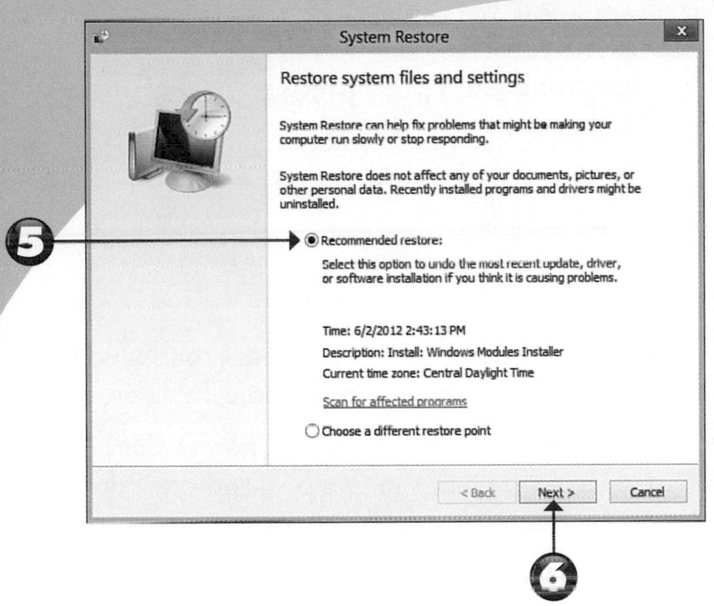

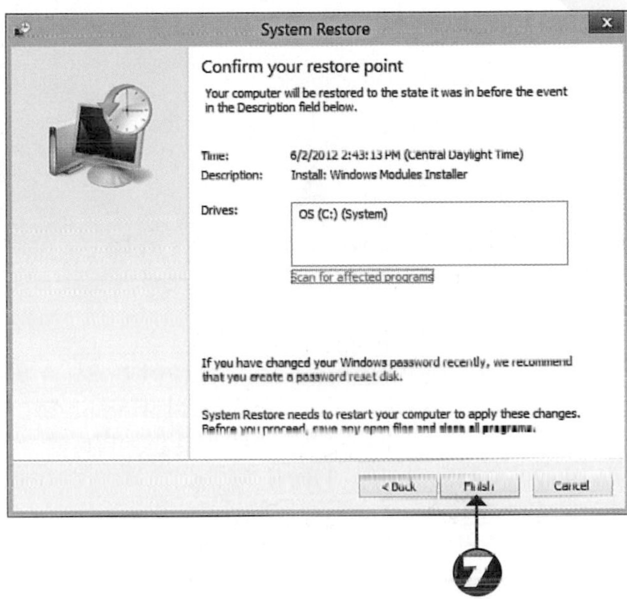

5 When the System Restore window appears, accept the recommended restore point or check **Choose a Different Restore Point** and select a different point.

6 Click the **Next** button.

7 When the Confirm Your Restore Point screen appears, click the **Finish** button to begin the restore process.

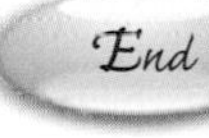

TIP

Refreshing System Files New to Windows 8 is the ability to "refresh" your system with the current versions of important system files, in case those files become damaged or deleted. To use the Refresh utility, go to the PC Settings page, select the **General** tab, scroll to the Refresh Your PC Without Affecting Your Files section, and click **Get Started**. ■

TIP

Resetting Your System In the event of a catastrophic system problem, you can reset your system to its factory-fresh condition by wiping clean the hard disk and reinstalling Windows from scratch. To use this Reset PC utility, go to the PC Settings page, select the **General** tab, scroll to the Reset Your PC and Start Over section, and click **Get Started**. Note, however, that this option will delete all the programs and files on your computer. ■

Glossary

A

add-in board A device that plugs in to a desktop computer's system unit and provides auxiliary functions. (Also called a *card*.)

address The location of an Internet host. An email address might take the form johndoe@xyz.com; a web address might look like www.xyztech.com. See also *URL*.

all-in-one computer A desktop computer where the system unit, monitor, and speakers are housed in a single unit. Often the monitor of such a system has s touchscreen display.

app See *application*.

application A computer program designed for a specific task or use, such as word processing, accounting, or missile guidance.

attachment A file, such as a Word document or graphics image, attached to an email message.

B

backup A copy of important data files.

boot The process of turning on your computer system.

broadband A high-speed Internet connection; it's faster than the older dial-up connection.

browser A program, such as Internet Explorer, that translates the Hypertext Markup Language (HTML) of the Web into viewable web pages.

bug An error in a software program or the hardware.

burner A device that writes CD-ROMs or DVD-ROMs.

C

cable modem A high-speed, broadband Internet connection via digital cable TV lines.

card Also called an *add-in board*, this is a device that plugs in to a desktop computer's system unit and provides auxiliary functions.

CD-R (compact disc recordable) A type of CD drive that lets you record only once onto a disc, which can then be read by any CD-ROM drive or audio CD player.

CD-ROM (compact disc read-only memory) A CD that can be used to store computer data. A CD-ROM, similar to an audio CD, stores data in a form readable by a laser, resulting in a storage device of great capacity and quick accessibility.

CD-RW (compact disc rewritable) A type of CD that can be recorded, erased, and rewritten to by the user, multiple times.

computer A programmable device that can store, retrieve, and process data.

CPU (central processing unit) The group of circuits that direct the entire computer system by (1) interpreting and executing program instruction and (2) coordinating the interaction of input, output, and storage devices.

cursor The highlighted area or pointer that tracks with the movement of your mouse or arrow keys onscreen.

D

data Information—on a computer, in digital format.

database A program for arranging facts in the computer and retrieving them—the computer equivalent of a filing system.

desktop The graphical user interface within Windows that runs older pre-Windows 8 apps.

desktop computer A personal computer designed for use on a typical office desktop. A traditional desktop computer system consists of a system unit, monitor, keyboard, mouse, and speakers.

device A computer file that represents some object—physical or nonphysical—installed on your system.

disk A device that stores data in magnetic or optical format.

disk drive A mechanism for retrieving information stored on a magnetic disk. The drive rotates the disk at high speed and reads the data with a magnetic head similar to those used in tape recorders.

domain The identifying portion of an Internet address. In email addresses, the domain name follows the @ sign; in website addresses, the domain name follows the www.

download A way to transfer files, graphics, or other information from the Internet to your computer.

dpi (dots per inch) A measurement of printer resolution; the more dots per inch, the higher the resolution.

driver A support file that tells a program how to interact with a specific hardware device, such as a hard disk controller or video display card.

DSL (digital subscriber line) A high-speed Internet connection that uses the ultra-high frequency portion of ordinary telephone lines, allowing users to send and receive voice and data on the same line at the same time.

DVD An optical disc, similar to a CD, that can hold a minimum of 4.7GB, enough for a full-length movie.

E

email Electronic mail; a means of corresponding with other computer users over the Internet through digital messages.

encryption A method of encoding files so only the recipient can read the information.

Ethernet The most common computer networking protocol; Ethernet is used to network, or hook together, computers so they can share information.

executable file A program you run on your computer system.

F

favorite A bookmarked site in Internet Explorer.

file Any group of data treated as a single entity by the computer, such as a word processor document, a program, or a database.

File Explorer The Windows folder used to navigate and display files and folders on your computer system. Previously known as Windows Explorer.

FiOS A type of broadband Internet service delivered over fiber-optic cable.

firewall Computer hardware or software with special security features to safeguard a computer connected to a network or to the Internet.

FireWire A high speed bus used to connect digital devices, such as digital cameras and video cameras, to a computer system. Also known as *i.LINK* and *IEEE-1394*.

folder A way to group files on a disk; each folder can contain multiple files or other folders (called *subfolders*). Folders are sometimes called *directories*.

freeware Free software available over the Internet. This is in contrast with *shareware*, which is available freely but usually asks the user to send payment for using the software.

G

gigabyte (GB) One billion bytes.

graphics Pictures, photographs, and clip art.

H

hard disk A sealed cartridge containing a magnetic storage disk(s) that holds much more memory than removable disks—up to 2 terabytes or more.

hardware The physical equipment, as opposed to the programs and procedures, used in computing.

home page The first or main page of a website.

HomeGroup A small network of computers all running Windows.

hover *See mouse over.*

hybrid computer A portable computer that combines the functionality of a touchscreen tablet and traditional notebook PC.

hyperlink A connection between two tagged elements in a web page, or separate sites, that makes it possible to click from one to the other.

I–J

icon A graphic symbol on the display screen that represents a file, peripheral, or some other object or function.

instant messaging Text-based, real-time one-on-one communication over the Internet.

Internet The global network of networks that connects millions of computers and other devices around the world.

Internet service provider (ISP) A company that provides end-user access to the Internet via its central computers and local access lines.

K–L

keyboard The typewriter-like device used to type instructions to a personal computer.

kilobyte (KB) A unit of measure for data storage or transmission equivalent to 1024 bytes; often rounded to 1000.

LAN (local-area network) A system that enables users to connect PCs to one another or to minicomputers or mainframes.

laptop A portable computer small enough to operate on one's lap. Also known as a *notebook* computer.

LCD (liquid crystal display) A flat-screen display where images are created by light transmitted through a layer of liquid crystals.

library A kind of virtual folder that doesn't physically exist on your hard disk but instead points to files and folders placed within it.

M–N

megabyte (MB) One million bytes.

megahertz (MHz) A measure of microprocessing speed; 1MHz equals 1 million electrical cycles per second.

memory Temporary electronic storage for data and instructions, via electronic impulses on a chip.

Metro The name Microsoft used during Windows 8's development phase to refer to the operating system's new flat, tiled interface.

microprocessor A complete central processing unit assembled on a single silicon chip.

modem (modulator demodulator) A device capable of converting a digital signal into an analog signal, which can be transmitted via a telephone line, reconverted, and then "read" by another computer.

monitor The display device on a computer, similar to a television screen.

motherboard Typically the largest printed circuit board in a computer, housing the CPU chip and controlling circuitry.

mouse A small handheld input device connected to a computer and featuring one or more button-style switches. When moved around on a flat surface, the mouse causes a symbol on the computer screen to make corresponding movements.

mouse over The act of selecting an item by placing your cursor over an icon without clicking.

network An interconnected group of computers.

notebook computer A portable computer with all components (including keyboard, screen, and touchpad) contained in a single unit. Notebook PCs can typically be operated via either battery or wall power.

O–P

operating system A sequence of programming codes that instructs a computer about its various parts and peripherals and how to operate them. Operating systems, such as Windows, deal only with the workings of the hardware and are separate from software programs.

parallel A type of external port used to connect printers and other similar devices; typically not found on newer PCs.

path The collection of folders and subfolders (listed in order of hierarchy) that hold a particular file.

peripheral A device connected to the computer that provides communication or auxiliary functions.

phishing The act of trying to "fish" for personal information via means of a deliberately deceptive email or website.

pixel The individual picture elements that combine to create a video image.

Plug and Play (PnP) Hardware that includes its manufacturer and model information in its ROM, enabling Windows to recognize it immediately upon startup and install the necessary drivers if not already set up.

pop-up A small browser window, typically without menus or other navigational elements, that opens seemingly of its own accord when you visit or leave another website.

port An interface on a computer to which you can connect a device, either internally or externally.

printer The piece of computer hardware that creates hard copy printouts of documents.

Q–R

RAM (random-access memory) A temporary storage space in which data can be held on a chip rather than being stored on disk or tape. The contents of RAM can be accessed or altered at any time during a session but will be lost when the computer is turned off.

resolution The degree of clarity an image displays, typically expressed by the number of horizontal and vertical pixels or the number of dots per inch (dpi).

ribbon A toolbar-like collection of action buttons, used in many newer Windows programs.

ROM (read-only memory) A type of chip memory, the contents of which have been permanently recorded in a computer by the manufacturer and cannot be altered by the user.

root The main directory or folder on a disk.

router A piece of hardware or software that handles the connection between two or more networks.

S

scanner A device that converts paper documents or photos into a format that can be viewed on a computer and manipulated by the user.

screensaver A display of moving designs on your computer screen when you haven't typed or moved the mouse for a while.

serial A type of external port used to connect communication devices; typically not found on newer PCs.

server The central computer in a network, providing a service or data access to client computers on the network.

shareware A software program distributed on the honor system; providers make their programs freely accessible over the Internet, with the understanding that those who use them will send payment to the provider after using them. See also *freeware*.

snaps The mouse actions that enable you to maximize and "snap" windows to either side of the screen.

software The programs and procedures, as opposed to the physical equipment, used in computing.

spam Junk email. As a verb, it means to send thousands of copies of a junk email message.

spreadsheet A program that performs mathematical operations on numbers arranged in large arrays; used mainly for accounting and other record keeping.

spyware Software used to surreptitiously monitor computer use (that is, spy on other users).

system unit The part of a desktop computer system that looks like a big beige or black box. The system unit typically contains the microprocessor, system memory, hard disk drive, floppy disk drives, and various cards.

T-U-V

tablet computer A small, handheld computer with no keyboard or mouse, operated solely via its touchscreen display.

terabyte (TB) One trillion bytes.

touchscreen display A computer display that is touch sensitive and can be operated with a touch of the finger.

trackpad The pointing device used on most notebook PCs, in lieu of an external mouse.

ultrabook A type of small and thin notebook computer with no built-in CD/DVD drive and a smaller display.

upgrade To add a new or improved peripheral or part to your system hardware. Also to install a newer version of an existing piece of software.

upload The act of copying a file from a personal computer to a website or Internet server. The opposite of *download*.

URL (uniform resource locator) The address that identifies a web page to a browser. Also known as a *web address*.

USB (universal serial bus) An external bus standard that supports data transfer rates of up to 4.8Gbps; an individual computer can connect up to 127 peripheral devices via USB.

virus A computer program segment or string of code that can attach itself to another program or file, reproduce itself, and spread from one computer to another. Viruses can destroy or change data and in other ways sabotage computer systems.

W-X-Y-Z

web page An HTML file, containing text, graphics, and/or mini-applications, viewed with a web browser.

website An organized, linked collection of web pages stored on an Internet server and read using a web browser. The opening page of a site is called a *home page*.

Wi-Fi The radio frequency (RF)-based technology used for home and small business wireless networks and for most public wireless Internet connections. It operates at 11Mbps (802.11b), 54Mbps (802.11g), or 600Mbps (802.11n). Short for "wireless fidelity."

window A portion of the screen display used to view simultaneously a different part of the file in use or a part of a different file than the one in use.

Windows The generic name for all versions of Microsoft's graphical operating system.

Windows Explorer See *File Explorer*.

Windows Store Microsoft's online store that offers Windows 8-specific apps for sale and download.

World Wide Web (WWW) A vast network of information, particularly business, commercial, and government resources, that uses a hypertext system for quickly transmitting graphics, sound, and video over the Internet.

Zip file A file that has been compressed for easier transmission.

A

B

D

E

G

H

I-J

K

L

M

O

P-Q

T

U